Modern PyQt

Create GUI Applications for Project Management, Computer Vision, and Data Analysis

Joshua Willman

Apress®

Modern PyQt

Joshua Willman
Hampton, VA, USA

ISBN-13 (pbk): 978-1-4842-6602-1   ISBN-13 (electronic): 978-1-4842-6603-8
https://doi.org/10.1007/978-1-4842-6603-8

Managing Director, Apress Media LLC: Welmoed Spahr
Acquisitions Editor: Celestin Suresh John
Development Editor: Rita Fernando
Coordinating Editor: Divya Modi

Cover designed by eStudioCalamar

Cover image designed by Pixabay

Distributed to the book trade worldwide by Springer Science+Business Media New York, 1 New York Plaza, Suite 4600, New York, NY 10004-1562, USA. Phone 1-800-SPRINGER, fax (201) 348-4505, e-mail orders-ny@springer-sbm.com, or visit www.springeronline.com. Apress Media, LLC is a California LLC and the sole member (owner) is Springer Science + Business Media Finance Inc (SSBM Finance Inc). SSBM Finance Inc is a **Delaware** corporation.

For information on translations, please e-mail booktranslations@springernature.com; for reprint, paperback, or audio rights, please e-mail bookpermissions@springernature.com.

Apress titles may be purchased in bulk for academic, corporate, or promotional use. eBook versions and licenses are also available for most titles. For more information, reference our Print and eBook Bulk Sales web page at http://www.apress.com/bulk-sales.

Any source code or other supplementary material referenced by the author in this book is available to readers on GitHub via the book's product page, located at www.apress.com/9781484266021. For more detailed information, please visit http://www.apress.com/source-code.

Printed on acid-free paper

To those who make me laugh

Valorie, Jason, Jazzmin, Teesha, Evelyn, Kalani

Table of Contents

About the Author

Joshua Willman began using Python in 2015 when he needed to build neural networks using machine learning libraries for image classification. While building large image datasets for his research, he needed to build a program that would simplify the workload and labeling process, which introduced him to PyQt. Since then, he has tried to dive into everything that is Python.

He currently works as a Python developer, building projects to help others learn more about coding in Python for game development, AI, and machine learning. Recently, he set up the site redhuli.io to explore his and others' interests in utilizing programming for creativity.

He is also the author of *Beginning PyQt: A Hands-on Approach to GUI Programming*.

About the Technical Reviewer

Lentin Joseph is an author, roboticist, and robotics entrepreneur from India. He runs a robotics software company called Qbotics Labs in Kochi, Kerala. He has 10 years of experience in the robotics domain, primarily in Robot Operating System (ROS), OpenCV, and PCL.

He has authored several books on ROS, namely, *Learning Robotics Using Python*, first and second editions; *Mastering ROS for Robotics Programming*, first and second editions; *ROS Robotics Projects*, first and second editions; and *Robot Operating System (ROS) for Absolute Beginners*.

He has obtained his master's in robotics and automation from India and also worked at the Robotics Institute, CMU, United States. He is also a TEDx speaker.

Acknowledgments

A few simple words can mean a lot to a person. They can be the little bit of hope that lets them know everything will be okay.

I first want to thank Apress Media LLC for giving me another opportunity to write, to learn, and to improve my creativity and skills.

To the community of Python, PyQt, and Qt programmers, thank you for your support and assistance.

To Adrian Rosebrock at PyImageSearch, thank you for your help, words of encouragement, and the knowledge you continue to share with others.

To Lentin Joseph, thank you for your help and support.

To Rita Fernando, thank you for your insight and help.

To Divya Modi, I am not even sure if words are enough to express how grateful I am for your patience. I owe you my deepest debt of gratitude.

To Christine Nieuwoudt, Callum Butler, and Giulio Mazzella, thank you for being the friends I needed so much while away from home.

To Andrea Cotman, Aaron Rountree, Vinita Acklin, and Malik Ranger, thank you for being the friends I need who make me miss home.

To my mother, Valorie Payne, thank you for your love and support and always being there when I need you.

To my sisters, Jazzmin and Teesha Payne, and my brother, Jason Willman, I love and miss all of you. P.S. Teesha, thank you for your help while writing this book.

To my wife, Lijing Ye (叶丽晶), once again I have to thank you for supporting me while I disappeared to write. I know it wasn't easy, and I thank you for always being supportive. <3

To my daughter, Kalani, thank you for running up to hug me when I came home in the evening. It means the world to me.

To everyone who picks up this book, thank you for reading, programming, and continuing to learn. Without you, this wouldn't be possible.

Introduction

When setting out to write this book, I didn't realize that data was the underlying theme the whole time. In everything we do now, data can be extracted. Our habits can be analyzed and models created to improve the ways in which we live. Data can be used to train and teach intelligent computer systems to think and make predictions. As we continue to add to the heaps of data that already exist, our understanding of the world continues to grow.

We understand what data is – a collection of numbers, names, words, and other types of information. Data can either be organized or jumbled and left up to us to clean and discern any meaning. The question this book aims to answer is how do we access and manipulate the information hidden within. That is the beauty of PyQt and graphical user interfaces (GUIs). We can create any application that visualizes and works with various kinds of data, including text, images, video, audio, or anything else. With PyQt, you can also easily leverage the power of existing Python modules in your applications.

That is what this book focuses on, showing you how to get started creating the different tools you need to interact with the data you collect. In *Modern PyQt*, we will begin to take a look at some of the ideas related to various fields and technologies that are being used in business and research today. Topics related to business and project management, data science, artificial intelligence (AI) and machine learning, computer vision, and more are introduced.

PyQt is an amazing tool for creating desktop, mobile, and embedded applications. *Modern PyQt* focuses on creating desktop applications for Mac, Windows, and Linux platforms. There are so many modules and classes to cover that it is impossible to cram them all into a single text. This guide aims to create a foundation for getting you started in building your own GUI applications.

Who Should Read This Book

This guide is intended for intermediate-level Python programmers or above with experience developing and coding GUIs. *Modern PyQt* is created both for GUI developers who have used PyQt before and are looking for assistance in building applications and for programmers who have experience using other toolkits, such as Tkinter or wxPython, and the concepts they have learned can be carried over for developing applications with PyQt.

The Focus of This Book

It must be stressed that this book is not an introduction to UI or GUI development, PyQt, or Python. You won't find a section that explains how to code in Python or lists all of the PyQt classes. There is an overview of PyQt in Chapter 1, but if this is your first time creating GUIs, it is recommended that you don't rely on *Modern PyQt* for teaching the basics. More focus is given on the creation of applications and features that will enhance the capabilities of GUIs.

About the Code

Each chapter contains example programs, projects, or both. Examples are designed to introduce each chapter's programming concepts. Projects will work toward creating either a complete application or the foundation for a program that you can modify and improve by adding your own features.

There are a few occasions when you will come across mathematical formulas. Variables representing vectors and matrices are set in boldface to follow typographical conventions.

Installing Applications in This Book

This book uses the current version of Python, version 3.8. The only exception is in Chapter 9, when you may need to roll back to an earlier version of Python to use the PyInstaller module.

As of this writing, the version for PyQt is version 5.15. Applications in this book will work on Python versions 3.5 and higher.

Various chapters will require you to install different Python or PyQt packages to run the code. There are numerous ways to install Python packages, such as installing from source, in a virtual environment, or using package managers or tools such as Anaconda. To keep a uniform method for installation throughout this book, the **Python Package**

Installer (pip) is used. pip installs packages from the **Python Package Index (PyPI)**. This method will be followed unless otherwise stated in the text. If you prefer a different method, there are tons of tutorials on the Internet to assist you.

pip should already come with Python, but if you find that you don't have pip installed on your computer, information about installing the package manager for your specific platform can be found at `https://pip.pypa.io/en/stable/`. More information about installing pip for Linux can also be found in the documentation.

One final thing to note is that this text installs packages using pip3 instead of pip. With Python 2 recently no longer supported, pip3 is only used to ensure that the Python 3 environment is being used. You can still use pip instead of pip3.

How This Book Is Organized

To give the breakdown on how to get started creating desktop applications with PyQt, **Chapter 1** will walk you through many of the fundamental concepts that you will probably need when creating an application. Not all topics are covered, only the crucial ones for getting you started. From there, **Chapter 2** will give you the lowdown on creating applications that use the drag and drop mechanism.

Chapters 3, **4**, **5**, and **6** focus on working with data. **Chapter 3** introduces techniques for visualizing and analyzing 2D data using PyQt and Matplotlib. In **Chapter 4**, you will get to work with PyQt's SQL classes. Computer vision is a relatively new field that works with visual data, including images and videos. **Chapter 5** will create GUIs that integrate the OpenCV library for computer vision applications. In **Chapter 6**, you'll be introduced to the PyQt module for working with 3D data.

From there, **Chapter 7** will briefly introduce the Python and PyQt classes for networking. **Chapter 8** will explore how to create a chatbot. To wrap everything up, **Chapter 9** will demonstrate how to create executable files from your PyQt applications.

Links to the Source Code

The source code and datasets used in *Modern PyQt* can be found on GitHub via the book's product page, located at `www.apress.com/9781484266021`.

Reader Feedback

Your feedback, questions, and comments are very important. If you would like to take a moment to let me know your thoughts about the book or ask any questions you may have, you can send comments to the following address: redhuli.comments@gmail.com.

You can also follow me on Twitter at `https://twitter.com/RedHuli`.

CHAPTER 1

Overview of PyQt5

Hello! Welcome to *Modern PyQt*! When you build an application, whether for desktop, mobile, or embedded devices, your goal is to create a seamless experience for the user. If you are designing a program for others to use, then you should always consider how the user might interact with the software to solve their problems. Applications such as web browsers, word processors, and video players are all created to enrich the end user's life, helping them achieve some task simply and efficiently.

Some programs are designed to perform a minimal number of tasks, such as the clock on your computer. Others bundle together a multitude of features that allow people to interact with machines in unique ways. An example of this is photo editing software. What these applications generally have in common is some kind of **user interface** (**UI**), a visual window into the happenings in human–machine interactions, providing feedback to the user and assisting in the human's decision-making process.

We still continue to use command-line interfaces to interact with our computers. However, humans have naturally steered more and more to UIs that use visual controls rather than textual prompts. These types of UIs, known as **graphical user interfaces** (**GUIs**), utilize a computer's graphical capabilities to create visual windows, menus, and other elements for a user to interact with computers. Good GUI design blends these visual components with intuitive design to improve functionality and a user's experience.

In *Modern PyQt*, we will focus on building GUI desktop applications with the Python programming language and the PyQt toolkit. Recent years have seen an increase in the number of both skilled and novice programmers using Python. Its uses are widespread, being employed in general programming, web development, data science, machine learning, game development, and more. So it's no wonder that Python also includes libraries for UI development.

© Joshua Willman 2021
J. Willman, *Modern PyQt*, https://doi.org/10.1007/978-1-4842-6603-8_1

In this chapter, you will

- Find out about PyQt.

- See how to install and get started using PyQt5.

- Be introduced to some key concepts in PyQt through two practical applications:

    - Pomodoro Timer

    - Basic User Manager GUI

Note   This text wastes no time getting into building GUIs. Hopefully, you have some prior experience with Python and have built user interfaces with PyQt or have used some other UI development toolkit before, such as Tkinter or wxPython. While the chapter is an overview of PyQt, this section only glosses over many of the fundamental topics necessary for getting started with PyQt and building UIs. Take a moment to review the fundamentals of PyQt if it is needed. Subsequent chapters and topics will be handled at a much slower pace.

What Is PyQt?

With the PyQt framework, you have tools at your disposal for building UIs that can work with SQL databases, 2D and 3D graphics, network communication, multimedia, and so much more.

However, PyQt is in fact a set of Python bindings that make it possible to use The Qt Company's Qt application framework. The cross-platform C++ development toolkit, Qt, actually contains everything you need for building applications on Windows, MacOS, Linux, Android, and embedded systems.

This means that by combining Python with Qt, you get the advantages of the C++ toolkit for making applications, such as the collection of GUI widgets and the ease of creating flexible UIs and reusable software elements, along with the simplicity and large collection of modules that already exist with Python. PyQt is like the glue holding them both together.

At the time of publication, the latest version of PyQt5 is version 5.15. PyQt4 also exists, but as of this writing, no more releases will be made for version 4.

To learn more about PyQt, which is maintained by Riverbank Computing Limited, check out `www.riverbankcomputing.com/software/pyqt/`.

If you are interested in learning more about the Qt framework, then have a look at the Qt documentation at `https://doc.qt.io/`.

Note   PyQt contains many of Qt's classes. However, there are some examples when a class does not exist in the PyQt library. One notable example is the Qt QList class. PyQt does not contain this class and rather takes full advantage of the `list` data structure in Python.

Installing PyQt5

Before you install PyQt, take a moment to ensure that Python v3.5 or higher is already installed on your computer. The easiest way to check your version of Python is to enter the following command into the command line for Windows or terminal for MacOS or Linux:

```
$ python --version
```

If you find that your version needs to be updated or that you don't have Python, the simplest way to get the latest version is to go to `https://python.org/downloads/` and find the installer for your OS.

Like Python, there are also a few ways to download PyQt5. PyQt has both a General Public License (GPL) and a commercial version. For this guide, we will take a look at how to install the latest GPL version of PyQt5 with wheels and the `pip` package installer. Enter the following command into your shell:

```
$ pip3 install PyQt5
```

The wheel that supports both your platform and your version of Python will be downloaded from the Python Package Index (PyPI) repository. The PyQt5 wheel already includes the parts of Qt that you need as well as the `sip` module. `sip` is simply a tool that connects the Qt software written in C++ to Python.

For Linux users (specifically Ubuntu), run the following command instead to install PyQt:

```
$ sudo apt install python3-pyqt5
```

Note   For more information about installing PyQt5, please refer to the "Introduction."

To ensure that PyQt5 is properly installed, enter `python3` into the command line to open the Python interpreter. Then input

```
>>> import PyQt5
```

If there are no errors, then you are ready to start making your own UI applications. For further information about installing PyQt5, have a look at

`www.riverbankcomputing.com/static/Docs/PyQt5/installation.html`.

Also, if you are ever curious to know what version of PyQt5 you have installed on your computer, enter the following two lines into the Python shell:

```
>>> from PyQt5.Qt import PYQT_VERSION_STR
>>> print("PyQt version:", PYQT_VERSION_STR)
```

Finally, if you want to find out the path to PyQt on your system or see a list of the PyQt5 modules you have installed, use the Python `help()` function:

```
>>> import PyQt5
>>> help(PyQt5)
```

After you get PyQt5 installed, you are ready to move on to this chapter's first application – the Pomodoro Timer.

Project 1.1: Pomodoro Timer

Given the number of distractions and challenges we all face trying to manage work, family, and personal projects, creating a desktop application for time management as the first project in this book seemed like the best thing to do.

The Pomodoro Technique [1] designed by Francesco Cirillo is a technique used to increase your focus and productivity when trying to complete assignments or meet deadlines. Choosing to use a Pomodoro Timer can help to give a task your full, undivided attention. The timer you will be coding can be seen in Figure 1-1.

---

[1]More information about the Pomodoro Technique can be found at `https://francescocirillo.com/pages/pomodoro-technique`

A tomato-shaped kitchen timer was originally used by Cirillo. Rather than tackling an assignment head-on for hours, this technique breaks the tasks into intervals, typically 25 minutes long (or one *pomodoro*). Each session of working is broken up by a short period of rest.

The typical process of the Pomodoro Technique consists of the following six steps:

1. Choose a task that you would like to finish.

2. Set the Pomodoro Timer for 25 minutes.

3. Work solely on that task until the timer rings.

4. After the timer rings, make a checkmark on a piece of paper.

5. Take a short break. You could go outside, meditate, or do some push-ups.

6. Once you have completed four Pomodoro cycles, you deserve a longer break. This time could be 20, or even 30, minutes if you need. (For this application, the long break's timer is set to 15 minutes.) Reset your checkmarks, and then return back to working on the task or start a new one.

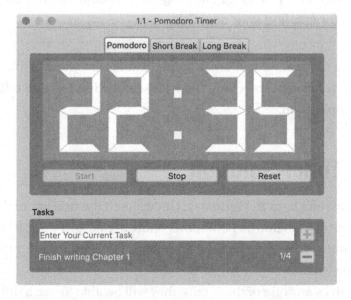

Figure 1-1. *The Pomodoro Timer GUI displaying the different tabs, Pomodoro, Short Break, and Long Break. The QLCDNumber widget displays the current tab's remaining time. The bottom of the GUI also gives the user a field for inputting their current task and recording the number of pomodoro cycles*

This project will introduce a number of the primary tools and concepts you will need to create your own GUIs with Python and PyQt. The Pomodoro Timer GUI demonstrates the following concepts:

- How to use PyQt modules and widget classes for creating graphical user interfaces

- The layout management classes, including QHBoxLayout and QVBoxLayout

- The use of container classes for organizing groups of widgets

- PyQt's signal and slot mechanism for event handling

- How to edit the appearance of widgets with Qt Style Sheets

- The QTimer class and event loops

- Using other Qt classes such as Qt and QIcon

Note   The first program in this chapter is a long one, but don't get discouraged. The hope is that you will continue following along and find out what this application has to offer. By building this program yourself, you will be introduced to some new ideas for creating your own GUIs.

In the following section, we will break apart the different widgets that comprise the interface, discuss the layout, take a look at the code in Listing 1-1, and talk about the logic behind the application.

Pomodoro Timer Solution

Take a moment and refer back to Figure 1-1. Underneath the title bar of the window, you should notice three tabs labeled as Pomodoro, Short Break, and Long Break. Each tab has its own time limit – 25 minutes for the Pomodoro tab, 5 minutes for the Short Break, and 15 for the Long Break.

When a user clicks any one of these tabs, they will be able to use a different timer. Each tab is distinguishable by a different color (visual attributes of widgets can be modified using Qt Style Sheets). The user can then choose to start, stop, or reset the current timer using the QPushButtons. After the user clicks the Start button, it is disabled until either Stop or Reset is clicked. When a user switches to a different tab, that tab's settings and widgets are reset.

The upper portion of the GUI that contains the tabs, timers, and buttons is separate from the lower portion, where the user can input their current task and see how many pomodoros they have completed. If four cycles are completed, a message will be displayed in the task bar urging the user to take a longer break. The widgets for each section are grouped together using container widgets and then organized using various layout managers.

All of these points and more will be broken down in the "Explanation" section.

The design for the application created in Listing 1-1 was influenced by some of the different Pomodoro Timers that can be found on the Internet.

Listing 1-1. Code for the Pomodoro Timer application

```python
# pomodoro.py
# Import necessary modules
import sys
from PyQt5.QtWidgets import (QApplication, QWidget, QLCDNumber,
QPushButton, QLabel, QLineEdit, QGroupBox, QTabWidget, QVBoxLayout,
QHBoxLayout)
from PyQt5.QtCore import Qt, QTimer
from PyQt5.QtGui import QIcon
from PomodoroStyleSheet import style_sheet

# Global variables for each timer
POMODORO_TIME = 1500000 # 25 mins in milliseconds
SHORT_BREAK_TIME = 300000 # 5 mins in milliseconds
LONG_BREAK_TIME = 900000 # 15 mins in milliseconds

class PomodoroTimer(QWidget):

    def __init__(self): # Create default constructor
        super().__init__()
        self.initializeUI()
```

```python
    def initializeUI(self):
        """Initialize the window and display its contents to the screen."""
        self.setMinimumSize(500, 400)
        self.setWindowTitle("1.1 - Pomodoro Timer")
        self.setWindowIcon(QIcon("images/tomato.png"))

        self.pomodoro_limit = POMODORO_TIME
        self.short_break_limit = SHORT_BREAK_TIME
        self.long_break_limit = LONG_BREAK_TIME

        self.setupTabsAndWidgets()

        # Variables related to the current tabs and widgets displayed in
        the GUI's window
        self.current_tab_selected = 0
        self.current_start_button = self.pomodoro_start_button
        self.current_stop_button = self.pomodoro_stop_button
        self.current_reset_button = self.pomodoro_reset_button
        self.current_time_limit = self.pomodoro_limit
        self.current_lcd = self.pomodoro_lcd

        # Variables related to user's current task
        self.task_is_set = False
        self.number_of_tasks = 0
        self.task_complete_counter = 0

        # Create timer object
        self.timer = QTimer(self)
        self.timer.timeout.connect(self.updateTimer)

        self.show()

    def setupTabsAndWidgets(self):
        """Set up the tab bar for the different pomodoro stages: pomodoro,
        short break, long break."""
        # Create the tab bar and the QWidgets (containers) for each tab
        self.tab_bar = QTabWidget(self)
```

```python
self.pomodoro_tab = QWidget()
self.pomodoro_tab.setObjectName("Pomodoro")
self.short_break_tab = QWidget()
self.short_break_tab.setObjectName("ShortBreak")
self.long_break_tab = QWidget()
self.long_break_tab.setObjectName("LongBreak")

self.tab_bar.addTab(self.pomodoro_tab, "Pomodoro")
self.tab_bar.addTab(self.short_break_tab, "Short Break")
self.tab_bar.addTab(self.long_break_tab, "Long Break")

self.tab_bar.currentChanged.connect(self.tabsSwitched)

# Call the functions that contain the widgets for each tab
self.pomodoroTab()
self.shortBreakTab()
self.longBreakTab()

# Create the line edit and button widgets and layout for Pomodoro
Taskbar
self.enter_task_lineedit = QLineEdit()
self.enter_task_lineedit.setClearButtonEnabled(True)
self.enter_task_lineedit.setPlaceholderText("Enter Your Current Task")

confirm_task_button = QPushButton(QIcon("images/plus.png"), None)
confirm_task_button.setObjectName("ConfirmButton")
confirm_task_button.clicked.connect(self.addTaskToTaskbar)

task_entry_h_box = QHBoxLayout()
task_entry_h_box.addWidget(self.enter_task_lineedit)
task_entry_h_box.addWidget(confirm_task_button)

self.tasks_v_box = QVBoxLayout()

task_v_box = QVBoxLayout()
task_v_box.addLayout(task_entry_h_box)
task_v_box.addLayout(self.tasks_v_box)
```

```python
        # Container for taskbar
        task_bar_gb = QGroupBox("Tasks")
        task_bar_gb.setLayout(task_v_box)

        # Create and set layout for the main window
        main_v_box = QVBoxLayout()
        main_v_box.addWidget(self.tab_bar)
        main_v_box.addWidget(task_bar_gb)
        self.setLayout(main_v_box)

    def pomodoroTab(self):
        """Set up the Pomodoro tab, widgets and layout."""
        # Convert starting time to display on timer
        start_time = self.calculateDisplayTime(self.pomodoro_limit)

        self.pomodoro_lcd = QLCDNumber()
        self.pomodoro_lcd.setObjectName("PomodoroLCD")
        self.pomodoro_lcd.setSegmentStyle(QLCDNumber.Filled)
        self.pomodoro_lcd.display(start_time)

        self.pomodoro_start_button = QPushButton("Start")
        self.pomodoro_start_button.clicked.connect(self.startCountDown)

        self.pomodoro_stop_button = QPushButton("Stop")
        self.pomodoro_stop_button.clicked.connect(self.stopCountDown)

        self.pomodoro_reset_button = QPushButton("Reset")
        self.pomodoro_reset_button.clicked.connect(self.resetCountDown)

        button_h_box = QHBoxLayout() # Horizontal layout for buttons
        button_h_box.addWidget(self.pomodoro_start_button)
        button_h_box.addWidget(self.pomodoro_stop_button)
        button_h_box.addWidget(self.pomodoro_reset_button)

        # Create and set layout for the pomodoro tab
        v_box = QVBoxLayout()
        v_box.addWidget(self.pomodoro_lcd)
        v_box.addLayout(button_h_box)
        self.pomodoro_tab.setLayout(v_box)
```

```python
def shortBreakTab(self):
    """Set up the short break tab, widgets and layout."""
    # Convert starting time to display on timer
    start_time = self.calculateDisplayTime(self.short_break_limit)

    self.short_break_lcd = QLCDNumber()
    self.short_break_lcd.setObjectName("ShortLCD")
    self.short_break_lcd.setSegmentStyle(QLCDNumber.Filled)
    self.short_break_lcd.display(start_time)

    self.short_start_button = QPushButton("Start")
    self.short_start_button.clicked.connect(self.startCountDown)

    self.short_stop_button = QPushButton("Stop")
    self.short_stop_button.clicked.connect(self.stopCountDown)

    self.short_reset_button = QPushButton("Reset")
    self.short_reset_button.clicked.connect(self.resetCountDown)

    button_h_box = QHBoxLayout() # Horizontal layout for buttons
    button_h_box.addWidget(self.short_start_button)
    button_h_box.addWidget(self.short_stop_button)
    button_h_box.addWidget(self.short_reset_button)

    # Create and set layout for the short break tab
    v_box = QVBoxLayout()
    v_box.addWidget(self.short_break_lcd)
    v_box.addLayout(button_h_box)
    self.short_break_tab.setLayout(v_box)

def longBreakTab(self):
    """Set up the long break tab, widgets and layout."""
    # Convert starting time to display on timer
    start_time = self.calculateDisplayTime(self.long_break_limit)

    self.long_break_lcd = QLCDNumber()
    self.long_break_lcd.setObjectName("LongLCD")
    self.long_break_lcd.setSegmentStyle(QLCDNumber.Filled)
    self.long_break_lcd.display(start_time)
```

```python
        self.long_start_button = QPushButton("Start")
        self.long_start_button.clicked.connect(self.startCountDown)

        self.long_stop_button = QPushButton("Stop")
        self.long_stop_button.clicked.connect(self.stopCountDown)

        self.long_reset_button = QPushButton("Reset")
        self.long_reset_button.clicked.connect(self.resetCountDown)

        button_h_box = QHBoxLayout() # Horizontal layout for buttons
        button_h_box.addWidget(self.long_start_button)
        button_h_box.addWidget(self.long_stop_button)
        button_h_box.addWidget(self.long_reset_button)

        # Create and set layout for the long break tab
        v_box = QVBoxLayout()
        v_box.addWidget(self.long_break_lcd)
        v_box.addLayout(button_h_box)
        self.long_break_tab.setLayout(v_box)

    def startCountDown(self):
        """Starts the timer. If the current tab's time is 00:00, reset the
        time if user pushes the start button."""
        self.current_start_button.setEnabled(False)

        # Used to reset counter_label if user has already has completed
        four pomodoro cycles
        if self.task_is_set == True and self.task_complete_counter == 0:
            self.counter_label.setText("{}/4".format(self.task_complete_
            counter))

        remaining_time = self.calculateDisplayTime(self.current_time_limit)
        if remaining_time == "00:00":
            self.resetCountDown()
            self.timer.start(1000)
        else:
            self.timer.start(1000)
```

```python
def stopCountDown(self):
    """If the timer is already running, then stop the timer."""
    if self.timer.isActive() != False:
        self.timer.stop()
        self.current_start_button.setEnabled(True)

def resetCountDown(self):
    """Resets the time for the current tab when the reset button is
    selected."""
    self.stopCountDown() # Stop countdown if timer is running

    # Reset time for currently selected tab
    if self.current_tab_selected == 0: # Pomodoro tab
        self.pomodoro_limit = POMODORO_TIME
        self.current_time_limit = self.pomodoro_limit
        reset_time = self.calculateDisplayTime(self.current_time_limit)

    elif self.current_tab_selected == 1: # Short break tab
        self.short_break_limit = SHORT_BREAK_TIME
        self.current_time_limit = self.short_break_limit
        reset_time = self.calculateDisplayTime(self.current_time_limit)

    elif self.current_tab_selected == 2: # Long break tab
        self.long_break_limit = LONG_BREAK_TIME
        self.current_time_limit = self.long_break_limit
        reset_time = self.calculateDisplayTime(self.current_time_limit)

    self.current_lcd.display(reset_time)

def updateTimer(self):
    """Updates the timer and the current QLCDNumber widget. Also,
    update the task counter if a task is set."""
    remaining_time = self.calculateDisplayTime(self.current_time_limit)

    if remaining_time == "00:00":
        self.stopCountDown()
        self.current_lcd.display(remaining_time)
```

```python
        if self.current_tab_selected == 0 and self.task_is_set == True:
            self.task_complete_counter += 1
            if self.task_complete_counter == 4:
                self.counter_label.setText("Time for a long break.
                {}/4".format(self.task_complete_counter))
                self.task_complete_counter = 0
            elif self.task_complete_counter < 4:
                self.counter_label.setText("{}/4".format(self.task_
                complete_counter))
    else:
        # Update the current timer by decreasing the current running
        time by one second
        self.current_time_limit -= 1000
        self.current_lcd.display(remaining_time)

def tabsSwitched(self, index):
    """Depending upon which tab the user is currently looking at, the
    information for that tab needs to be updated. This function updates
    the different variables that keep track of the timer, buttons, lcds
    and other widgets, and update them accordingly."""
    self.current_tab_selected = index
    self.stopCountDown()

    # Reset variables, time and widgets depending upon which tab is the
    current_tab_selected
    if self.current_tab_selected == 0: # Pomodoro tab
        self.current_start_button = self.pomodoro_start_button
        self.current_stop_button = self.pomodoro_stop_button
        self.current_reset_button = self.pomodoro_reset_button
        self.pomodoro_limit = POMODORO_TIME
        self.current_time_limit = self.pomodoro_limit

        reset_time = self.calculateDisplayTime(self.current_time_limit)
        self.current_lcd = self.pomodoro_lcd
        self.current_lcd.display(reset_time)
```

```python
        elif self.current_tab_selected == 1: # Short break tab
            self.current_start_button = self.short_start_button
            self.current_stop_button = self.short_stop_button
            self.current_reset_button = self.short_reset_button
            self.short_break_limit = SHORT_BREAK_TIME
            self.current_time_limit = self.short_break_limit

            reset_time = self.calculateDisplayTime(self.current_time_limit)
            self.current_lcd = self.short_break_lcd
            self.current_lcd.display(reset_time)

        elif self.current_tab_selected == 2: # Long break tab
            self.current_start_button = self.long_start_button
            self.current_stop_button = self.long_stop_button
            self.current_reset_button = self.long_reset_button
            self.long_break_limit = LONG_BREAK_TIME
            self.current_time_limit = self.long_break_limit

            reset_time = self.calculateDisplayTime(self.current_time_limit)
            self.current_lcd = self.long_break_lcd
            self.current_lcd.display(reset_time)

    def addTaskToTaskbar(self):
        """When the user clicks the plus button, the widgets for the new
        task will be added to the task bar. Only one task is allowed to be
        entered at a time."""
        text = self.enter_task_lineedit.text()
        self.enter_task_lineedit.clear()

        # Change number_of_tasks if you want to ask more tasks to the task bar
        if text != "" and self.number_of_tasks != 1:
            self.enter_task_lineedit.setReadOnly(True)
            self.task_is_set = True
            new_task = QLabel(text)

            self.counter_label = QLabel("{}/4".format(self.task_complete_
            counter))
            self.counter_label.setAlignment(Qt.AlignRight)
```

```python
        cancel_task_button = QPushButton(QIcon("images/minus.png"), None)
        cancel_task_button.setMaximumWidth(24)
        cancel_task_button.clicked.connect(self.clearCurrentTask)

        self.new_task_h_box = QHBoxLayout()
        self.new_task_h_box.addWidget(new_task)
        self.new_task_h_box.addWidget(self.counter_label)
        self.new_task_h_box.addWidget(cancel_task_button)

        self.tasks_v_box.addLayout(self.new_task_h_box)
        self.number_of_tasks += 1

    def clearCurrentTask(self):
        """Delete the current task, and reset variables and widgets related
        to tasks."""
        # Remove items from parent widget by setting the argument value in
        setParent() to None
        self.new_task.setParent(None)
        self.counter_label.setParent(None)
        self.cancel_task_button.setParent(None)

        self.number_of_tasks -= 1
        self.task_is_set = False
        self.task_complete_counter = 0

        self.enter_task_lineedit.setReadOnly(False)

    def convertTotalTime(self, time_in_milli):
        """Convert time to milliseconds."""
        minutes = (time_in_milli / (1000 * 60)) % 60
        seconds = (time_in_milli / 1000) % 60
        return int(minutes), int(seconds)

    def calculateDisplayTime(self, time):
        """Calculate the time that should be displayed in the QLCDNumber
        widget."""
        minutes, seconds = self.convertTotalTime(time)
        amount_of_time = "{:02d}:{:02d}".format(minutes, seconds)
        return amount_of_time
```

```python
# Run main event loop
if __name__ == '__main__':
    app = QApplication(sys.argv)
    app.setStyleSheet(style_sheet)
    window = PomodoroTimer()
    sys.exit(app.exec_())
```

The resulting GUI can be seen in both Figures 1-1 and 1-2. The different timers can be accessed by clicking a timer's corresponding tab in the tab bar at the top of the window.

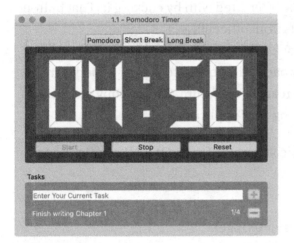 

Figure 1-2. *The left image displays the tab used for short breaks, while the right image shows the tab for long breaks*

Explanation

A graphical user interface can be composed of many different components working together to achieve some goal. The Pomodoro Timer created in Listing 1-1 is a good example of an application that is comprised of different PyQt widgets and classes that change and update depending upon the user's actions.

Let's begin by taking a look at the basic parts you will need just to create an empty GUI window with Python and PyQt.

Creating an Empty Window

In order to follow along with the code written in this book, you will definitely need a basic understanding of the **Object-Oriented Programming (OOP)** paradigm. Rather than writing a program that works sequentially to perform a task, OOP builds relationships between objects with their own properties and behaviors. Each object has relationships with other objects. With GUIs, these objects are the widgets created from classes – which are the templates for what an object can do and its attributes – and can inherit properties and behaviors from a parent class.

When you create an **instance** of a class, such as a QPushButton widget, you are essentially creating a button object that can be interacted with by clicking it. That button not only has its own methods but also inherits from other classes.

The example code in Listing 1-2 takes a look at how to get started using PyQt classes to build an empty window with the OOP approach. The code also acts as a good starting point for any program that you may want to create in the future. Simply copy and paste the code into a Python script and begin creating your application.

Listing 1-2. Code demonstrating the basic structure for PyQt GUI applications

```python
# Import necessary modules
import sys
from PyQt5.QtWidgets import QApplication, QWidget

class ExampleClass(QWidget):

    def __init__(self): # Create default constructor
        super().__init__()
        self.initializeUI()

    def initializeUI(self):
        """Initialize the window and display its contents to the screen."""
        self.setGeometry(100, 100, 500, 400)
        self.setWindowTitle('Empty Window in PyQt')
        self.show()

if __name__ == '__main__':
    app = QApplication(sys.argv)
    window = ExampleClass()
    sys.exit(app.exec_())
```

First, we need to `import` a couple of plugins, `sys` and `PyQt5`. The `sys` module can be used to pass command-line arguments to our applications and safely exit a program.

The UI elements you need to create desktop-like applications are found in the `QtWidgets` module. From `QtWidgets`, let's import `QApplication` and `QWidget`. The **QApplication** class manages an application's main event loop, flow, initialization, and finalization of widgets and provides session management. Only one instance of QApplication is allowed per program. **QWidget** is the base class for all user interface objects.

The functionality of Qt classes can be extended using Python classes. **Subclassing** Qt classes allows you to create classes that inherit properties and methods from a parent class. Since the class created, `ExampleClass`, inherits from `QWidget`, we also have access to QWidget's different properties and methods. The default constructor for `ExampleClass` is created using `__init__()`, and we use `super()` to inherit from our `QWidget` class. An example of subclassing the QPushButton widget class can be seen in Chapter 2.

Next in `initializeUI()`, the size and location of the window is set with `setGeometry()`, and the window's title is assigned with `setWindowTitle()`. The `show()` method is necessary for displaying the window to the screen.

Finally, we create the `QApplication` instance before creating any other objects in our user interface. We create an instance of the `ExampleClass` which will generate and display the GUI's window. Lastly, we begin the main event loop with `app.exec_()`.

Before going further, we should take a look at how PyQt's modules and classes are used in the Pomodoro Timer.

PyQt Modules and Classes

The Qt framework has a number of modules and classes[2] for building a variety of different graphical applications.

For the Pomodoro Timer GUI, we need to import

- `QtWidgets` – Contains the traditional user interface components primarily for desktop applications

- `QtCore` – Consists of essential non-GUI functions, such as communication between widgets and threading

- `QtGui` – Provides the classes for graphics, basic imaging, fonts, and more

---

[2] `www.riverbankcomputing.com/static/Docs/PyQt5/sip-classes.html`.

These are but a few of the modules that we will be taking a look at throughout this guide.

There are hundreds of PyQt classes, and the Pomodoro Timer uses only a few of them, including QWidget, QPushButton, QLabel, and QLineEdit. Each class contains its own attributes and methods. For example, the following bit of code from Listing 1-1 demonstrates how to create a QLineEdit widget for the Pomodoro Timer and alter a few of its properties, such as enabling a clear button to be displayed if text is entered into the input field of the widget and setting placeholder text:

```
self.enter_task_lineedit = QLineEdit() # Create object
# A few methods of the QLineEdit class
self.enter_task_lineedit.setClearButtonEnabled(True)
self.enter_task_lineedit.setPlaceholderText("Enter Your Current Task")
```

Other examples that can be seen in this application include setting the maximum width of a QPushButton with setMaximumWidth() or modifying the appearance of the segments in QLCDNumber's display using setSegmentStyle().

Classes Qt and QIcon are also included in the Pomodoro Timer. The Qt class contains numerous miscellaneous identifiers from the Qt framework. QIcon can be used for setting an icon in a GUI's title bar or on widgets, such as QPushButtons. An example of setting the icon in the Pomodoro Timer's title bar is shown in the following:

```
self.setWindowIcon(QIcon("images/tomato.png"))
```

The result can be seen in Figure 1-3.

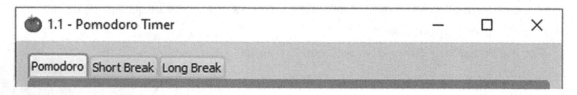

Figure 1-3. *An icon can be seen in the title bar of the window on Windows and Linux. For Mac users, the icon will not be displayed due to MacOS guidelines*

The Pomodoro Timer uses three separate QLCDNumber objects for each of the different countdown timers – pomodoro_lcd, short_break_lcd and long_break_lcd. The different timers can be seen in Figures 1-1 and 1-2. These timers are controlled using their respective start, stop, and reset QPushButton objects. All of these widgets are separated and organized using the QTabWidget class, which acts as a container.

Using Container Classes in PyQt

Container classes act as a means to arrange and control groups of widgets. This can be useful for managing similar widgets or organizing objects to help the user navigate their way around the GUI or simply to add decoration and space between widgets. QFrame, QGroupBox, QStackedWidget, and QTabWidget are just some of the container classes, and each one has unique features for controlling groups of objects. Widgets grouped inside a container also need to be arranged using a layout manager which will be discussed a little later in this chapter.

For our project, the `PomodoroTimer` class inherits from `QWidget`. After setting the window's minimum size and window title and icon in `initializeUI()`, we need to create a number of variables for keeping track of which tab the user is currently viewing as well as the user's current task. If the user switches to another tab, we will need to update the variables.

When the program begins, the user will always start on the Pomodoro tab. Therefore, the following variables from Listing 1-1 are initialized to begin with values related to this tab:

```
# Each tab has an index value. The first tab is 0.
self.current_tab_selected = 0
self.current_start_button = self.pomodoro_start_button
self.current_stop_button = self.pomodoro_stop_button
self.current_reset_button = self.pomodoro_reset_button
self.current_time_limit = self.pomodoro_limit
self.current_lcd = self.pomodoro_lcd
```

Other variables, `task_is_set`, `number_of_tasks`, and `task_complete_counter`, are also instantiated. Since there is no task created when the program begins, `task_is_set` equals `False`.

The next step is to set up the tab bar and each tab in the `setupTabsAndWidgets()` method. To use `QTabWidget`, we first create an instance of the tab widget, `tab_bar`, and create the `QWidget` containers for each tab, also referred to as a page. The following snippets of code from Listing 1-1 show how to set up the tab widget:

```
self.tab_bar = QTabWidget(self)
self.pomodoro_tab = QWidget()
```

Next, we add the tab to `tab_bar` with `addTab()` and give the tab a name:

```
self.tab_bar.addTab(self.pomodoro_tab, "Pomodoro")
```

Then, we call the functions that contain the widgets for each page:

```
self.pomodoroTab()
```

This process is repeated for `short_break_tab` and `long_break_tab`. In the `pomodoroTab()` method, the `QLCDNumber` and `QPushButton` objects are created. We begin by calling `calculateDisplayTime()` to convert the `pomodoro_limit` from 1500000 milliseconds to a more readable 25:00 (minutes and seconds). The value returned, `start_time`, is shown in the `QLCDNumber` object using `display()`. Other tabs are also similarly structured.

Although these tabs are alike, three separate methods with their own display and button widgets are created. This ensures that the correct tab has ownership of only the widgets related to its page.

Finally, let's take a brief look at where the user can enter the task that they are currently working on. In the task bar, users can enter text into the `QLineEdit` widget, `enter_task_lineedit`. If `task_is_set` is `True`, then every time the Pomodoro timer (not the timers for the Short Break or Long Break) reaches 0, the `QLabel` widgets in the task bar will reflect these situations accordingly.

All of these widgets are added to the `task_bar_bg` `QGroupBox` container. You can assign a label to a QGroupBox object that is visible to the user. The following code from Listing 1-1 shows how:

```
task_bar_gb = QGroupBox("Tasks")
```

In order to know when to update the `QLCDNumber` displays and other widgets, we need a way to keep track of the time that has passed since starting a timer.

The QTimer Class

Whenever you begin running your application, `QApplication.exec_()` begins the main event loop. Inside of this loop is where all of your program's event checking, updating of widgets, and other tasks occur. We can take advantage of this loop to create timers for processing events at regular intervals or after a specified amount of time has passed.

QTimer is the main PyQt class for creating regular timers. For the Pomodoro Timer, we create a `timer` instance that is a child of the `PomodoroTimer` class. This is done by passing `self` as an argument to the timer. We can use `timeout()` to call a method to perform some task when the time reaches zero. In this case, timeout() calls updateTimer(), and the current_lcd will then be updated to reflect the time remaining for the current_tab_selected. The following bit of code from Listing 1-1 shows this process. Check out the "Event Handling with Signals and Slots" section to learn more about signals and slots and connect():

```
self.timer = QTimer(self) # Create timer object
self.timer.timeout.connect(self.updateTimer) # Connect the QTimer's signal,
timeout(), to a slot
```

When the user clicks the Start button in any of the tabs, the timer begins running. The timer in Listing 1-1 is set to time out every 1000 milliseconds, or one second. This is handled in startCountDown():

```
self.timer.start(1000)
```

So the basic pattern for using a QTimer object is to

1.   Create an instance of QTimer.

2.   Connect the timer to timeout().

3.   start() the timer.

The updateTimer() method in the Pomodoro Timer is also used to keep track of how many pomodoros have been completed. If the user has finished four cycles, a label is displayed in the window advising them to take a longer break.

Only one timer is created for this application, and it is shared between the three different tabs. timer is started, stopped, and reset as needed and depending upon the current_tab_selected.

Layout Management

Layout management is the manner in which we decide to arrange widgets in the application's window. PyQt provides a few different layout manager classes for organizing widgets – QBoxLayout, QGridLayout, and QFormLayout. While these classes each have their own rules, they are useful for handling sizing and positioning of widgets; resizing, adding, or removing widgets; and using the space within a window efficiently. PyQt also allows for nested layouts, giving you better control and more versatility for arranging objects.

QBoxLayout can be divided into two subclasses:

1. QHBoxLayout for arranging widgets horizontally in the window

2. QVBoxLayout for organizing widgets vertically in the window

The Pomodoro Timer application uses a combination of these two classes to organize its widgets. Let's take a look at a simplified version from Listing 1-1 of how we create a nested layout using both the QHBoxLayout and QVBoxLayout classes in the Pomodoro tab:

```
button_h_box = QHBoxLayout() # Horizontal box layout
# Add widgets to a layout using addWidget()
button_h_box.addWidget(self.pomodoro_start_button)

# Create vertical box layout for the pomodoro tab
v_box = QVBoxLayout()
v_box.addWidget(self.pomodoro_lcd)
v_box.addLayout(button_h_box) # Nested layout
self.pomodoro_tab.setLayout(v_box)
```

This bit of code is simplified in order to only show the main steps for creating the layout managers and adding widgets to the correct layout. Use addWidget() to add widgets to a layout; use addLayout() to create nested layouts. Depending upon what manager you are using, the methods may change for adding widgets to a layout. However, the procedure is still the same:

1. Create a layout manager object.

2. Add widgets and other layouts (if necessary) to the current layout. There are also methods available for adding spacing and stretching to a layout such as addSpacing().

3. Set the layout of the widget. This widget could possibly be a container widget or the main window.

Widgets in the Pomodoro Timer for each tab as well as the task bar at the bottom of the window are added to layouts in a similar fashion.

Event Handling with Signals and Slots

GUIs are designed to be responsive. When a user clicks a button, types on the keyboard, or when a timer times out, these actions signal **events** and must be handled by the application. These events can often lead the program to modify its behavior. Event handling in PyQt is performed with the signals and slots mechanism and with special event handlers.

Signals are the events that are triggered when a button is clicked or a tab is switched. **Slots** are the methods that perform defined actions in response to the signal. Slots can be built-in PyQt functions or Python methods created specifically for the application. The `connect()` method associates the emitted signal with its intended slot. An example of connecting to a signal from Listing 1-1 is accomplished by

```
self.tab_bar.currentChanged.connect(self.tabsSwitched)
```

The Pomodoro Timer needs to handle events caused when

- The user switches tabs. The `tab_bar` uses the `currentChanged()` signal to update the variables and widgets related to the `current_tab_selected` in the `tabsSwitched()` slot.

- The Start, Stop, or Reset button is clicked on any of the pages. These buttons all emit the `clicked()` signal. Start buttons are connected to the `startCountDown()` slot and begin the timer. Stop buttons are connected to `stopCountDown()` and stop the timer. Reset is connected to `resetCountDown()` and resets the timer and LCD display for the current tab.

- The buttons for adding or deleting tasks in the task bar are clicked. The `confirm_task_button` sends a signal that is connected to `addTaskToTaskbar()`. This adds a task in the task bar only if the user has entered text in `enter_task_lineedit`. If a task exists, then the user can delete that task using the `cancel_task_button`.

- The timer times out. The `timeout()` signal is connected to `updateTimer()`. The slot first checks if the `remaining_time` is 00:00. If it is, the appropriate variables and widgets are updated. If not, the `current_time_limit` is decreased by 1000 milliseconds and updated in the `current_lcd_display`.

While you can use built-in signals and slots, you can also customize your own in PyQt. You have already seen in this project how to create custom slots.

PyQt also delivers events to widgets using predefined event handlers. One example is the show() method for displaying the window. Event handlers are used for responding to mouse movements, the pressing of keys, window operations, and more. An example of customizing event handlers is demonstrated in Chapter 2.

Qt Style Sheets

The last tool we are going to consider is useful for customizing the look and feel of your applications. PyQt uses the QStyle class to mimic the appearance of your platform. A single application created using PyQt will look different on Windows, Mac, or Linux without you having to write any additional code. However, you can still modify the look of a GUI by either creating a custom style or using **Qt Style Sheets** and applying customized styles on top of a widget's current style.

The format for Qt Style Sheets resembles that of HTML Cascading Style Sheets (CSS) and is adapted for use in GUI programs. You can apply style sheets either to an entire QApplication or individual widgets using the setStyleSheet() method.

When we imported modules at the beginning of Listing 1-1, you might have noticed the following line of code:

```
from PomodoroStyleSheet import style_sheet
```

PomodoroStyleSheet is simply a Python script that contains the style_sheet for the Pomodoro Timer. The style sheet code can be seen in Listing 1-3. For information about where the styles are applied, have a look at the comments in the code. Comments in CSS begin with /* and end with */.

To apply the style sheet in Listing 1-1, we use

```
app.setStyleSheet(style_sheet)
```

With Qt Style Sheets, you are able to add quite a bit of customization to your applications. For more information or examples about Qt Style Sheets, refer to https://doc.qt.io/qt-5/stylesheet.html.

Note   This project illustrates how detailed a style sheet can get. Programs in later chapters will only use style sheets for minor instances and will leave the task of stylizing them up to you.

Listing 1-3. The CSS code for the style sheet used in the Pomodoro Timer project[3]

```
# PomodoroStyleSheet.py
# Style sheet for the Pomodoro Timer GUI
style_sheet = """
    QWidget{
        background-color: #D8D3D3 /* background for main window */
    }

    QTabWidget:pane{ /* The tab widget frame */
        border-top: 0px /* width of 0 pixels */
    }

    QTabBar:tab{ /* Style the tabs using tab sub-control and QTabBar */
        /* Add gradient look to the colors of each tab */
        background: qlineargradient(x1: 0, y1: 0, x2: 0, y2: 1,
                        stop: 0 #E1E1E1, stop: 0.4 #DDDDDD,
                        stop: 0.5 #D8D8D8, stop: 1.0 #D3D3D3);
        border: 2px solid #C4C4C3;
        border-bottom-color: #C2C7CB;
        border-top-left-radius: 4px;
        border-top-right-radius: 4px;
        min-width: 8ex;
        padding: 2px;
    }
```

---

[3]Parts of the style sheet were influenced by https://doc.qt.io/qt-5/stylesheet-examples.html.

```
QTabBar:tab:selected, QTabBar:tab:hover {
    /* Use same color scheme for selected tab, and other tabs when the
    user hovers over them */
    background: qlineargradient(x1: 0, y1: 0, x2: 0, y2: 1,
                    stop: 0 #FAFAFA, stop: 0.4 #F4F4F4,
                    stop: 0.5 #E7E7E7, stop: 1.0 #FAFAFA);
}

QTabBar:tab:selected {
    border-color: #9B9B9B;
    border-bottom-color: #C2C7CB; /* Same as pane color */
}

QTabBar:tab:!selected {
    margin-top: 2px; /* Make non-selected tabs look smaller when not
    selected */
}

QWidget#Pomodoro{ /* Pomodoro tab container widget */
    background-color: #EF635C;
    border: 1px solid #EF635C;
    border-radius: 4px;
}

QWidget#ShortBreak{ /* Short break tab container widget */
    background-color: #398AB5;
    border: 1px solid #398AB5;
    border-radius: 4px;
}

QWidget#LongBreak{ /* Long break tab container widget */
    background-color: #55A992;
    border: 1px solid #55A992;
    border-radius: 4px;
}
```

```
QLCDNumber#PomodoroLCD{
    background-color: #F48B86;
    color: #FFFFFF;
    border: 2px solid #F48B86;
    border-radius: 4px;
}

QLCDNumber#ShortLCD{
    background-color: #5CAFDC;
    color: #FFFFFF;
    border: 2px solid #5CAFDC;
    border-radius: 4px;
}

QLCDNumber#LongLCD{
    background-color: #6DD4B7;
    color: #FFFFFF;
    border: 2px solid #6DD4B7;
    border-radius: 4px;
}

QPushButton{ /* General look of QPushButtons */
    background-color: #E1E1E1;
    border: 2px solid #C4C4C3;
    border-radius: 4px;
}

QPushButton:hover{
    background-color: #F8F4F4
}

QPushButton:pressed{
    background-color: #E9E9E9;
    border: 2px solid #C4C4C3;
    border-radius: 4px;
}
```

```
    QPushButton:disabled{
        background-color: #D8D3D3;
        border: 2px solid #C4C4C3;
        border-radius: 4px;
    }

    QGroupBox{ /* Style for Pomodoro task bar */
        background-color: #EF635C;
        border: 2px solid #EF635C;
        border-radius: 4px;
        margin-top: 3ex
    }

    QGroupBox:title{
        subcontrol-origin: margin;
        padding: 2px;
    }

    QLineEdit{
        background-color: #FFFFFF
    }

    QLabel{
        background-color: #EF635C;
        color: #FFFFFF
    }
"""
```

Changing the appearance of widgets can be very useful for helping a user differentiate between objects and widget states and for more easily navigating around the GUI. With style sheets, you can change a widget's properties, pseudostates, and subcontrols. Some of the properties that can be modified include a widget's background and foreground colors, fonts, border width and style, or margins. To change the subcontrols of a complex widget, be sure to specify the subcontrol you want to adjust in the style sheet. For example, to restrict changes only to an unselected tab of QTabBar in Listing 1-3, you can use

```
QTabBar:tab:!selected {/* Other CSS code */}
```

In Listing 1-1, the `setObjectName()` method is included after selecting widgets to give each object a specific name, for example:

```
self.pomodoro_lcd.setObjectName("PomodoroLCD")
```

The object name can be used in the style sheet in Listing 1-3 to apply properties only to that particular widget:

```
QLCDNumber#PomodoroLCD{/* Other CSS code */}
```

For this chapter's next project, we are going to take a look at a few other important concepts, namely, creating menus, dialog boxes, and Qt's model/view paradigm.

Project 1.2: User Manager Application

There are many applications that exist for managing the personal data of their clients. The general UI allows users to view and modify their individual information. Meanwhile, administrators who manage the application may be given extra privileges that allow them to view, edit, and update a client's information, assign and create groups for organizing clients, and even disable others' accounts.

This information can be presented to the administrator in a number of formats. For the User Manager GUI shown in Figure 1-4, you will take a look at building a simple interface that demonstrates how to create tables using PyQt and Python classes. This project is just the foundation for what could be a much larger project.

In the next couple of sections, you will learn about

- PyQt's model/view architecture and classes for working with data

- Using menus and the `QAction` class

- The difference between windows and dialogs and how to use `QDialog`

- Other widget and layout classes, particularly `QComboBox` and `QFormLayout`

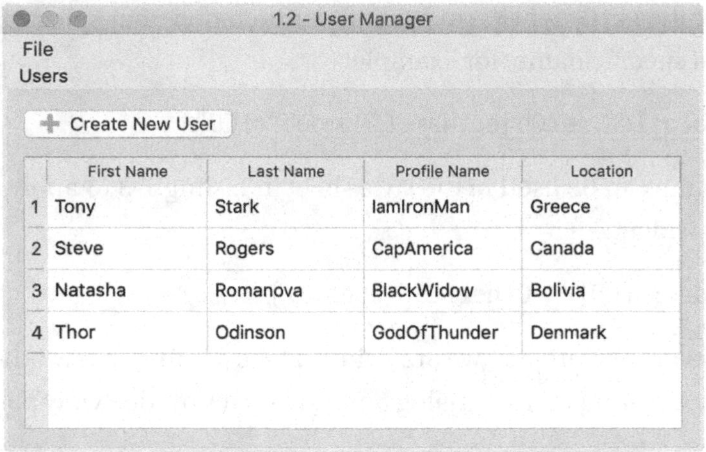

Figure 1-4. *The User Manager GUI*

User Manager Application Solution

When the user opens the application, they are presented with a window similar to Figure 1-4. However, the table will be empty. Listing 1-4 shows how to create a table and add information into its rows and columns.

The user can click the Create New User button in the window. This will open up a separate dialog box, shown in Figure 1-6, where the user can input their information using QLineEdit and QComboBox widgets. After the user is finished entering data into the table, they can choose to save the data or quit the program using the actions in the File menu.

Listing 1-4. Code for the User Manager application

```
# user_manager.py
# Import necessary modules
import sys, csv
from PyQt5.QtWidgets import (QApplication, QMainWindow, QPushButton,
QLineEdit, QComboBox, QGroupBox, QTableView, QHeaderView, QHBoxLayout,
QFormLayout, QVBoxLayout, QDialog, QFileDialog, QAction)
from PyQt5.QtGui import QIcon, QStandardItem, QStandardItemModel
from PyQt5.QtCore import Qt
```

```
style_sheet = """
    QGroupBox:title{
        subcontrol-origin: margin;
        padding: 0 10px;
    } """

class UserManager(QMainWindow):

    def __init__(self):
        super().__init__()
        self.initializeUI()

    def initializeUI(self):
        """Initialize the window and display its contents to the screen. """
        self.setGeometry(100, 100, 500, 300)
        self.setWindowTitle('1.2 - User Manager')

        self.setupModelView()
        self.setupMenu()
        self.show()

    def setupModelView(self):
        """Set up widgets, and standard item model and table view."""
        user_gb = QGroupBox("Users")

        new_user_button = QPushButton(QIcon("images/plus.png"), "Create New
User")
        new_user_button.setMaximumWidth(160)
        new_user_button.clicked.connect(self.createNewUserDialog)

        self.list_of_table_headers = ["First Name", "Last Name", "Profile
Name", "Location"]

        self.model = QStandardItemModel()
        self.model.setHorizontalHeaderLabels(self.list_of_table_headers)

        table_view = QTableView()
        table_view.setModel(self.model)
        table_view.horizontalHeader().setSectionResizeMode(QHeaderView.
Stretch)
```

```python
        # Set initial row and column values
        self.model.setRowCount(0)
        self.model.setColumnCount(4)

        v_box = QVBoxLayout()
        v_box.addWidget(new_user_button, Qt.AlignLeft)
        v_box.addWidget(table_view)

        user_gb.setLayout(v_box)
        self.setCentralWidget(user_gb)

    def setupMenu(self):
        """Set up menubar."""
        # Create actions for file menu
        save_act = QAction('Save', self)
        save_act.setShortcut('Ctrl+S')
        save_act.triggered.connect(self.saveTableToFile)

        exit_act = QAction('Exit', self)
        exit_act.setShortcut('Ctrl+Q')
        exit_act.triggered.connect(self.close)

        # Create menubar
        menu_bar = self.menuBar()
        # For MacOS users, places menu bar in main window
        menu_bar.setNativeMenuBar(False)

        # Create file menu and add actions
        file_menu = menu_bar.addMenu('File')
        file_menu.addAction(save_act)
        file_menu.addSeparator()
        file_menu.addAction(exit_act)

    def createNewUserDialog(self):
        """Set up the dialog box that allows the user to enter new user
        information."""
        self.new_user_dialog = QDialog(self)
        self.new_user_dialog.setWindowTitle("Create New User")
        self.new_user_dialog.setModal(True)
```

```python
        self.enter_first_line = QLineEdit()
        self.enter_last_line = QLineEdit()
        self.display_name_line = QLineEdit()

        locations_list = ["Select Location...", "Algeria", "Argentina",
        "Bolivia", "Canada", "Denmark", "Greece", "Iran", "Liberia", "New
        Zealand", "Qatar", "Uganda"]

        self.location_cb = QComboBox()
        self.location_cb.addItems(locations_list)

        create_button = QPushButton("Create User")
        create_button.clicked.connect(self.addNewUserToTable)
        cancel_button = QPushButton("Cancel")
        cancel_button.clicked.connect(self.new_user_dialog.reject)

        button_h_box = QHBoxLayout()
        button_h_box.addWidget(create_button)
        button_h_box.addSpacing(15)
        button_h_box.addWidget(cancel_button)

        # Add widgets to form layout
        dialog_form = QFormLayout()
        dialog_form.setFormAlignment(Qt.AlignLeft)
        dialog_form.setFieldGrowthPolicy(QFormLayout.ExpandingFieldsGrow)
        dialog_form.addRow("First name", self.enter_first_line)
        dialog_form.addRow("Last name", self.enter_last_line)
        dialog_form.addRow("Display Name", self.display_name_line)
        dialog_form.addRow("Location", self.location_cb)
        dialog_form.addItem(button_h_box)

        self.new_user_dialog.setLayout(dialog_form)

        # Restrict the size of the dialog in relation to the size of the
        dialog_form's sizeHint()
        self.new_user_dialog.setMaximumSize(dialog_form.sizeHint())
        self.new_user_dialog.show()
```

```python
    def addNewUserToTable(self):
        """Add information from input widgets in dialog box to a list. If a
        widget is empty, append None to the list. Finally, add a new row to
        the table."""
        new_user_info_list = []

        if self.enter_first_line.text() != "":
            new_user_info_list.append(QStandardItem(self.enter_first_line.
            text()))
        else:
            new_user_info_list.append(None)
        if self.enter_last_line.text() != "":
            new_user_info_list.append(QStandardItem(self.enter_last_line.
            text()))
        else:
            new_user_info_list.append(None)
        if self.display_name_line.text() != "":
            new_user_info_list.append(QStandardItem(self.display_name_line.
            text()))
        else:
            new_user_info_list.append(None)
        if self.location_cb.currentIndex() != 0:
            new_user_info_list.append(QStandardItem(self.location_
            cb.currentText()))
        else:
            new_user_info_list.append(None)

        # Add a new row to the model
        self.model.appendRow(new_user_info_list)
        self.new_user_dialog.close()

    def saveTableToFile(self):
        """Save user information to a csv file."""
        file_name, _ = QFileDialog.getSaveFileName(self, 'Save Table', "",
        "CSV Files (*.csv)")
```

```
    # If file_name exists and there is at least one row in the table,
    then save
    if file_name and self.model.rowCount() != 0:
        with open(file_name, "w") as csv_wf:
            user_writer = csv.writer(csv_wf, delimiter=',')
            user_writer.writerow(self.list_of_table_headers)

            # Iterate through each row and column in the table for row
            in range(self.model.rowCount()):
                current_row_list = []
                for column in range(self.model.columnCount()):
                    item = str(self.model.data(self.model.index(row,
                    column)))
                    current_row_list.append(item)
                user_writer.writerow(current_row_list)

if __name__ == '__main__':
    app = QApplication(sys.argv)
    app.setStyleSheet(style_sheet)
    window = UserManager()
    sys.exit(app.exec_())
```

The completed User Manager's interface can be seen in Figure 1-4.

Explanation

We begin by importing the Python and PyQt5 packages. The csv module provides classes for reading and writing tabular data in Comma-Separated Values (CSV) format.

From QtWidgets, we import classes for widgets such as QLineEdit and QComboBox; QTableView and QHeaderView for creating and working with tables; layout classes including QFormLayout; classes for building windows and menus, QMainWindow and QAction; and QDialog and QFileDialog for creating dialog boxes.

The QtGui module contains the classes QStandardItem and QStandardItemModel needed for using Qt's model/view paradigm for arranging and displaying data.

The next step is to begin building the constructor for the UserManager class. This time, our class will inherit from QMainWindow, not QWidget. First, initialize the window's location and size on your computer with setGeometry(). Then use setWindowTitle() to set the GUI's title. show() will display the window on the user's screen.

To create the GUI's tabular view, this application uses Qt's model/view programming architecture.

Qt's Model/View Architecture

PyQt provides three convenience widgets for presenting data to a user in QTableWidget, QListWidget, and QTreeWidget. Whether you want to display information in a table, in a list, or in a hierarchical format using trees, these classes already contain all the basic functionality you need for working with data.

However, if you want more control and customizability for both the appearance and editing of data in larger projects or need to display data using different formats at the same time, then you should consider Qt's model/view architecture. **Model/view programming** separates the work for handling data among three components and gives more flexibility to developers for how they present the data. The three components are

- **Model** – Responsible for communicating with the data source, accessing data, and linking the data with view and delegate classes

- **View** – Handles displaying data to the user using a list, table, or tree format, retrieving data from the model, and working with input from the user

- **Delegate** – In charge of painting data items and providing editor widgets in the view. Reports back to the model if data has been edited in the view, allowing the model to update the data source

The User Manager program uses the QStandardItemModel model class and the QTableView view class. For this GUI, the default delegate class, QStyledItemDelegate, is used.

In the setupModelView() method, the user_gb QGroupBox will contain all of the main window's widgets. If the user clicks the new_user_button, it will send a signal that calls the createNewUserDialog() slot.

Building the model/view table is straightforward. First, create a model object:

```
self.model = QStandardItemModel()
```

You can also create labels for both the horizontal and vertical headers. To set the horizontal header's labels, use setHorizontalHeaderLabels(). This method accepts a Python iterable object as an argument.

Next, we can create the view object and set the model using setModel():

```
table_view = QTableView()
table_view.setModel(self.model)
```

You can also make the horizontal and vertical headers resize to fit the view and set the number of rows and columns of the table. Items can be added to the table using QStandardItem. Examples of how to append items and rows to the table can be seen in the program's addNewUserToTable() method.

Finally, QVBoxLayout is utilized to organize the widgets in user_gb. When using QMainWindow, use setCentralWidget() to set the main window's widget. The central widget must be set for the QMainWindow class.

This example only demonstrates QTableView, but there are also QListView, QTreeView, and many other model and delegate classes. More detailed information related to model/view programming can be found at https://doc.qt.io/qt-5/model-view-programming.html.

Creating Menus

The more complex a GUI becomes, the more widgets and features you will need to add to the application's window. If you are not careful, your GUI can become crowded with too many features. Thankfully, menus are a great way for organizing and tracking down all of those components.

There are handful of menu types that you can employ, such as menu bars, toolbars, context menus, and dock widgets, each with their own special purposes. By creating a class that inherits from QMainWindow, developers have access to these classes and the framework for easily building and managing a GUI's main window.

The User Manager's setupMenu() method illustrates how to create a simple menu bar. Since menus consist of a collection of items for opening and saving files, undoing actions, or closing an application, we need a way to manage all of these different tasks. Luckily, the QAction class defines actions for menus and toolbars and does the managing for us. For this project, we only need to create the foundation for the menu bar.

The following code creates the save_act QAction in the menu, sets the shortcut hot keys, and connects the action to the saveTableToFile() slot when the user triggers the signal in the menu bar:

```
save_act = QAction('Save', self)
save_act.setShortcut('Ctrl+S')
save_act.triggered.connect(self.saveTableToFile)
```

We can create the `menu_bar` object using `menuBar()` and individual menus in the menu bar with `addMenu()`. To add our save action to the File menu, use the `addAction()` method. The `save_act` triggers the `saveTableToFile()` slot, opening up a dialog box to enter a `file_name`. If `file_name` is not empty and there is at least one row in the table, then `csv.writer()` writes each row to the output file using CSV format. An example of the output file is shown in Figure 1-5.

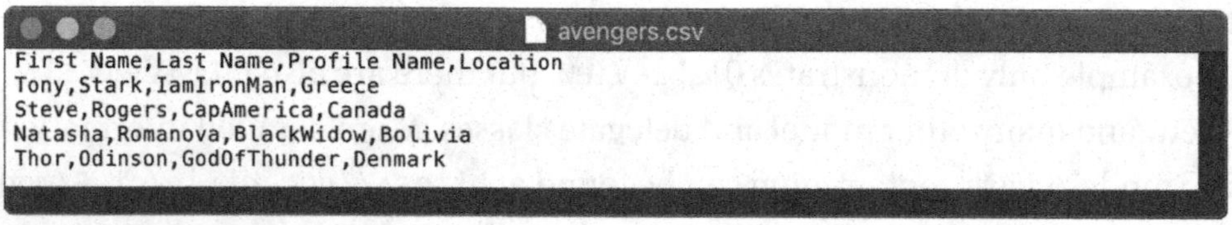

avengers.csv

```
First Name,Last Name,Profile Name,Location
Tony,Stark,IamIronMan,Greece
Steve,Rogers,CapAmerica,Canada
Natasha,Romanova,BlackWidow,Bolivia
Thor,Odinson,GodOfThunder,Denmark
```

Figure 1-5. *Output file for the User Manager using CSV format*

Windows and Dialog Boxes

With Qt, any widget that is not placed inside of a parent widget is considered a **window**. The main window of an application can consist of a menu bar, a status bar, and other widgets and serves as the principal interface that the user sees. **Dialog boxes** are useful for prompting the user for feedback about how to handle a situation; they are the small pop-ups that you see when you close an application or when an error is encountered.

PyQt has some built-in dialogs for handling different circumstances. QMessageBox creates general dialogs to display information to the user and get their feedback through buttons. QFileDialog is useful for selecting local files or directories on your computer. The QDialog class is the base class for all dialog boxes and can be used to create custom dialogs. Other dialog classes will be introduced throughout the book.

Dialog boxes can be either **modal**, where the user cannot interact with the rest of the program until the box is closed, or **modeless**, where interaction is not blocked even if the dialog is still open.

When the `new_user_button` is clicked in the main window, a dialog box like the one in Figure 1-6 is shown to the user. The `QDialog` object is created in the `createNewUserDialog()` method:

```
self.new_user_dialog = QDialog(self)
```

Passing `self` as an argument makes the dialog box a child of the parent window.

Figure 1-6. *The dialog box for entering a new user's information*

The QLabel, QLineEdit, and QComboBox widgets are instantiated and arranged in the dialog using a combination of QFormLayout and QHBoxLayout. Adding multiple items to a QComboBox is simple with addItems() and Python lists. The drop-down list can be seen in Figure 1-7.

Widgets are added to a QFormLayout as a combination of a label and an object using addRow(). For example, the First name label and corresponding widget are added by

```
dialog_form.addRow("First name", self.enter_first_line)
```

The buttons, Create User and Cancel, are added to the bottom of the dialog with the addItem() method. If the Create User button is clicked, then text from the input widgets is added to a list, and that list is added to the table using appendRow(). The dialog box is then closed.

Figure 1-7. *Example of a drop-down QComboBox for the Create New User dialog*

Summary

PyQt is a great toolkit for making cross-platform graphical user interface applications. By combining the simplicity of Python code and the vast number of modules that already exist with the large number of widgets and customizability found in Qt, you are able to create some unique programs.

In this chapter, you took a look at two different projects to help summarize some of the main concepts for creating interfaces with PyQt. The first application, the Pomodoro Timer, demonstrates how you can use PyQt's signals and slots to create widgets that communicate and update their states or appearance based upon events caused either by the user or the application's internal workings. You were also introduced to a number of useful PyQt modules and classes for layout management, containers, creating timers, and styling widgets.

The second GUI application introduced a few key ideas that we will expound upon in further chapters as we go over SQL databases and data analysis topics, especially the model/view paradigm and creating menus.

Of course, there are still plenty of topics that were not covered in this chapter. In Chapter 2, we will continue to explore the idea of creating GUIs for managing projects using PyQt's drag and drop mechanics.

CHAPTER 2

Creating GUIs for Project Management

We all have projects that need our time and attention. Some of these tasks may be personal, perhaps finding time to write a novel or learning a new programming language. Others may be work related, such as helping to build your company's website or launching a new product. To organize and prioritize assignments, we need some way to keep track of their progress.

An important thing to remember is that all of those projects are only temporary ventures. They have a beginning and an end. By managing different resources – time, manpower, financial, risk, and others – you or your company can hope to create unique services, products, or results.

Project management allows us to apply our knowledge, skills, and tools to these projects so that we can meet defined goals. Thankfully, modern technology has given us new ways to better utilize our time and assets. Existing applications already help us to formulate our ideas, begin working on different steps of the plan, collaborate, manage teams and assign tasks to specific members, track progress and provide feedback, and see it all through until completion.

The general process for project management is as follows:

1. Conceptualize and initiate the project.

2. Define and plan the project by setting goals, creating a schedule, and communicating with others, if necessary.

3. Execute the steps needed to create the project as sketched out in the plan, and allow for some leeway when needed.

4. Monitor, control, and provide feedback about the performance and quality of the project.

5. Complete the project and maintain or update.

© Joshua Willman 2021
J. Willman, *Modern PyQt*, https://doi.org/10.1007/978-1-4842-6603-8_2

The user interfaces created for project management applications come in an array of different styles. They may include buttons, tables, charts or graphs, calendars, and an assortment of other features that allow for team members to keep track of a project's progress. One feature that is key to many intuitive and responsive GUIs, especially for project management applications, is the drag and drop mechanism.

This chapter begins to examine and use this important tool to give you ideas about how to apply it to your own desktop and mobile applications. You will

- Understand how to apply drag and drop using PyQt in order to

    - Drag and drop images from your computer onto PyQt widgets.

    - Drag and drop widgets onto other PyQt objects.

    - Build a simple project management GUI.

- Learn about the `QDrag` and `QMimeData` classes.

- Find out how to subclass PyQt widget classes.

- See how to reimplement PyQt event handlers.

While this chapter does discuss some of the topics that pertain to project management, the main focus is on the drag and drop system using PyQt. Project management serves as the backdrop to help us visualize and code examples where drag and drop operations can be applied.

The Basics of Drag and Drop

With the **drag and drop** mechanism, virtual objects can be "grabbed" using the pointer and dragged across the screen onto a new location, where the objects are then dropped, bringing about some predefined action. If designed correctly, this creates an intuitive interface that can speed up the time it takes to complete repetitive tasks. Common drag and drop examples include

- Moving or copying files between folders or directories

- Selecting and dragging text

- Rearranging widgets in a GUI to customize its layout

- Dragging a color, or some other attribute, onto a graphical object to change its appearance

- Rearranging the tabs in a web browser

GUIs can often suffer if there are no clear indications about which items are draggable or where objects can be dropped. A well-designed GUI that uses drag and drop will give clear visual cues about objects that can be grabbed, relay feedback to the user that an object is being dragged, and indicate the location of drop zones. A few frequently used graphical prompts are

- Using distinct colors, outlines, or borders to identify drag and drop choices.

- Adding textual notes on target locations.

- Specifying particular state styles for when an item is being dragged. This can be accomplished using style sheets.

- Changing the look of the mouse cursor when hovering over an object that can be dragged.

- Displaying drop zones using placeholder visuals after a user begins dragging an item. Placeholder locations can be outlined with dashed or dotted lines.

Of course, these are only some of the visual options you could use in your own programs. One important thing to remember is to always use consistent cues throughout your application.

Drag and Drop with PyQt

Drag and drop provides an intuitive mechanism for copying or moving information from one window to another or even within the same window. For the applications created using PyQt, many of the widgets already contain some support for drag and drop operations. For example, QTextEdit objects already support drag and drop for plain text, rich text, and HTML formats. In addition, the item views that are part of Qt's model/view framework and graphics view classes also include drag and drop functionality.

45

For some widgets, enabling drag and drop is as simple as calling two methods, setAcceptDrops() and setDragEnabled(), and setting their values equal to True. This is illustrated in the Listing 2-1 for QTableWidget.

Listing 2-1. Simple code to set up drag and drop capabilities

```
table_widget = QTableWidget()
table_widget.setAcceptDrops(True)
table_widget.setDragEnabled(True)
```

However, not all widgets inherit these methods. For example, you can call setAcceptDrops() on QLabel objects, but there is no setDragEnabled() function. For situations like these, if the widget you want to use lacks drag or drop functionality (or you want to modify these behaviors), then you may need to reimplement certain event handlers.

Since drag is normally initiated when a user clicks an item, you will need to consider modifying the following functions:

- mousePressEvent() – Event triggered when the user clicks a widget

- mouseMoveEvent() – Used when a widget is moved

- mouseReleaseEvent() – Event generated when the mouse button is released

The following are for handling events as drag and drop actions enter the target area:

- dragEnterEvent() – Event called as the dragging action is in progress and the mouse enters the target widget

- dragMoveEvent() – Used when drag is in progress and the cursor enters the target widget or when the cursor moves inside of the widget

- dragLeaveEvent() – Called when a drag is in progress and the mouse leaves the area of the target widget

- dropEvent() – Event called when the dragged object is dropped on the target widget

When data is finally dropped onto the target area, the developer needs to decide how to handle the event. If the data is accepted, then use Qt.DropAction flags to decide whether the data is moved from the source to the target with Qt.MoveAction or copied with Qt.CopyAction or select some other action. Otherwise, if the item is not accepted, then use functions such as ignore() or set setAccepted() to False to reject the drag and drop operation.

The QDrag and QMimeData Classes

Since we will be creating our own drag and drop features in this chapter, it is important to learn a little about the QDrag and QMimeData classes. The data that can be moved in or between applications can take on various formats: plain or formatted text, documents, images, videos, sound files, color data, and more. In order to determine what kind of data is moving around, the Multipurpose Internet Mail Extensions (MIME) format is used to identify an object's content type.

The **QMimeData** class acts as the container that is used to link the type of data stored in the clipboard or transferred using drag and drop with its compatible MIME type. QMimeData handles the different data types and allows for data to be safely moved and copied between and within applications.

What **QDrag** does is provide support for transferring QMimeData objects using drag and drop operations. The drag and drop system in PyQt revolves around the QDrag class. In Listing 2-2, you can see how the QDrag object takes ownership of the QMimeData object with setMimeData().

Listing 2-2. Setting up QDrag and QMimeData

```
drag = QDrag(self) # Create QDrag object
mimedata = QMimeData() # Create QMimeData object

mimedata.setText(self.text()) # Data type is plain text
drag.setMimeData(mimedata) # Assign mimedata
# exec_() begins the drag and drop operation with specified drop action(s)
drag.exec_(Qt.MoveAction)
```

If the dragged object is dropped onto a target area that accepts text data types, then the drop is accepted. Otherwise, the drop will fail.

In the following two sections, you will see how to create two separate example GUIs with drag and drop functionality, one that demonstrates how to accept drops from external sources and the other that shows how to create draggable items and drop zones using PyQt widgets.

Example 2.1: Drag and Drop Data from Other Sources

An important feature of many modern GUIs is the ability to drag data, such as text or images, into an application from other sources. This is a very common feature of web browsers, photo editing applications, and media players.

A good idea for smart GUI design is to inform the user of areas within the window where they can drag and drop, or even import, images or other types of data. It is important to clearly indicate a drop zone like in Figure 2-1. This can be achieved using a variety of different techniques. For the following example in Listing 2-3, you will see how to

- Subclass PyQt widgets to give them drag and drop capabilities.

- Use Qt Style Sheets to create visual indicators of drop zones.

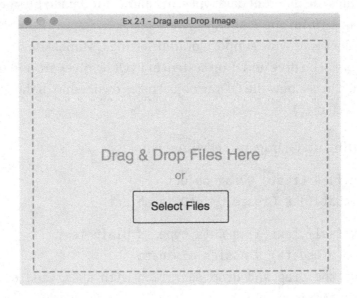

Figure 2-1. *Example of a QLabel widget that acts as a drop zone to display image files*

Since QLabel widgets can be used for displaying text, images, or movies, label objects are ideal for acting as drop areas.

Listing 2-3. Code that demonstrates how to drag images from other sources onto PyQt widgets

```python
# drag_drop_image.py
# Import necessary modules
import sys
from PyQt5.QtWidgets import (QApplication, QWidget, QLabel, QPushButton,
QVBoxLayout, QFileDialog)
from PyQt5.QtGui import QPixmap
from PyQt5.QtCore import Qt

style_sheet = """
    QLabel#TargetLabel{
        color: darkgrey;
        border: 2px dashed darkgrey;
        font: 24px 'Helvetica';
        qproperty-alignment: AlignCenter
    }

    QLabel{
        color: darkgrey;
        font: 18px 'Helvetica';
        qproperty-alignment: AlignCenter
    }

    QPushButton{
        border: 1px solid;
        border-radius: 3px;
        font: 18px 'Helvetica'
    }

    QPushButton:pressed{
        background-color: skyblue
    }"""

class TargetLabel(QLabel):

    def __init__(self):
        super().__init__()
```

```python
        # Create interface and layout
        self.setText("Drag & Drop Files Here")
        self.setObjectName("TargetLabel")

        self.or_label = QLabel("or")
        self.select_image_button = QPushButton("Select Files")
        self.select_image_button.setFixedSize(150, 50)
        self.select_image_button.clicked.connect(self.selectImageFile)

        label_v_box = QVBoxLayout()
        label_v_box.addStretch(3)
        label_v_box.addWidget(self.or_label)
        label_v_box.addWidget(self.select_image_button, 0, Qt.AlignCenter)
        label_v_box.addStretch(1)

        self.setLayout(label_v_box)

    def setPixmap(self, image):
        """Reimplement setPixmap() method so that images will appear on
        objects created from TargetLabel class. Hide other widgets."""
        # Method gets called on parent class. Otherwise, the image would
        not be seen.
        super().setPixmap(image)

        self.or_label.setVisible(False)
        self.select_image_button.setVisible(False)

    def selectImageFile(self):
        """Open an image file and display it on the label widget."""
        image_file, _ = QFileDialog.getOpenFileName(self, "Open Image", "",
            "JPG Files (*.jpeg *.jpg );;PNG Files (*.png);;Bitmap Files
            (*.bmp);;\
            GIF Files (*.gif)")

        if image_file:
            self.setPixmap(QPixmap(image_file))
            self.setScaledContents(True)

class DropTargetEx(QWidget):
```

```python
def __init__(self):
    super().__init__()
    self.initializeUI()

def initializeUI(self):
    """Initialize the window and display its contents to the screen. """
    self.setMinimumSize(500, 400)
    self.setWindowTitle("Ex 2.1 - Drag and Drop Image")
    self.setAcceptDrops(True)

    self.setupWidgets()
    self.show()

def setupWidgets(self):
    """Set up the label widget that will display the image after a
    drop, and the main layout."""
    self.target_label = TargetLabel()

    main_v_box = QVBoxLayout()
    main_v_box.addWidget(self.target_label)

    self.setLayout(main_v_box)

def dragEnterEvent(self, event):
    """Reimplement event handler to check the data type of an item
    being dragged onto the widget."""
    if event.mimeData().hasImage:
        event.setAccepted(True)
    else:
        event.setAccepted(False)

def dropEvent(self, event):
    """Reimplement event handler to handle when an item is dropped
    on the target. If the mimeData is an image, then the item is
    accepted."""
    if event.mimeData().hasImage:
        event.setDropAction(Qt.CopyAction)
        image_path = event.mimeData().urls()[0].toLocalFile()
        self.setImage(image_path)
```

```
            # Accept the drop action
            event.setAccepted(True)
        else:
            event.setAccepted(False)

    def setImage(self, image_file):
        """Set the label's pixmap when an item is dropped onto the target
        area."""
        self.target_label.setPixmap(QPixmap(image_file))
        self.target_label.setScaledContents(True)

if __name__ == '__main__':
    app = QApplication(sys.argv)
    app.setStyleSheet(style_sheet)
    window = DropTargetEx()
    sys.exit(app.exec_())
```

Figure 2-2 displays how the label will look after an image has been dropped onto it. Notice how the QLabel text and the QPushButton are hidden from view.

Figure 2-2. *The GUI displays an image that has been dropped onto the window using PyQt's drag and drop system*

Explanation

To get started, we are going to import sys and a few PyQt5 classes for the widgets and layouts that we need. Since we will be working with images in this example, we also need to import QPixmap from the QtGui module.

Next, let's set up a simple style sheet. If you look at Figure 2-1, you can see that there are a dashed border and text, "Drag & Drop Files Here," serving as indicators to the user that images can be dropped inside of this region. These are common methods used in many applications for indicating drop zones. Visual properties for other widgets are also applied in style_sheet.

There are two classes in this example, TargetLabel and DropTargetEx. The TargetLabel class inherits from QLabel, acts as a container for other widgets, and creates the visual cues for the drop area. We need to subclass QLabel in order to reimplement the setPixmap() method to display an image when one is dropped into the main window. If an image is dropped, then the text and button widgets are hidden by setting setVisible() to False.

Images can also be displayed in TargetLabel objects using the select_image_ button. This opens an instance of QFileDialog for the user to select local files.

The widgets in TargetLabel are all organized using a QVBoxLayout. In order to customize a layout, methods such as addStretch() can be used for adding stretchable space between widgets.

In DropTargetEx, the main window's attributes are assigned, and show() is used to display the GUI to the screen. Next, we instantiate the target_label object and arrange it in the main window in setupWidgets().

To enable drops on a widget, setAcceptDrops() needs to be set to True. The dragEnterEvent() and dropEvent() event handlers also need to be reimplemented. The dragEnterEvent() function can be used to inform PyQt about what kind of data a widget can accept. The following code from Listing 2-3 shows how to reimplement dragEnterEvent() so that our widget can only receive image data types:

```
def dragEnterEvent(self, event):
    # Check if the mimeData type from the drag event is an image. If so,
    accept the drop. Otherwise, ignore.
    if event.mimeData().hasImage:
      event.setAccepted(True)
    else:
      event.setAccepted(False)
```

In dropEvent(), if the mimeData() type is an image, then we want to copy the dropped image data from image_path. The type of drop action for the event in Listing 2-3 is assigned by

```
event.setDropAction(Qt.CopyAction)
```

The `target_label`'s pixmap is set by calling the reimplemented `setPixmap()` method. Finally, the image that is dragged into the window is scaled to fit the label's current size using `setScaledContents()`.

Example 2.2: Drag and Drop Widgets

In the first example, you saw how simple PyQt makes it to reimplement event handlers to add drag and drop functionality to widgets. Now we are going to take a look at how we can use those same ideas to create widgets that can be moved around within the same application window. Following along with this example will also make it easier to understand the Project Manager application later in this chapter.

Example 2.2 demonstrates the fundamental steps necessary for creating widgets that can be dragged and for building container classes that can receive data drops. The GUI for this program can be seen in Figure 2-3.

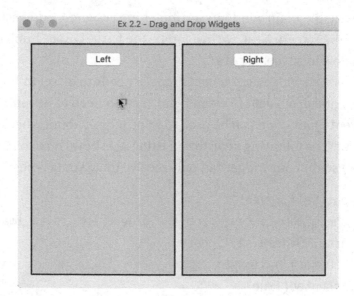

Figure 2-3. *The GUI window is made up of two containers that can handle QPushButton drops. The mouse pointer in the image is shown dragging a button into the left container. The small square under the pointer is the basic feedback that PyQt gives when a widget is being dragged*

For Listing 2-4, a simple program is created to help you understand how to subclass different PyQt classes in order to give them either drag or drop capabilities.

Listing 2-4. Demonstrates how to subclass PyQt classes and reimplement drag and drop event handlers

```python
# drag_drop_widget.py
# Import necessary modules
import sys
from PyQt5.QtWidgets import (QApplication, QWidget, QPushButton,
QHBoxLayout, QVBoxLayout, QFrame)
from PyQt5.QtGui import QDrag
from PyQt5.QtCore import Qt, QMimeData

style_sheet = """
    QFrame#Containers{
        background-color: lightgrey;
        border: 2px solid black
    }"""

# Class for objects that can be dragged
class DragButton(QPushButton):

    def __init__(self, text):
        super().__init__(text)
        self.setText(text)

    def mousePressEvent(self, event):
        """Reimplement the event handler when the object is pressed."""
        if event.button() == Qt.LeftButton:
            self.drag_start_postion = event.pos()

    def mouseMoveEvent(self, event):
        """Reimplement the event handler when the object is being dragged."""
        drag = QDrag(self) # Create drag object for MIME-based drag and drop
        mime_data = QMimeData()

        drag.setMimeData(mime_data)
        # Begins the drag and drop operation and sets the type of drop
        action
        drag.exec_(Qt.MoveAction)
```

```python
# Target: Where the dragged object is being dropped
class DropTargetWidget(QFrame):

    def __init__(self):
        super().__init__()
        # Enable drop events
        self.setAcceptDrops(True)
        self.setObjectName("Containers")

        # Create drop target class layout
        self.container_v_box = QVBoxLayout()
        self.container_v_box.setAlignment(Qt.AlignTop)
        self.setLayout(self.container_v_box)

    def addButton(self, button):
        """Add QPushButton widgets to container class layout."""
        self.container_v_box.addWidget(button, 0, Qt.AlignCenter)

    def dragEnterEvent(self, event):
        """Accept drag and drop operations when objects are dragged inside
        widget."""
        event.acceptProposedAction()

    def dropEvent(self, event):
        """Check the source of the mouse event. If the source (position of
        click on widget) does not already exist in the target widget then
        the drop is accepted."""
        event.setDropAction(Qt.MoveAction)
        source = event.source() # Source of the mouse event

        if source not in self.children():
            event.setAccepted(True)
            self.container_v_box.addWidget(source, 0, Qt.AlignCenter)
        else:
            event.setAccepted(False)

class DragDropWidgetsEx(QWidget):
```

```python
    def __init__(self):
        super().__init__()
        self.initializeUI()

    def initializeUI(self):
        """Initialize the window and display its contents to the screen. """
        self.setMinimumSize(500, 400)
        self.setWindowTitle("Ex 2.2 - Drag and Drop Widgets")

        self.setupWidgets()
        self.show()

    def setupWidgets(self):
        """Set up the left and right DropTargetWidget objects, add a single
        DragButton object to each one, and create the main layout for the
        GUI."""
        left_target = DropTargetWidget()
        left_label = DragButton("Left")
        left_target.addButton(left_label)

        right_target = DropTargetWidget()
        right_label = DragButton("Right")
        right_target.addButton(right_label)

        main_h_box = QHBoxLayout()
        main_h_box.addWidget(left_target)
        main_h_box.addWidget(right_target)

        self.setLayout(main_h_box)

if __name__ == '__main__':
    app = QApplication(sys.argv)
    app.setStyleSheet(style_sheet)
    window = DragDropWidgetsEx()
    sys.exit(app.exec_())
```

The drag and drop GUI can be seen in Figure 2-3.

Explanation

Let's begin by importing the classes we need from QtWidgets, QtGui, and QtCore.

For this example, we will also begin using the QDrag and QMimeData classes.

The Qt Style Sheet here is only used to make the QFrame widgets stand out visually from the window's background.

Creating Drag Widgets

The DragButton class that inherits from QPushButton sets up the properties and reimplements the basic event handler functions necessary for creating a widget that can be dragged. Objects created from this class will act as the draggable widgets in the GUI window. For this class, both the mousePressEvent() and mouseMoveEvent() functions are reimplemented so that we can distinguish between clicks and drags.

The mousePressEvent() function begins the drag and drop operation and stores the position of where the mouse clicks the widget. If the user begins dragging the mouse after clicking the DragButton object, then mouseMoveEvent() will create the QDrag and QMimeData objects, set the drag object's mime_data, and finally begin the drag and drop operation with exec_(). The specified drop action is Qt.MoveAction.

Creating Drop Targets

In Example 2.1, the entire main window acts as the drop area. Once an image is dropped in the window, the QLabel widget will update to display that image to the user. For this example, we will take a look at subclassing PyQt classes that will serve as drop areas. Multiple instances of this class can then be added to a single application to create separate drop areas.

The DropTargetWidget class inherits from QFrame. In the class constructor, setAcceptDrops() is set to True so that the class can receive data drops. Next, we create a simple layout, container_v_box. When the user adds buttons, either by using the class's addButton() method or by dropping buttons onto the DropTargetWidget object, they will be added to the layout.

Our next step is to reimplement the dragEnterEvent() and dropEvent() event handlers. You will typically use dragEnterEvent() to determine what kinds of data that the widget can receive. Here we use this function to accept the proposed action, which is Qt.MoveAction, without checking the type of data.

In dropEvent(), we use the source of the mouse event to determine whether or not to accept the drop. If the source of the drag and drop came from outside the widget, then add the source to the container_v_box layout and accept the move action. The results of a successful drag and drop can be seen in Figure 2-4.

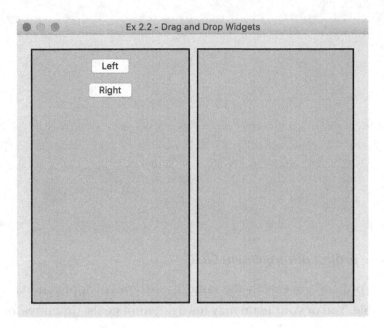

Figure 2-4. *Shows the results of dragging and dropping the Right QPushButton onto the left QFrame widget*

The last step is to create the DragDropWidgetsEx class to initialize and show the GUI window and set up the DropTargetWidget and DragButton objects.

Project 2.1: Project Management GUI

Project management applications are designed with ease of use in mind. Whether it's for keeping track of your to-do lists, ideas, or team projects, no user wants to be distracted by a chaotic interface. A simplistic layout, clearly defined widgets and other interactive elements, and intuitive mechanics such as drag and drop are important to project management GUIs like the one shown in Figure 2-5.

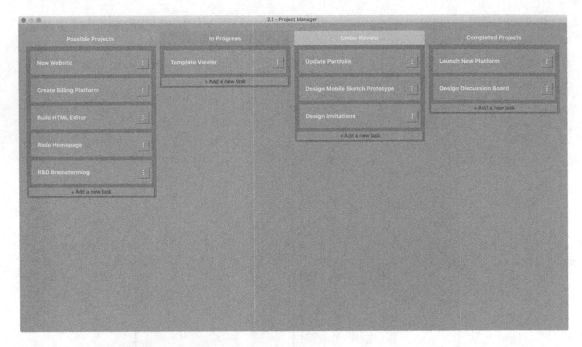

Figure 2-5. *The project management GUI*

Since no two projects are exactly the same, these types of applications are usually fairly customizable. You or your team may have different goals, timelines, or resources. Therefore, it is best that the different widgets that display information are updatable and can reflect changes back to the user.

Project Management GUI Solution

The interfaces of most project management GUIs are generally clutter-free. Each widget that is displayed only gives the necessary visual or textual information to let the user know only the essential details about a particular project such as the name, team members working on it, deadline, and current level of progress. Only when the user clicks a particular task will they be able to gain access to widgets that display more information or provide tools for editing the project, typically by either expanding the widget's size or opening a dialog box.

The project[1] found in Listing 2-5 focuses on only the essential requirements for getting started making this kind of application. By doing so, we can focus on getting many of the drag and drop mechanics working properly.

---

[1]Some of the features for this application are loosely based on Trello boards (`https://trello.com/`).

The window in Figure 2-5 displays four separate categories to represent the process a project might undergo, from conceptualization to execution, to review, and finally, completion. Different tasks can be added to a category using the button at the bottom of each section. Once a new task is created, the user can then add additional information about that task by opening up a different dialog box. This dialog can be accessed by clicking the QPushButton that appears next to each task's label. Also, tasks can be dragged and dropped between the different containers.

There are other features, such as deleting tasks or being able to create your own custom categories, that are left up to you to implement.

Listing 2-5. Code for the project management GUI

```python
# project_manager.py
# Import necessary modules
import sys
from PyQt5.QtWidgets import (QApplication, QWidget, QLabel, QFrame,
QPushButton, QLineEdit, QTextEdit, QHBoxLayout, QVBoxLayout, QDialog)
from PyQt5.QtCore import Qt, QMimeData, QSize
from PyQt5.QtGui import QDrag, QIcon, QPixmap, QPainter, QTextCursor
from ProjectManagerStyleSheet import style_sheet

class TaskWidget(QFrame):

    def __init__(self, title):
        super().__init__()
        self.setMinimumHeight(32)
        self.setObjectName("Task")
        self.title = title
        self.task_description = ""

        task_label = QLabel(title)
        task_label.setObjectName("TaskLabel")
        edit_task_button = QPushButton(QIcon("images/three_dots.png"), None)
        edit_task_button.setIconSize(QSize(28, 28))
        edit_task_button.setMaximumSize(30, 30)
        edit_task_button.clicked.connect(self.specifyTaskInfo)
```

```python
        task_h_box = QHBoxLayout()
        task_h_box.addWidget(task_label)
        task_h_box.addWidget(edit_task_button)
        self.setLayout(task_h_box)

    def specifyTaskInfo(self):
        """Create the dialog box where the user can write more information
        about their currently selected task."""
        self.task_info_dialog = QDialog(self)

        task_header = QLabel(self.title)
        task_header.setObjectName("TaskHeader")
        description_label = QLabel("Description")
        description_label.setObjectName("DescriptionLabel")

        self.enter_task_desc_text = QTextEdit()
        self.enter_task_desc_text.setText(self.task_description)
        # The cursor will appear at the end of the text edit input field
        self.enter_task_desc_text.moveCursor(QTextCursor.End)

        save_button = QPushButton("Save")
        save_button.clicked.connect(self.confirmTaskDescription)
        cancel_button = QPushButton("Cancel")
        cancel_button.clicked.connect(self.task_info_dialog.reject)

        # Create layout for the dialog's buttons
        button_h_box = QHBoxLayout()
        button_h_box.addWidget(save_button)
        button_h_box.addSpacing(15)
        button_h_box.addWidget(cancel_button)

        # Create layout and add widgets for the dialog box
        dialog_v_box = QVBoxLayout()
        dialog_v_box.addWidget(task_header)
        dialog_v_box.addWidget(description_label, Qt.AlignLeft)
        dialog_v_box.addWidget(self.enter_task_desc_text)
        dialog_v_box.addItem(button_h_box)
```

```python
    self.task_info_dialog.setLayout(dialog_v_box)
    self.task_info_dialog.show() # Display dialog box

def confirmTaskDescription(self):
    """When a user selects Save, save the info written in the text edit
    widget to the task_description variable."""
    text = self.enter_task_desc_text.toPlainText()

    if text == "":
        pass
    elif text != "":
        self.task_description = text

    self.task_info_dialog.close() # Close dialog box

def mousePressEvent(self, event):
    """Reimplement what happens when the user clicks on the widget."""
    if event.button() == Qt.LeftButton:
        self.drag_start_position = event.pos()

def mouseMoveEvent(self, event):
    """Reimplement how to handle the widget being dragged. Change the
    mouse icon when the user begins dragging the object."""
    drag = QDrag(self)
    # When the user begins dragging the object, change the cursor's
    # icon and set the drop action
    drag.setDragCursor(QPixmap("images/drag.png"), Qt.MoveAction)
    mime_data = QMimeData()
    drag.setMimeData(mime_data)

    # Create the QPainter object that will draw the widget being dragged
    pixmap = QPixmap(self.size()) # Get the size of the object
    painter = QPainter(pixmap) # Set the painter's pixmap
    # Draw the pixmap; grab() renders the widget into a pixmap
    # specified by rect()
    painter.drawPixmap(self.rect(), self.grab())
    painter.end()
```

```
        drag.setPixmap(pixmap) # Set the pixmap to represent the drag action
        drag.setHotSpot(event.pos())
        drag.exec_(Qt.MoveAction)

class TaskContainer(QWidget):

    def __init__(self, title, bg_color):
        super().__init__()
        self.setAcceptDrops(True)
        self.setObjectName("ContainerWidget")

        container_label = QLabel(title) # Container's title
        # Set the background color of the container's label
        container_label.setStyleSheet("background-color: {}".format(bg_
        color))
        container_frame = QFrame() # Main container to hold all TaskWidget
        objects
        container_frame.setObjectName("ContainerFrame")

        self.new_task_button = QPushButton("+ Add a new task")
        self.new_task_button.clicked.connect(self.createNewTask)

        self.tasks_v_box = QVBoxLayout()
        self.tasks_v_box.insertWidget(-1, self.new_task_button)
        container_frame.setLayout(self.tasks_v_box)

        # Main layout for container class
        container_v_box = QVBoxLayout()
        container_v_box.setSpacing(0) # No space between widgets
        container_v_box.setAlignment(Qt.AlignTop)
        container_v_box.addWidget(container_label)
        container_v_box.addWidget(container_frame)
        container_v_box.setContentsMargins(0, 0, 0, 0)

        self.setLayout(container_v_box)

    def createNewTask(self):
        """Set up the dialog box that allows the user to create a new
        task."""
        self.new_task_dialog = QDialog(self)
```

```python
        self.new_task_dialog.setWindowTitle("Create New Task")
        self.new_task_dialog.setModal(True) # Create a modal dialog

        self.enter_task_line = QLineEdit()
        self.enter_task_line.setPlaceholderText("Enter a title for this
        task...")

        self.add_task_button = QPushButton("Add Task")
        self.add_task_button.clicked.connect(self.confirmTask)
        cancel_button = QPushButton("Cancel")
        cancel_button.clicked.connect(self.new_task_dialog.reject)

        # Create layout for the dialog's buttons
        button_h_box = QHBoxLayout()
        button_h_box.addWidget(self.add_task_button)
        button_h_box.addSpacing(15)
        button_h_box.addWidget(cancel_button)

        # Create layout and add widgets for the dialog box
        dialog_v_box = QVBoxLayout()
        dialog_v_box.addWidget(self.enter_task_line)
        dialog_v_box.addItem(button_h_box)

        self.new_task_dialog.setLayout(dialog_v_box)
        self.new_task_dialog.show()

    def confirmTask(self):
        """If a user clicks Add Task in the dialog box, create a new
        TaskWidget object and insert it into the container's layout."""
        if self.enter_task_line.text() != "":
            new_task = TaskWidget(self.enter_task_line.text())
            self.tasks_v_box.insertWidget(0, new_task, 0)
        self.new_task_dialog.close()

    def dragEnterEvent(self, event):
        """Accept the dragging event onto the widget."""
        event.setAccepted(True)
```

```python
    def dropEvent(self, event):
        """Check the source of the mouse event. If the source does not
        already exist in the target widget then the drop is allowed."""
        event.setDropAction(Qt.MoveAction)
        source = event.source()

        if source not in self.children():
            event.setAccepted(True)
            self.tasks_v_box.addWidget(source)
        else:
            event.setAccepted(False)

        # Whenever a widget is dropped, ensure new_task_button stays at the
        bottom of the container
        self.tasks_v_box.insertWidget(-1, self.new_task_button)

class ProjectManager(QWidget):

    def __init__(self):
        super().__init__()
        self.initializeUI()

    def initializeUI(self):
        """Initialize the window and display its contents to the screen. """
        self.setMinimumSize(800, 400)
        self.showMaximized()
        self.setWindowTitle('2.1 - Project Manager')

        self.setupWidgets()
        self.show()

    def setupWidgets(self):
        """Set up the containers and main layout for the window."""
        possible_container = TaskContainer("Possible Projects", "#0AC2E4")
        # Blue
        progress_container = TaskContainer("In Progress", "#F88A20") # Orange
        review_container = TaskContainer("Under Review", "#E7CA5F") # Yellow
        completed_container = TaskContainer("Completed Projects",
        "#10C94E") # Green
```

```
        main_h_box = QHBoxLayout()
        main_h_box.addWidget(possible_container)
        main_h_box.addWidget(progress_container)
        main_h_box.addWidget(review_container)
        main_h_box.addWidget(completed_container)

        self.setLayout(main_h_box)

if __name__ == '__main__':
    app = QApplication(sys.argv)
    app.setStyleSheet(style_sheet)
    window = ProjectManager()
    sys.exit(app.exec_())
```

The complete application's GUI is shown in Figure 2-5.

Explanation

For this project, we will use many of the concepts learned in the previous examples. Similar to Example 2.2, one Python class will be used for handling the drop operations, and another class will act as the target area for drop actions.

To begin, import the widget, layout, and dialog classes from the QtWidgets module. The QDrag and QMimeData classes will be used for creating the drag and drop mechanics and transferring data between widgets in the application, respectively.

Other classes we need to include are QIcon and QSize for setting and adjusting the size of icons, QPixmap and QPainter for recreating and drawing an image of the widget the user is dragging on the screen, and QTextCursor for interacting with the cursor in the QTextEdit widgets. Finally, we import the style_sheet for the GUI from ProjectManagerStyleSheet.

Let's begin with the TaskWidget class that inherits from QFrame and functions as a draggable widget. The container consists of two widgets: task_label for displaying a task's title and edit_task_button that the user can click to open a dialog box.

The edit_task_button's clicked() signal is connected to the specifyTaskInfo() slot. This opens a QDialog object for the user to enter description text into a QTextEdit widget. The dialog box can be seen in Figure 2-6. If the user clicks the Save button in the dialog, the text they entered will be saved to the task_description variable in confirmTaskDescription(). The next time a user opens this dialog, they then can pick up where they left off and make new changes or add notes to the description.

Figure 2-6. *Dialog box for users to enter more detailed information about specific tasks*

This class reimplements the mousePressEvent() and mouseMoveEvent() functions similar to Example 2.2. However, there are some notable differences. When the user begins dragging the widget, the mouse cursor's icon will change to let the user know they have begun moving the widget. This is accomplished using the setDragCursor() method in the following code from Listing 2-5:

```
drag.setDragCursor(QPixmap("images/drag.png"), Qt.MoveAction)
```

Also, this program demonstrates how to display an image of the selected TaskWidget object while it is being dragged. Figure 2-7 illustrates both the changed drag cursor icon and the visual feedback for the current task being dragged. Refer to the code and comments in mouseMoveEvent() to see how to use the QPixmap and QPainter classes to create this type of feedback.

If you begin dragging a widget, the mouse will automatically snap to its top-left corner. To avoid this, you can set the mouse's hot spot using the setHotSpot() method. For the project in Listing 2-5, the hot spot reflects the position of the drag event (where the mouse clicked the widget):

```
drag.setHotSpot(event.pos())
```

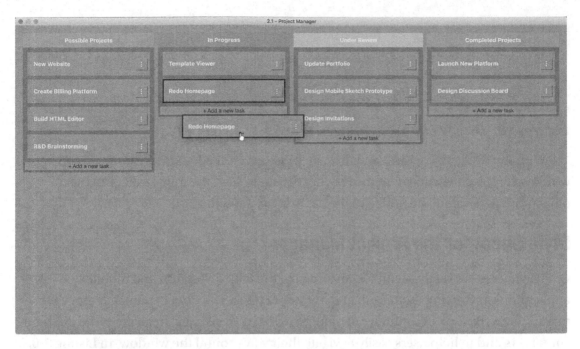

Figure 2-7. *Visual feedback for drag and drop operations can be given to the user in different ways. Changing the mouse cursor's icon, displaying an image of the widget while it is being dragged, and using style sheets to indicate that an object can be dragged are just a few of the methods utilized in the Project Manager GUI*

TaskContainer instances act as the drop areas for the TaskWidget objects. When the application first begins, the containers will be empty except for the new_task_button. Rather than use addWidget() to append the widget to the layout, the button is added to the layout using insertWidget(). In the next bit of code from Listing 2-5, the -1 argument makes certain that the new_task_button will always appear at the bottom of a TaskContainer:

```
self.tasks_v_box.insertWidget(-1, self.new_task_button)
```

When the user wants to add a new task by clicking the new_task_button, a dialog box, shown in Figure 2-8, appears. The user can then enter a task's title and click Add Task to send a signal to the confirmTask() slot where a new TaskWidget object will be created. The event handlers dragEnterEvent() and dropEvent() are reimplemented much like in Example 2.2.

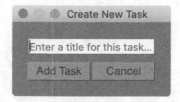

Figure 2-8. *Dialog box for creating new tasks*

With the draggable widget and drop area classes created, the class for the main window can be constructed. In the `ProjectManager` class, the four `TaskContainer` objects are generated and added to the `main_h_box` layout.

Style Sheet for the Project Manager

Qt Style Sheets are really useful for customizing the look of desktop and mobile applications and giving them fresh and unique designs. The project management GUI manipulates the look of a number of different widgets to visually break apart the different containers and to help users easily navigate their way around the window. In Listing 2-6, you can find the CSS code as well as comments to help you better understand the modifications made to the different PyQt classes.

Listing 2-6. The code for the style sheet of the Project Manager application

```
# ProjectManagerStyleSheet.py
# Style sheet for the Project Manager GUI
style_sheet = """
    QWidget{ /* Main window's background color */
        background-color: #ACADAD
    }

    QFrame#ContainerFrame{ /* Style border for TaskContainer class */
        background-color: #8B8E96;
        border-bottom-left-radius: 4px;
        border-bottom-right-radius: 4px
    }

    QFrame:hover#Task{ /* Indicate that the object is interactive and can
    be dragged when the user hovers over it*/
        border: 3px solid #2B2B2B
    }
```

```
QLabel#TaskHeader{ /* Style header for dialog box */
    background-color: #8B8E96;
    qproperty-alignment: AlignLeft;
    padding: 0px 0px;
}

QLabel#TaskLabel{ /* Set alignment for QLabel in TaskWidget class */
    qproperty-alignment: AlignLeft;
}

QLabel#DescriptionLabel{ /* Style for label in dialog box */
    background-color: #8B8E96;
    qproperty-alignment: AlignLeft;
    padding: 0px 0px;
    font: 13px
}

QLabel{ /* Style for QLabel objects for TaskContainer's title */
    color: #EFEFEF;
    qproperty-alignment: AlignCenter;
    border-top-left-radius: 4px; border-top-right-radius: 4px;
    padding: 10px 0px;
    font: bold 15px
}

QPushButton{
    color: #4E4C4C;
    font: 14px 'Helvetica'
}

QPushButton#Task{
    color: #EFEFEF
}

QDialog{
    background-color: #8B8E96
}
```

```
QLineEdit{
    background-color: #FFFFFF
}

QTextEdit{
    background-color: #FFFFFF
}"""
```

The `style_sheet` is imported by the project management GUI in Listing 2-3 and then applied to the application by

```
app.setStyleSheet(style_sheet)
```

Summary

The drag and drop mechanism is an important feature included in many desktop and mobile applications. The process of selecting files, images or text, either from within a program or from external sources or applying commands and tools at a specific location within a GUI is made simpler with intuitive drag and drop controls. Drag and drop takes advantage of how humans generally interact with computers through point and click actions and mouse movements and combines them with the visual context and cues provided by graphics, to create smoother and more user-friendly interfaces.

In this chapter, we saw how to use drag and drop for moving images from your local system onto PyQt applications. We also learned how to subclass PyQt classes and reimplement event handlers in order to drag and drop widgets back and forth between PyQt classes. These ideas were applied to the concept of project management applications as these types of UIs need to be customizable and accessible to a wide range of users with potentially different technical skill levels.

The core class for drag and drop used by PyQt is QDrag. This class can be combined with QMimeData to make it possible to transfer any type of information between applications safely using drag and drop. One of the benefits of working with MIME data is that drag and drop actions are not simply limited to text or images. With PyQt, you can also create your own data types. For more information about how to do this, check out `https://doc.qt.io/qt-5/dnd.html`.

In the next chapter, we will begin taking a look at additional PyQt modules designed for creating charts and graphs to visualize and analyze data.

## CHAPTER 3

Data Visualization and Analysis

Unless you have been living under a rock for the last few decades, then you know just how important collecting and understanding data has become. The evolution of **data science**, the field of study interested in extracting knowledge and patterns from data, continues to spread its reach and permeate into a majority of other industries.

Our world continues to find new uses for data, from Internet search algorithms to product recommendation, image and speech recognition, and more. The applications we can create from studying and understanding data seem endless. However, data often does not come in a nice package with a pretty bow on top. It is often unstructured and hard for the human brain to comprehend if not organized and presented visually.

Data visualization allows us to see data presented in visual form, helping us to gain insight and make effective decisions based on the patterns within the information. This process makes it much easier for humans to discern relationships between variables when viewed graphically with charts, tables, and graphs. There are already a few programming languages available for working with data, including Python, Java, SQL, and R.

In this chapter, we will explore some of the tools provided by PyQt for creating 2D charts for visualizing and analyzing data. While some basic data visualization concepts are covered in this chapter, the main focus is to serve as an introduction to GUI development for data visualization with PyQt. Some of the topics covered in this chapter include

- Learning about and installing the PyQtChart module for creating 2D charts

- Creating various GUIs for data visualization using public datasets

- Seeing various techniques for modifying the appearance of charts

J. Willman, *Modern PyQt*, https://doi.org/10.1007/978-1-4842-6603-8_3

- Utilizing `PyQtChart` classes for performing linear regression

- Taking a look at two other libraries often used for data science with Python – NumPy and Matplotlib

- Building a data visualization GUI that combines PyQt and Matplotlib

Before moving on to creating charts, it is important to understand the steps necessary for collecting, processing, visualizing, and analyzing data.

Steps for Data Analysis

Data analysis is the process of collecting, cleaning, shaping, and modeling data with the purpose of discovering useful information that can be used in decision-making processes. Data visualization is but one part of the whole operation.

A number of data analysis tools already exist for processing, visualizing, and manipulating data, as well as analyzing correlations between datasets. The general process for data analysis is illustrated in Figure 3-1. While the process for a single project is generally cyclical, problems, such as having insufficient amounts of data or incorrectly processing data, can cause a researcher to repeat previous steps.

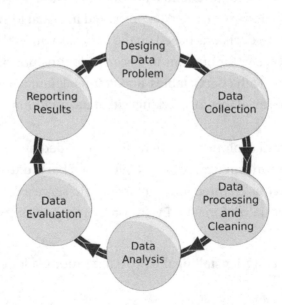

Figure 3-1.   *Depiction of the data analysis process*

Different texts may view the process of building data analysis projects in slightly different ways, but the general process is as follows:

- Designing Data Problem – Establish the purpose and the parameters for collecting data. Decide what problem your project is looking to solve, what kind of data you will need, and identify possible sources for collecting data.

- Data Collection – Gather the information based on guidelines set in the previous step. Possible data sources may include databases or scraping from websites.

- Data Processing and Cleaning – This step includes organizing, managing, and storing your data. After processing, you can begin to clean the data by removing empty spaces, duplicates, or errors.

- Data Analysis – With the data cleaned, you can begin exploring the data and testing different analysis and visualization techniques to look for patterns and new questions to better understand the underlying data. Different statistical techniques may also be needed to identify relationships in the data. You may also need to return to previous steps for further data collection or cleaning.

- Data Evaluation – Dive further into the data to answer the questions specific to your problem. Evaluate your prediction models and assure accurate results.

- Reporting Results – Relay and present the results of analysis to others. This may involve the use of data visualization techniques to help others see the relationships in the data. In many cases, this step could also involve deploying your model for use by others. With the project complete, return back to designing a new data problem.

With a basic understanding of the data analysis process, let's move on and begin seeing how we can use PyQt to help us visualize our own datasets.

The PyQtChart Module

The Qt library includes an extensive library for creating charts – Qt Chart. The **PyQtChart** module is a set of Python bindings that allow you to seamlessly integrate 2D charts into your Python programs. With PyQtChart, you can create customizable and interactive GUIs for data visualization. The charts and graphs are created using the Qt Graphics View Framework, enabling developers to include animation, incorporate interactive elements, and create dynamic plots.

In the upcoming sections in this chapter, you will see how to install the PyQtChart module and then get started building interfaces for working with data.

Note   If you are interested in visualizing data in 3D, PyQt also includes a set of bindings for the Qt Data Visualization library, which we will explore in Chapter 6.

For more information about the Riverbank Computing's PyQtChart module, have a look at `https://riverbankcomputing.com/software/pyqtchart`.

If you are interested in finding out more about the Qt Company's Qt Chart library or would like some examples of other ways that you can use Qt Chart, check out `https://doc.qt.io/qt-5/qtcharts-index.html`.

Overview of Chart Types

PyQtChart provides a number of easy-to-use classes for building charts. When you are creating data-centric applications, the QChart class can be used to display different types of information, presented by employing one of the different chart types listed in Table 3-1.

Each of the chart types inherits from one of the many QAbstractSeries derived classes. Once data has been added to a series class instance, the data can be visualized using QChart. Different kinds of series can be displayed in a single chart. When utilizing datasets, you can also consider using model mapper classes, such as QDataWidgetMapper, as a data source for creating editable charts.

Table 3-1. *The PyQtChart module's chart types. The classes needed to create the different chart types are also included in the table*

Chart Types	Description	PyQtChart Classes
Area chart	Based on line charts with the area under the line filled in. Useful for emphasizing the scale of difference between groups.	QAreaSeries; boundaries between lines are created with QLineSeries.
Bar chart	Represents data using horizontal or vertical bars. Can also create horizontal or stacked bar charts. Useful for comparing discrete values.	QBarSet to create one set of bars; then use QBarSeries, QBarHorizontalSeries, or QStackedBarSeries.
Box plot	Represents data as quartiles with whiskers (box-and-whisker charts) to visualize variations and outliers in the data values.	QBoxSet to create a single box-and-whisker item and then QBoxPlotSeries.
Candlestick chart	Represents data as boxes where the tails of the boxes depict high and low fluctuations in the data. Typically used in financial charts.	QCandlestickSet to create a candlestick and then QCandlestickSeries.
Line chart, spline chart	Represents data as a series of data points joined by a line. Useful for comparing continuous values.	QLineSeries, QSplineSeries.
Scatter plot	Displays data as a collection of points. Useful for showing the existence of a relationship between two variables.	QScatterSeries.
Pie chart	Represents data as a pie divided into slices. Useful for displaying the share of each part in relation to the total value.	QPieSeries; add slices using QPieSlice.
Polar plot	Displays data in a circular graph, where a series is represented by a closed curve from the center. Placement of data points is based on the radial distance and angle from the pole (the center).	Use QPolarChart, which inherits from QChart and includes support for line, spline, and scatter series.

More information about the different chart types can be found at https://doc.qt.io/qt-5/qtcharts-overview.html.

Installing PyQtChart

The PyQt framework has a number of add-ons that are not installed at the same time you install PyQt5. PyQtChart for visualizing 2D data happens to be one of them, and installing the module is thankfully very simple.

To obtain the PyQtChart module from the PyPI repository, open up your computer's shell and enter

```
$ pip3 install PyQtChart
```

After the installation is complete, go into the Python shell by entering `python3` in the command line. Then enter

```
>>> import PyQt5.QtChart
```

If no errors appear, then you are ready to start using PyQt's PyQtChart module in your own applications.

Example 3.1: Creating a Simple Chart

To get started, we will first see how to create a simple line chart, shown in Figure 3-2, using the PyQtChart module. Line charts are very useful for visualizing how one variable (represented on the vertical y-axis and referred to as the dependent variable) changes with respect to another (represented on the horizontal x-axis and denoted as the independent variable). Line graphs are great for depicting continuous values typically related to time. By looking at the slope of the line for any given segment, the user can understand the direction of the trends in the data.

By the end of this example, you will understand how to

- Create a simple chart using `QChart` and `QChartView`.

- Add data to a `PyQtChart` series, namely, `QLineSeries`.

- Set up the chart's axes, legend, and other chart-related features.

- Load real data from CSV-formatted files for data visualization.

With a few modifications to the program in Listing 3-1, such as the path to the file name, the columns selected for independent and dependent variables, and the values displayed in the axes, this example can be quickly adapted to your own data visualization projects.

Quick Glance at the Dataset

Rather than creating synthetic data for the examples found in this chapter, a better approach may be to actually show how to collect and utilize public datasets for data visualization. The step-by-step process for setting up and viewing data using PyQtChart is covered in the "Explanation" section of this example.

Before you begin creating a chart, you need to decide which chart type you want to use. This data will be represented in a **series** – a related set of data items. You can think of a series as a column you select from a dataset. For this example, we will use the QLineSeries class to represent our series of data.

Let's take a look at the data we will visualize using PyQt in Table 3-2. Governments are able to pay for development projects, education, healthcare, infrastructure, and other goods and services through public spending. For an early-industrialized country, such as Sweden, a portion of their public spending as a percentage of GDP focused on social spending,[1] and the amount spent increased over time. Rapid growth in the late twentieth century can be associated with the intensity of funding for education and healthcare.

Note   The datasets for this chapter can be found on GitHub at the link in the "Introduction."

Table 3-2.   *The header row and the first five rows in the social_spending_sweden. csv file. The Code column for each country is included in the original dataset*

Entity	Code	Year	SocialExpenditureGDP(%)
Sweden	SWE	1880	0.72
Sweden	SWE	1890	0.85
Sweden	SWE	1900	0.85
Sweden	SWE	1910	1.03
Sweden	SWE	1920	1.14

---

[1]The data used for this example is permitted under the CC BY license. More information can be found in Esteban Ortiz-Ospina (2016). "Government Spending." Published online at OurWorldInData.org. Retrieved from https://ourworldindata.org/government-spending [online resource].

This trend of increased public social expenditure with relation to time can be seen in both the data in Table 3-2 and the line chart in Figure 3-2. Values in the Year column will act as the independent variable, and values in the SocialExpenditureGDP(%) column will serve as the dependent variable for our chart.

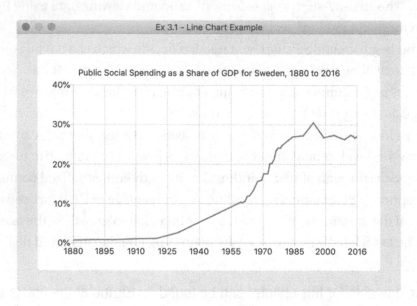

Figure 3-2. *A simple line chart displaying the growth in public social spending in Sweden from 1880 to 2016*

To understand how you can create the chart shown in Figure 3-2 from an actual dataset, follow along with Listing 3-1 and the "Explanation" section.

Listing 3-1. Code for plotting a simple line chart in PyQt

```
# simple_line_chart.py
# Import necessary modules
import sys, csv
from PyQt5.QtWidgets import QApplication, QWidget, QVBoxLayout
from PyQt5.QtChart import QChart, QChartView, QLineSeries, QValueAxis
from PyQt5.QtCore import Qt
from PyQt5.QtGui import QPainter

class DisplayGraph(QWidget):
```

```python
def __init__(self):
    super().__init__()
    self.initializeUI()

def initializeUI(self):
    """Initialize the window and display its contents."""
    self.setMinimumSize(600, 400)
    self.setWindowTitle("Ex 3.1 - Line Chart Example")

    self.setupChart()
    self.show()

def setupChart(self):
    """Set up the GUI's graph line series type, chart instance, chart
    axes, and chart view widget."""
    # Collect x and y data values from the CSV file
    x_values, y_values = self.loadCSVFile()

    # Create chart object
    chart = QChart()
    chart.setTitle("Public Social Spending as a Share of GDP for
    Sweden, 1880 to 2016")
    chart.setAnimationOptions(QChart.SeriesAnimations)
    chart.legend().hide() # Hide the chart's legend

    line_series = QLineSeries() # Using line charts for this example

    # Loop through corresponding x and y values and add them to the
    line chart
    for value in range(0, self.row_count - 1):
        line_series.append(x_values[value], y_values[value])
    chart.addSeries(line_series) # Add line series to chart instance

    # Specify parameters for the x and y axes
    axis_x = QValueAxis()
    axis_x.setLabelFormat("%i")
    axis_x.setTickCount(10)
    axis_x.setRange(1880, 2016)
    chart.addAxis(axis_x, Qt.AlignBottom)
    line_series.attachAxis(axis_x)
```

```python
        axis_y = QValueAxis()
        axis_y.setLabelFormat("%i" + "%")
        axis_y.setRange(0, 40)
        chart.addAxis(axis_y, Qt.AlignLeft)
        line_series.attachAxis(axis_y)

        # Create QChartView object for displaying the chart
        chart_view = QChartView(chart)
        chart_view.setRenderHint(QPainter.Antialiasing)

        # Create layout and set the layout for the window
        v_box = QVBoxLayout()
        v_box.addWidget(chart_view)
        self.setLayout(v_box)

    def loadCSVFile(self):
        """Load data from CSV file for the line chart.
        Select and store x and y values into Python list objects.
        Return the x_values and y_values lists."""
        x_values, y_values = [], []
        file_name = "files/social_spending_sweden.csv"

        with open(file_name, "r") as csv_f:
            reader = csv.reader(csv_f)
            header_labels = next(reader) # Skip header row

            for row in reader:
                x = int(row[2])
                x_values.append(x)
                y = float(row[3])
                y_values.append(y)

            # Count the number of rows in the CSV file. Reset the reader's
            # current position back to the top of the file
            csv_f.seek(0)
            self.row_count = len(list(reader))
        return x_values, y_values
```

```python
if __name__ == "__main__":
    app = QApplication(sys.argv)
    window = DisplayGraph()
    sys.exit(app.exec_())
```

The GUI for this simple example can be seen in Figure 3-2.

Explanation

For this program, let's first import the Python and PyQt classes we need for creating GUIs, including sys, QApplication, QWidget, a layout class (in this case QVBoxLayout), and Qt. In addition to these classes, we also need to import csv for working with CSV data files.

The QtChart module contains all of the classes you need for creating 2D charts and graphs. Let's import QChart and QChartView. The QChart class handles the graphical representation of the series used in your applications as well as other related objects, including axes and the legend. The QChartView class is a convenience class that can also be used as a standalone widget for displaying charts.

Depending upon the needs of your application, you can either

- Create a simple QChartView object.

- Create an instance of QChart and display the data by adding the chart to a QChartView object.

- Create a QChart, which inherits from QGraphicsWidget, and show the chart in a QGraphicsScene. This has the advantage of providing more tools for modifying your application graphically, but may not be necessary if you are only looking for a way to simply visualize data.

We will use QLineSeries to create the line series and QValueAxis to manipulate the chart's axes. QPainter is the class used for drawing PyQt objects.

With the classes we need imported, we can now begin initializing the window for the application in the DisplayGraph class.

Creating a Chart

The general process for visualizing data using QChart is as follows:

1. Create a `QChart` object.

2. Instantiate the series, such as `QLineSeries` or `QSplineSeries`, for visualizing data in the chart and add data to the series.

3. Add the series to the chart instance.

4. Specify the parameters for the chart's axes. This can be done either by using the `createDefaultAxes()` method (shown in Example 3.2) or stating the boundaries explicitly.

5. Create a view to display the chart, such as `QChartView` or a `QGraphicsScene`.

In the `setupChart()` function, we initially load the data points from the CSV file. We'll take a look at how the `loadCSVFile()` function works later in this section. Following this step, create the `chart` object. Use `setTitle()` to create the `chart`'s title. Since QChart inherits from Qt's graphics classes, you can incorporate animations into your charts. Use the `setAnimationOptions()` function to use the built-in animations.

A legend is an area in a chart that explains the different symbols, markings, and other graphical elements in a chart. In PyQt, the legend is an object that can be referenced by the chart. The easiest way to achieve this is by calling the reference to the legend like in the following line of code:

```
chart.legend().setAlignment(Qt.AlignRight)
```

This will place the legend to the right of the chart. The QLegend class also includes other methods for setting the color, marker shape, border style, and more.

The next step is to create the series for the chart type and add points using `append()`, shown in Listing 3-2.

Listing 3-2. Adding points to a series

```
line_series = QLineSeries()
line_series.append(1, 2)
line_series.append(3, -3)
```

The quickest way to add lots of points is to use a for loop. After all of the points have been appended to the series, you can add the series to the chart in Listing 3-1 using addSeries():

```
chart.addSeries(line_series)
```

Project 3.1 shows you how to add multiple series to a single chart. With the series added, you are now ready to create the axes. There are a few different classes provided for creating an axis, including ones for numeric values, categories, bar categories, dates and times, and logarithmic values. The following bit of code demonstrates how to create the x-axis in Listing 3-1. The y-axis is set up in a similar manner:

```
axis_x = QValueAxis() # Create value axis instance
axis_x.setLabelFormat("%i") # Display integer values
axis_x.setTickCount(10) # Number of grid lines drawn
axis_x.setRange(1880, 2016) # Set the axis' range
chart.addAxis(axis_x, Qt.AlignBottom) # Add the axis to the chart
line_series.attachAxis(axis_x) # Attach the axis to the series
```

The last step is to create the QChartView object so we can view the chart and add the view widget to the layout:

```
chart_view = QChartView(chart) # Add chart to view
```

Loading Data from CSV Files

We took a brief look at writing information stored in PyQt tables to CSV-formatted files in Chapter 1. In this example, you can see how to read information from files using the reader() function.

With reader(), you can iterate over the lines in a file. For this application, we need some way to select specific columns for the independent and dependent variables and then store those values into lists. Selecting specific columns can be done by specifying the column's index value while iterating over the file's contents:

```
for row in reader: # For each row in the file
    # Look at items in the third column; index starts at 0
    x = int(row[2])
```

The `csv` module also includes classes for working with information from a file using Python dictionaries – `DictReader` and `DictWriter`. If you choose to use either one of these methods, you will need to specify the column's header value rather than the index value.

Note   The data found in this chapter has already been cleaned up to fit the needs of the examples. Knowing this, data is read from the files without performing checks for null or missing data to keep more focus on creating GUI applications.

More information about working with CSV files in Python can be found at `https:// docs.python.org/3/library/csv.html`.

Project 3.1: Data Visualization GUI

Now that we have seen how to visualize a single data series with QChart, we can move on to visualizing multiple series on the same chart. This project, shown in Figure 3-3, will take what you have learned in Example 3.1 and build upon that knowledge to show you more possibilities with PyQtChart.

It can be useful to plot multiple lines in a single chart to compare the trends between different series. For this application, you will

- Plot multiple series in a single `QChart` instance.

- Learn how to use different built-in Qt themes and styles to customize the look of your charts.

- See how to visualize data in a table using Qt's model/view framework.

- Find out how to subclass `QChartView` to implement scroll and drag features.

The program in this section demonstrates how you could begin building your own application to fit a user's data visualization needs.

Quick Glance at the Dataset

This project uses the same source of data used in Example 3.1 and also focuses on studying the relationship between public social spending and time. However, this application also visualizes the information for a number of different countries.

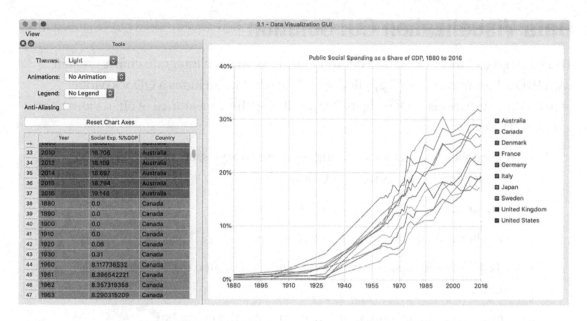

Figure 3-3. *GUI application for visualizing multiple series of data in the same chart. The dock widget on the left side contains widgets for changing different visual parameters of the chart and a table for viewing the values for the different series*

Table 3-3 presents a few examples of the different countries listed in the data file. We will be using the Entity, Year, and SocialExpenditureGDP(%) columns. The values in the Entity column will be used for differentiating the different line series and for the labels in the chart's legend.

Table 3-3. *Sample data from social_spending_simplified.csv displaying the header row and five randomly selected rows. Row Value is included in the table only as a reference for locating the row in the CSV file*

Row Value	Entity	Code	Year	SocialExpenditureGDP(%)
12	Australia	AUS	1964	5.976754619
48	Canada	CAN	1963	8.290315209
114	France	FRA	1978	19.45212529
201	Japan	JPN	1900	0.17
281	United Kingdom	GBR	1965	11.0674075

Let's take a moment to better understand the different components of the GUI's main window.

Data Visualization GUI Solution

The main goal of this project is to demonstrate how you can integrate charts created with PyQtChart into your GUI applications. The window includes a QDockWidget which contains various PyQt widgets[2] for modifying the appearance of charts and chart features. These include

- QComboBox widgets for selecting different Qt Styles, animation styles, and legend locations in the window

- QCheckBox for turning on and off antialiasing

- QPushButton for resetting the chart's axes

- QTableView for displaying color-coded data related to the plotted line series

The dock widget can be hidden or retrieved using the menu bar.

In this project, you will see how to create a different line series for each of the different countries represented in the dataset. Each country is represented by a different color in the chart. Also, similar to Example 3.1, with some small modifications to the program in Listing 3-3, you can also deploy the application for viewing other datasets.

Listing 3-3. Code for the data visualization application

```
# data_visualization.py
# Import necessary modules
import sys, csv, random
from PyQt5.QtWidgets import (QApplication, QMainWindow, QWidget,
QPushButton, QComboBox, QCheckBox, QFormLayout, QDockWidget, QTableView,
QHeaderView, QGraphicsView)
from PyQt5.QtChart import QChart, QChartView, QLineSeries, QValueAxis
from PyQt5.QtCore import Qt
from PyQt5.QtGui import QPainter, QColor, QStandardItemModel, QStandardItem

class ChartView(QChartView):
```

---

[2]Parts of this GUI are adapted from the Qt Chart Themes Example found on the https://doc.qt.io/ website.

```python
def __init__(self, chart):
    super().__init__(chart)
    self.chart = chart

    # Starting position for mouse press event
    self.start_pos = None

def wheelEvent(self, event):
    """Reimplement the scroll wheel on the mouse for zooming in and out
    on the chart."""
    zoom_factor = 1.0 # Simple way to control the total amount zoomed
    in or out
    scale_factor = 1.10 # How much to scale into or out of the chart

    if event.angleDelta().y() >= 120 and zoom_factor < 3.0:
        zoom_factor *= 1.25
        self.chart.zoom(scale_factor)
    elif event.angleDelta().y() <= -120 and zoom_factor > 0.5:
        zoom_factor *= 0.8
        self.chart.zoom(1 / scale_factor)

def mousePressEvent(self, event):
    """If the mouse button is pressed, change the mouse cursor and get
    the coordinates of the click."""
    if event.button() == Qt.LeftButton:
        self.setDragMode(QGraphicsView.ScrollHandDrag)
        self.start_pos = event.pos()

def mouseMoveEvent(self, event):
    """Reimplement the mouseMoveEvent so that the user can scroll the
    chart area."""
    if (event.buttons() == Qt.LeftButton):
        delta = self.start_pos - event.pos()
        self.chart.scroll(delta.x(), -delta.y())
        self.start_pos = event.pos()

def mouseReleaseEvent(self, event):
    self.setDragMode(QGraphicsView.NoDrag) # Don't display mouse cursor
```

```python
class MainWindow(QMainWindow):

    def __init__(self):
        super().__init__()
        self.initializeUI()

    def initializeUI(self):
        """Initialize the window and display its contents."""
        self.setMinimumSize(1200, 600)
        self.setWindowTitle("3.1 - Data Visualization GUI")

        self.setupChart()
        self.setupToolsDockWidget()
        self.setupMenu()
        self.show()

    def setupChart(self):
        """Set up the GUI's graph series type, chart instance, chart axes,
        and chart view widget."""
        random.seed(50) # Create seed for random numbers

        # Create the model instance and set the headers
        self.model = QStandardItemModel()
        self.model.setColumnCount(3)
        self.model.setHorizontalHeaderLabels(["Year", "Social Exp. %GDP",
        "Country"])

        # Collect x and y data values and labels from the CSV file
        xy_data_and_labels = self.loadCSVFile()

        # Create the individual lists for x, y and labels values
        x_values, y_values, labels = [], [], []
        # Append items to the corresponding lists
        for item in range(len(xy_data_and_labels)):
            x_values.append(xy_data_and_labels[item][0])
            y_values.append(xy_data_and_labels[item][1])
            labels.append(xy_data_and_labels[item][2])
```

```
# Remove all duplicates from the labels list using list comprehension.
# This list will be used to create the labels in the chart's legend.
set_of_labels = []
[set_of_labels.append(x) for x in labels if x not in set_of_labels]

# Create chart object
self.chart = QChart()
self.chart.setTitle("Public Social Spending as a Share of GDP, 1880
to 2016")
self.chart.legend().hide() # Hide legend at the start

# Specify parameters for the x and y axes
self.axis_x = QValueAxis()
self.axis_x.setLabelFormat("%i")
self.axis_x.setTickCount(10)
self.axis_x.setRange(1880, 2016)
self.chart.addAxis(self.axis_x, Qt.AlignBottom)

self.axis_y = QValueAxis()
self.axis_y.setLabelFormat("%i" + "%")
self.axis_y.setRange(0, 40)
self.chart.addAxis(self.axis_y, Qt.AlignLeft)

# Create a Python dict to associate the labels with the individual
line series
series_dict = {}

for label in set_of_labels:
    # Create labels from data and add them to a Python dictionary
    series_label = 'series_{}'.format(label)
    series_dict[series_label] = label # Create label value for each
    line series

# For each of the keys in the dict, create a line series
for keys in series_dict.keys():
    # Use get() to access the corresponding value for a key
    label = series_dict.get(keys)
```

```python
            # Create line series instance and set its name and color values
            line_series = QLineSeries()
            line_series.setName(label)
            line_series.setColor(QColor(random.randint(10, 254), random.
            randint(10, 254), random.randint(10, 254)))

            # Append x and y coordinates to the series
            for value in range(len(xy_data_and_labels)):
                if line_series.name() == xy_data_and_labels[value][2]:
                    line_series.append(x_values[value], y_values[value])

                    # Create and add items to the model (for displaying in
                    the table)
                    items = [QStandardItem(str(item)) for item in xy_data_
                    and_labels[value]]
                    color = line_series.pen().color()
                    for item in items:
                        item.setBackground(color)
                    self.model.insertRow(value, items)

        self.chart.addSeries(line_series)
        line_series.attachAxis(self.axis_x)
        line_series.attachAxis(self.axis_y)

    # Create QChartView object for displaying the chart
    self.chart_view = ChartView(self.chart)
    self.setCentralWidget(self.chart_view)

def setupMenu(self):
    """Create a simple menu to manage the dock widget."""
    menu_bar = self.menuBar()
    menu_bar.setNativeMenuBar(False)

    # Create view menu and add actions
    view_menu = menu_bar.addMenu('View')
    view_menu.addAction(self.toggle_dock_tools_act)
```

```python
def setupToolsDockWidget(self):
    """Set up the dock widget that displays different tools and themes
    for interacting with the chart. Also displays the data values in a
    table view object."""
    tools_dock = QDockWidget()
    tools_dock.setWindowTitle("Tools")
    tools_dock.setMinimumWidth(400)
    tools_dock.setAllowedAreas(Qt.LeftDockWidgetArea |
    Qt.RightDockWidgetArea)

    # Create widgets for dock widget area
    themes_cb = QComboBox()
    themes_cb.addItems(["Light", "Cerulean Blue", "Dark", "Sand Brown",
    "NCS Blue", "High Contrast", "Icy Blue", "Qt"])
    themes_cb.currentTextChanged.connect(self.changeChartTheme)

    self.animations_cb = QComboBox()
    self.animations_cb.addItem("No Animation", QChart.NoAnimation)
    self.animations_cb.addItem("Grid Animation", QChart.
    GridAxisAnimations)
    self.animations_cb.addItem("Series Animation", QChart.
    SeriesAnimations)
    self.animations_cb.addItem("All Animations", QChart.AllAnimations)
    self.animations_cb.currentIndexChanged.connect(self.
    changeAnimations)

    self.legend_cb = QComboBox()
    self.legend_cb.addItem("No Legend")
    self.legend_cb.addItem("Align Left", Qt.AlignLeft)
    self.legend_cb.addItem("Align Top", Qt.AlignTop)
    self.legend_cb.addItem("Align Right", Qt.AlignRight)
    self.legend_cb.addItem("Align Bottom", Qt.AlignBottom)
    self.legend_cb.currentTextChanged.connect(self.changeLegend)

    self.antialiasing_check_box = QCheckBox()
    self.antialiasing_check_box.toggled.connect(self.
    toggleAntialiasing)
```

```python
        reset_button = QPushButton("Reset Chart Axes")
        reset_button.clicked.connect(self.resetChartZoom)

        # Create table view and set its model
        data_table_view = QTableView()
        data_table_view.setModel(self.model)
        data_table_view.horizontalHeader().setSectionResizeMode(QHeaderVie
        w.Stretch)
        data_table_view.verticalHeader().setSectionResizeMode(QHeaderView.
        Stretch)

        dock_form = QFormLayout()
        dock_form.setAlignment(Qt.AlignTop)
        dock_form.addRow("Themes:", themes_cb)
        dock_form.addRow("Animations:", self.animations_cb)
        dock_form.addRow("Legend:", self.legend_cb)
        dock_form.addRow("Anti-Aliasing", self.antialiasing_check_box)
        dock_form.addRow(reset_button)
        dock_form.addRow(data_table_view)

        # Create QWidget object to act as a container for dock widgets
        tools_container = QWidget()
        tools_container.setLayout(dock_form)
        tools_dock.setWidget(tools_container)

        self.addDockWidget(Qt.LeftDockWidgetArea, tools_dock)
        # Handles the visibility of the dock widget
        self.toggle_dock_tools_act = tools_dock.toggleViewAction()

    def changeChartTheme(self, text):
        """Slot for changing the theme of the chart. The charts themes are
        represented by numerical values specified by the Qt library."""
        themes_dict = {"Light": 0, "Cerulean Blue": 1, "Dark": 2, "Sand
        Brown": 3, "NCS Blue": 4, "High Contrast": 5, "Icy Blue": 6, "Qt": 7}
        theme = themes_dict.get(text)
        if theme == 0:
            self.setupChart()
        else:
            self.chart.setTheme(theme)
```

```python
def changeAnimations(self):
    """Slot for changing the animation style of the chart."""
    animation = QChart.AnimationOptions(
        self.animations_cb.itemData(self.animations_cb.currentIndex()))
    self.chart.setAnimationOptions(animation)

def changeLegend(self, text):
    """Slot for turning off the legend, or changing its location."""
    alignment = self.legend_cb.itemData(self.legend_cb.currentIndex())

    if text == "No Legend":
        self.chart.legend().hide()
    else:
        self.chart.legend().setAlignment(Qt.Alignment(alignment))
        self.chart.legend().show()

def toggleAntialiasing(self, state):
    """If self.antialiasing_check_box.isChecked() is True, turn on
    antialiasing."""
    if state:
        self.chart_view.setRenderHint(QPainter.Antialiasing, on=True)
    else:
        self.chart_view.setRenderHint(QPainter.Antialiasing, on=False)

def resetChartZoom(self):
    """Reset the chart and the axes."""
    self.chart.zoomReset()
    self.axis_x.setRange(1880, 2016)
    self.axis_y.setRange(0, 40)

def loadCSVFile(self):
    """Load data from CSV file for the chart.
    Select and store x and y values and labels into Python list objects.
    Return the xy_data_and_labels list."""
    file_name = "files/social_spending_simplified.csv"

    with open(file_name, "r") as csv_f:
        reader = csv.reader(csv_f)
        header_labels = next(reader)
```

```
                    row_values = [] # Store current row values
                    xy_data_and_labels = [] # Store all values

                    for i, row in enumerate(reader):
                        x = int(row[2])
                        y = float(row[3])
                        label = row[0]

                        row_values.append(x)
                        row_values.append(y)
                        row_values.append(label)

                        # Add row_values to xy_data_and_labels, then reset row_
                        values
                        xy_data_and_labels.append(row_values)
                        row_values = []

                return xy_data_and_labels

if __name__ == "__main__":
    app = QApplication(sys.argv)
    window = MainWindow()
    sys.exit(app.exec_())
```

The data visualization GUI can be seen in Figure 3-3.

Explanation

To start, let's first import the Python and PyQt5 modules that we need. A number of widget classes are needed from QtWidgets for creating the GUI's window. QGraphicsView is only used in this application to display a drag hand in QChartView as visual feedback to the user.

QTableView is imported so that we can view data from a model, QStandardItemModel, using Qt's model/view paradigm. You can refer to the section titled "Qt's Model/View Architecture" in Chapter 1 for a refresher. In order to add items to the model, QStandardItem also needs to be imported from the QtGui module.

Implementing Dragging and Scrolling in QChartView

Before we get into setting up the application's main class for displaying the GUI window, let's take a look at the `ChartView` class which subclasses `QChartView`. By subclassing `QChartView`, we are able to modify the class's event handlers to implement drag and scroll features specifically in the `QChartView` area of the window.

In the `ChartView` class constructor, `chart` is included as a parameter so that we have access to a few QChart class functions, mainly, `zoom()` and `scroll()`. In this class, the following events are reimplemented:

- `wheelEvent()` – Use the scroll wheel on the mouse to zoom in or out on the chart. Manage how much the user can scroll into or out of the chart area. `angleDelta()` refers to how much the wheel has rotated in eighths of a degree. Since most mouse types rotate in steps of 15 degrees, we use a factor of 120 to determine if we should zoom or not (i.e., 120 units * 1/8 = 15 degrees). Depending upon the direction of the wheel, the chart's zoom is based on the `scale_factor` value.

- `mousePressEvent()` – Display a hand to the user to indicate that dragging is enabled.

- `mouseMoveEvent()` – Drag the chart. Use `scroll()` to move around the chart area.

- `releaseMouseEvent()` – Hide the drag hand once the mouse button is released.

Figure 3-4 shows the results of dragging and scrolling around in the chart. You could also create dynamic charts that allow the user to add or remove values by clicking in the chart view region.

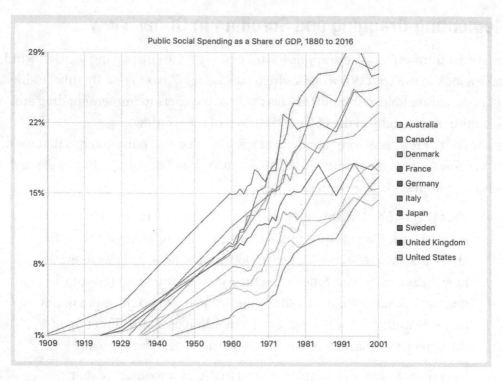

Figure 3-4. *An example of zooming and scrolling in the chart view*

Setting Up a Chart to Display Multiple Line Series

In the MainWindow class that inherits from QMainWindow, we set up the widgets and other parameters that will be displayed in the GUI. The setupChart() function is where we create the QStandardItemModel instance for accessing our data, call loadCSVFile() to load our data, and set up the QChart object, multiple QLineSeries instances, and the QChartView object for displaying the data.

The loadCSVFile() function has a few notable differences from Example 3.1. For starters, the data we need from each row is stored in a single list, xy_data_and_labels. The labels from the dataset need to be included in order to create separate line series and labels in the legend that pertain to each of the countries. With the dataset loaded, we then break down the larger list into its separate x_values, y_values, and corresponding country labels. This step is performed for better readability in Listing 3-2.

The purpose of set_of_labels is threefold: to create labels from the dataset that will be displayed in the legend, to create a separate line series for each of the labels, and to match the different values in the data based on their labels to their corresponding line series using line_series.name().

Once the data preparation is complete, the process for setting up the chart object, creating the axes, and visualizing the data is similar to Example 3.1, except this time we also need to account for the multiple line series. For each of the labels in set_of_labels, create a separate QLineSeries instance, and assign it a specific name and color using setName() and setColor().

Next, using a for loop, iterate through the items in xy_data_and_labels. If the name() corresponds to the label values in xy_data_and_labels at index 2, append the x and y coordinate values to the line_series. Also for each added value in the line_series, create a QStandardItem consisting of the data points and the label, and add the corresponding items into the model using insertRow(). The color for each item will be the same as the line_series.pen().color() and is set using the setBackground() method.

With the points and labels added to their respective line_series and all of the items added to the model, add the line_series to the chart and also attach the x and y axes to the series with attachAxis().

After iterating through the keys in the series_dict, create the QChartView instance and pass chart as an argument.

Changing Chart Themes, Animations, and More

The tools for changing the chart's theme, animation style, and legend location, toggling antialiasing on or off, and displaying our data are all located in the tools_dock QDockWidget. You can use the setAllowedAreas() method to specify where the dock widget can be placed in the window.

There are a few different widgets contained in the dock widget. These include

- themes_cb – A QComboBox for selecting between the different predefined QtChart themes. Items are appended to the combobox using addItems(). When an item is selected, a signal is sent to the changeChartTheme() slot. Since changing a theme overwrites the previous customizations you applied to charts, when the user selects the Light (default) theme, the original chart is recreated by calling setupChart(). Some examples of different chart themes are shown in Figure 3-5.

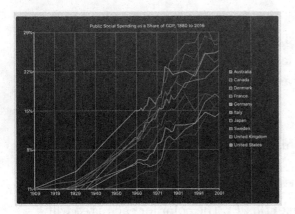 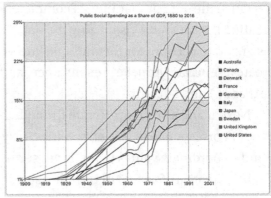

Figure 3-5. *Examples of a few of Qt's different built-in chart themes. These can be changed in the GUI by using the QComboBox located in the dock widget*

- animations_cb – A QComboBox for selecting the chart's animation style. The user can choose no animation or animations for the grid lines, series, or both. Items are added to the combobox by specifying the string to be displayed and the userData in the addItem() function. The userData specifies the role to be used if the item is selected in the combobox, such as QChart.NoAnimation. Using itemData(), we are able to retrieve that role and apply the correct animation type to the chart.

- legend_cb – A QComboBox for aligning the legend to different sides of the chart, set up in a similar manner as the animations_cb. An example is shown in Figure 3-6.

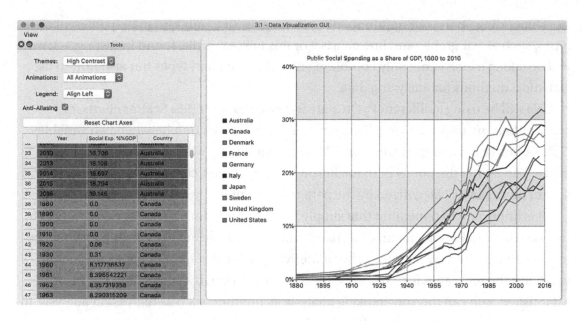

Figure 3-6. *Demonstration of aligning the legend to the left side of the chart*

- antialiasing_check_box – A QCheckBox for toggling antialiasing on or off depending upon the state of the widget.

- reset_button – A QPushButton that calls the resetChartZoom() slot when clicked() and resets the chart to its original settings using zoomReset(). Also it resets the chart's axes.

- data_table_view – A QTableView instance for displaying tabular data. The view's model is set using setModel().

Widgets are arranged in tools_dock using QFormLayout. The dock widget can be displayed or hidden by using the menu bar created in setupMenu().

We have seen in this project how to create multiple series of the same type and view them in a single chart. Next, we will see how to display series of different types in one chart.

Example 3.2: Combining Different Chart Types

You may often find that a single chart, or several charts spread out across multiple views, cannot clearly depict the relationship between two variables. Combining two or even more chart types in a single view can be helpful for analyzing data in different ways or visually validating the relationship between two variables. It is even possible to combine different types of data into one chart.

Depending upon your requirements, you may see fit to mix and match different chart types, such as bar graphs and line charts. For this next example, found in Listing 3-3, we will be taking a look at not only combining two different chart types but also how to use statistical methods for analyzing data.

We will be using a different PyQtChart series: QScatterSeries. Scatter charts, or scatter plots, are useful for visualizing and testing for correlation between two variables. Data points in a scatter plot with some kind of relationship will fall along a line or a curve. The tighter the points fit to the line, the stronger their correlation. Relationships in scatter plots can be categorized by the patterns present in the data.

It is important to remember that simply because a relationship is observed between two variables, it does not mean that changes in one variable are responsible for changes in the other. There may be some other underlying factor that has not been considered yet that is the real cause for what appears to be correlation. If a correlation has been established, you can then begin using analysis techniques, such as regression analysis, to assess the relationship between the variables in your data.

A Brief Introduction to Linear Regression

Statistical methods are often applied to visualized data to analyze and discover underlying patterns and trends. One commonly used statistical method is **regression analysis**. The goal of regression analysis is to understand or predict the values of a dependent variable based on some independent variables.

Imagine taking a set of plotted points and drawing a line through the middle of them. This line, often referred to as a **regression line** or **line of best fit**, represents the relationship between the independent variable and the dependent variable and can be used to make, with some degree of uncertainty, accurate predictions on new data. An example of a line of best fit can be seen in Figure 3-7.

For the purposes of this example, we will be using a basic regression analysis technique, **simple linear regression**, for establishing the causal relationship between our variables with a regression line. The equation of a line is represented by

$$\mathbf{Y} = a + b\mathbf{X}$$

where **Y** denotes the values for the dependent variable, **a** is the y-intercept, **b** is the slope of the line, and **X** denotes values for the independent variable. Using the independent and dependent variables in the dataset, we can calculate the values for the slope and the y-intercept and plot the line that best fits the data points. The resulting equation can then be used for prediction.

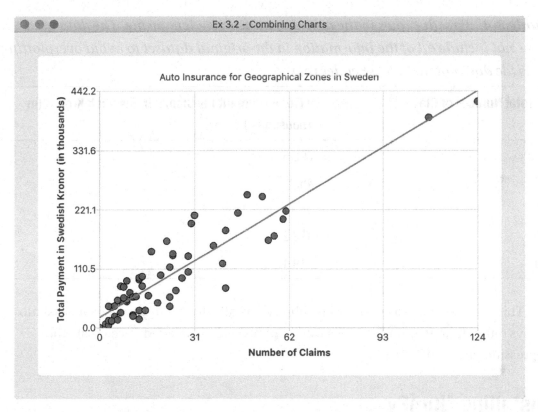

Figure 3-7. *Scatter plot showing payments vs. claims and the line of best fit for the Swedish insurance dataset*

Quick Glance at the Dataset

The Swedish Auto Insurance dataset[3] takes a look at the factors that may influence the possibility of a client making an auto insurance claim and, given the occurrence of an accident, the potential amount of the payout.

---

[3]More information about the original dataset can be found in Frees, E. (2009). Regression Modeling with Actuarial and Financial Applications (International Series on Actuarial Science). Cambridge: Cambridge University Press. doi:10.1017/CBO9780511814372.

For this example, we are going to plot the relationship between the number of insurance claims and the total amount paid in Swedish kronor. From Figure 3-7, it is evident that the payment amounts linearly increase with the number of claims for the different geographical areas in Sweden. Using the data points in the scatter plot (a few rows are listed in Table 3-4), we can then plot a regression line for predicting payout amounts given new claims.

Table 3-4. *First five rows in the auto_insurance_sweden.csv file. The data used does not include all of the information in the original dataset to avoid overplotting. This file does not include a header row*

x (Total Number of Claims)	y (Total Payment for Claims in Swedish Kronor (in Thousands))
108	392.5
19	46.2
13	15.7
124	422.2
40	119.4

This time, we will use a very useful library, NumPy, for arranging the datasets into arrays rather than Python lists. This will simplify the code needed to calculate the regression line in Listing 3-3.

Installing NumPy

NumPy is a widely used package for scientific computing in Python. The library allows you to easily format your data into arrays, which share some similarities to Python lists. However, NumPy arrays are homogeneous and make the task of managing and interacting with large amounts of data faster. NumPy also includes some mathematical functions for interacting with the arrays you create. More information about NumPy can be found at `https://numpy.org`.

If you do not already have NumPy installed on your device, you can download the wheel from the PyPI repository. To install NumPy, enter the following command into the command line:

```
$ pip3 install numpy
```

Next, let's verify that the installation worked correctly. You can either enter `import numpy` into the Python shell or use the `show` command:

```
$ pip3 show numpy
```

You can also use `show` to find out what version of NumPy you currently have installed. The current version as of this writing is 1.19. Upgrading to the current version of NumPy can be done with

```
$ pip3 install --upgrade numpy
```

With NumPy installed, you are ready to see how to create charts that combine different PyQtChart series types in Listing 3-4.

Listing 3-4. Code that demonstrates how to display different series types in the same QChart object

```python
# combine_charts.py
# Import necessary modules
import sys, csv
import numpy as np
from PyQt5.QtWidgets import QApplication, QWidget, QVBoxLayout
from PyQt5.QtChart import QChart, QChartView, QScatterSeries, QLineSeries
from PyQt5.QtCore import Qt
from PyQt5.QtGui import QColor

def linearRegression(x_values, y_values):
    """Find the regression line that fits best to the data.
    Calculate the values for m, the slope of a line, and b, the y-intercept
    in the equation Y = a + bX."""
    # Calculate the average values for x and y
    mean_x, mean_y = np.mean(x_values), np.mean(y_values)

    # Calculate the covariance and variance for the slope coefficient;
    # covariance_xy describes the linear relationship of the variables as
    # they change; variance_x calculates how far observed x_values differs
    # from the mean_x
    covariance_xy = np.sum((x_values - mean_x) * (y_values - mean_y))
    variance_x = np.sum((x_values - mean_x) ** 2)
```

```python
    # Calculate the slope, m, and the y-intercept, b
    b_slope = covariance_xy / variance_x
    a_intercept = mean_y - b_slope * mean_x

    return (a_intercept, b_slope)

class DisplayGraph(QWidget):

    def __init__(self):
        super().__init__()
        self.initializeUI()

    def initializeUI(self):
        """Initialize the window and display its contents."""
        self.setMinimumSize(700, 500)
        self.setWindowTitle("Ex 3.2 - Combining Charts")

        self.row_count = 0 # Number of rows in CSV file

        self.setupChart()
        self.show()

    def setupChart(self):
        """Set up the GUI's series and chart."""
        # Collect x and y data values from the CSV file
        x_values, y_values = self.loadCSVFile()

        # Get the largest x and y values; Used for setting the chart's axes
        x_max, y_max = max(x_values), max(y_values)

        # Create numpy arrays from the x and y values
        x_values = np.array(x_values)
        y_values = np.array(y_values)

        # Calculate the regression line
        coefficients = linearRegression(x_values, y_values)

        # Create chart object
        chart = QChart()
        chart.setTitle("Auto Insurance for Geographical Zones in Sweden")
        chart.legend().hide()
```

```python
# Create scatter series and add points to the series
scatter_series = QScatterSeries()
scatter_series.setName("DataPoints")
scatter_series.setMarkerSize(9.0)
scatter_series.hovered.connect(self.displayPointInfo)

for value in range(0, self.row_count - 1):
    scatter_series.append(x_values[value], y_values[value])
    scatter_series.setBorderColor(QColor('#000000'))

# Create line series and add points to the series
line_series = QLineSeries()
line_series.setName("RegressionLine")

# Calculate the regression line
for x in x_values:
    y_pred = coefficients[0] + coefficients[1] * x
    line_series.append(x, y_pred)

# Add both series to the chart and create x and y axes
chart.addSeries(scatter_series)
chart.addSeries(line_series)
chart.createDefaultAxes()

axis_x = chart.axes(Qt.Horizontal)
axis_x[0].setTitleText("Number of Claims")
axis_x[0].setRange(0, x_max)
axis_x[0].setLabelFormat("%i")

axis_y = chart.axes(Qt.Vertical)
axis_y[0].setTitleText("Total Payment in Swedish Kronor (in
thousands)")
axis_y[0].setRange(0, y_max + 20)

# Create QChartView object for displaying the chart
chart_view = QChartView(chart)

v_box = QVBoxLayout()
v_box.addWidget(chart_view)
self.setLayout(v_box)
```

```python
    def displayPointInfo(self, point):
        """Demonstration that series can be interacted with."""
        print("(X: {}, Y: {})".format(point.x(), point.y()))

    def loadCSVFile(self):
        """Load data from CSV file for the scatter chart.
        Select and store x and y values into Python list objects.
        Return the x_values and y_values lists."""
        x_values, y_values = [], []
        file_name = "files/auto_insurance_sweden.csv"

        with open(file_name, "r") as csv_f:
            reader = csv.reader(csv_f)
            for row in reader:
                x = float(row[0])
                x_values.append(x)
                y = float(row[1])
                y_values.append(y)

            # Count the number of rows in the CSV file. Reset the reader's
            # current position back to the top of the file
            csv_f.seek(0)
            self.row_count = len(list(reader))
        return x_values, y_values

if __name__ == "__main__":
    app = QApplication(sys.argv)
    window = DisplayGraph()
    sys.exit(app.exec_())
```

Figure 3-7 shows the graphical user interface for Example 3.2, displaying both the scatter plot data and the line of best fit.

Explanation

Let's get started by importing the modules and PyQt classes we need. A common practice is to import numpy and set its alias to np.

From the QtWidgets module, we need the basic classes to create a GUI window and set the layout. We also need to import QChart and QChartView to create the chart. This example will utilize both the QLineSeries and the QScatterSeries classes.

The linearRegression() function builds the equation for calculating the regression line that represents the relationship between the independent variable, x_values, and the dependent variable, y_values, in the dataset. You can refer back to this example's introduction and the code in Listing 3-3 to understand the fundamentals of the linear regression equation.

Next, we begin building the class for the GUI's main window, DisplayGraph. After initializing the main window's title and minimum size, let's set up the chart for visualizing our data. Using the loadCSVFile() function, create two Python lists, x_values and y_values, that will hold their respective x and y coordinate values. Refer to Table 3-5 to visualize a few rows from the dataset. For this example, x_values corresponds to column 0, the number of claims reported; y_values refers to column 1, the total insurance payment in Swedish kronor. This data will be used to create the points in the scatter plot.

We can now create our NumPy arrays for the x and y values. These arrays are passed as arguments to the linearRegression() function, which returns the coefficient values, a_intercept and b_slope, as a Python tuple. These values will be used to calculate the regression line for the QLineSeries, line_series. The relationship between the independent and dependent variables is summarized by the regression line on the graph with the equation

```
Total Payment = 19.994 + 3.414 * Number of Claims
```

After preparing the data for visualization and estimating the values for the linear regression equation, we can now create the QChart object, set its title, and hide the chart's legend. With QScatterSeries, we can visualize the relationship between the variables in the dataset. In a for loop, use the append() method to add all of the points to scatter_series.

When PyQt creates points in a scatter plot, bars in a bar graph, or any other graphical object in a chart, you can actually make them interactive using PyQt's signal and slot mechanism. For this program, the points added to the scatter series are connected to the displayPointInfo() slot using the built-in hovered() signal. When a user hovers over the points, their values will be printed in the shell window. This can be seen in Figure 3-8. Of course, this is just an example to demonstrate how to connect the objects in your graph using signals and slots. Using QPainter and other graphics classes, you could actually create visual objects that display the points or values of your data in the GUI window.

```
● ● ●              ch03_data_visualization — -bash — 80×24
(X: 4.0, Y: 38.1)
(X: 5.0, Y: 40.3)
(X: 5.0, Y: 40.3)
(X: 8.0, Y: 55.6)
(X: 8.0, Y: 55.6)
(X: 9.0, Y: 52.1)
(X: 9.0, Y: 52.1)
(X: 11.0, Y: 57.2)
(X: 48.0, Y: 248.1)
(X: 48.0, Y: 248.1)
```

Figure 3-8. *PyQt's signals and slots can be used to visualize the values of different points in the scatter plot*

We can now create the QLineSeries object for plotting the regression line. Using the coefficient values for the slope and y-intercept, we can calculate the predicted y values for the regression line. Adding two or more series to a QChart instance in Listing 3-4 is as easy as calling addSeries() multiple times on the same chart instance:

```
chart.addSeries(scatter_series)
chart.addSeries(line_series)
```

Unlike the previous two applications in this chapter, this example shows how to create a chart's axes using createDefaultAxes(), which creates axes based on the values in the series added to the chart. This function should be called after all series have been added. Axes created for the series are specific to the type of series. Call the axes() method and the Qt orientation to access and modify a specific axis. The following bit of code is found in Listing 3-4:

```
axis_x = chart.axes(Qt.Horizontal)
axis_x[0].setRange(0, x_max)
```

Finally, create an instance of QChartView and pass chart as an argument. Add chart_view to the window's layout and use show() to display the GUI on the screen.

Project 3.2: Visualizing Data with Matplotlib

In previous sections, we have focused mainly on using PyQtChart classes for data visualization. However, depending upon the requirements of your application, that is not your only choice for creating good-looking and interactive charts.

For this chapter's final project seen in Figure 3-9, you will take a look at Matplotlib, a commonly used graphing library for Python. Using Matplotlib instead of PyQtChart might be a better choice if you already have experience working with the library, want to make use of the extensive plotting tools that Matplotlib offers, or need to move an existing Matplotlib project into a PyQt application.

Before jumping into the solution, let's take a brief look at both the Matplotlib toolkit and the dataset we will be using this time around.

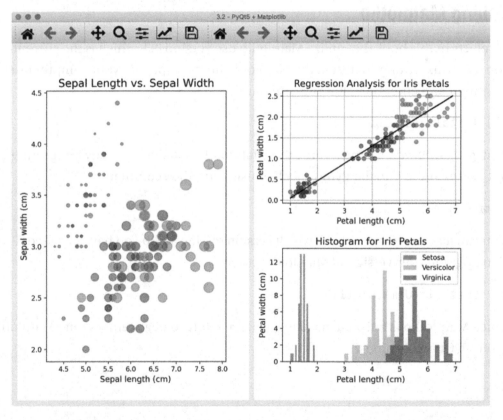

Figure 3-9. *PyQt application embedded with multiple Matplotlib canvases. The left figure displays the relationship between the sepal lengths and widths; the top-right figure shows the regression line for petal sizes; the bottom-right figure displays a histogram showing the distribution of iris petal sizes*

111

Introduction to Matplotlib

A popular library used with Python for data visualization already exists – **Matplotlib**. The framework, just like PyQtChart, includes tools for plotting data in different types of charts and figures. Also like PyQt, graphs created using Matplotlib can be fixed, dynamic, or interactive. There is also functionality included for 3D data visualization.

Matplotlib, which is built around NumPy arrays, also includes a number of significant features for working with different graphics backends, such as Qt, for rendering plots. This is the reason that you can embed Matplotlib plots in your PyQt applications with very little effort. The default backend for Matplotlib is Agg.

Check out `https://matplotlib.org` for more information.

Installing Matplotlib

Any projects in this book that utilize Matplotlib use version 3.3, which is the current edition as of this writing. To install the Matplotlib library, open up your computer's shell environment and enter the following command:

```
$ pip3 install matplotlib
```

If all goes well, you can next verify that Matplotlib installed correctly by entering `import matplotlib` into the Python shell or using the `show` command:

```
$ pip3 show matplotlib
```

You can also use `show` to check which version of Matplotlib you have installed. If you need to upgrade your version of Matplotlib, enter

```
$ pip3 install -U matplotlib
```

Once Matplotlib is finished installing, you are ready to begin embedding Matplotlib into your PyQt applications.

Quick Glance at the Dataset

For this chapter's final program, we will be using a well-known dataset – the Iris dataset[4] – for learning how to embed Matplotlib plots in PyQt5 applications. First presented in Ronald Fisher's research paper "The use of multiple measurements in taxonomic problems" in 1936, the dataset contains information about three classes of iris plants with 50 examples collected for each. The columns hold information related to both the sepal and petal lengths and widths for the different iris samples.

Table 3-5 lists a few rows selected from the Iris dataset.

Table 3-5. *Six selected rows in the iris.csv file (the first two rows from each variety of iris). The measurements for the parts of the irises are in centimeters*

sepal.length	sepal.width	petal.length	petal.width	variety
5.1	3.5	1.4	0.2	Setosa
4.9	3	1.4	0.2	Setosa
7	3.2	4.7	1.4	Versicolor
6.4	3.2	4.5	1.5	Versicolor
6.3	3.3	6	2.5	Virginica
5.8	2.7	5.1	1.9	Virginica

Visualizing Data with Matplotlib Solution

The following project in Listing 3-5 explores how to embed Matplotlib figures into PyQt applications for data visualization and analysis. You will also find out how to use different Matplotlib graphs, chiefly line charts, scatter plots, and histograms, for analyzing how to visualize the same dataset using varying techniques.

---

[4]More information about this dataset can be found in Dua, D. and Graff, C. (2019). UCI Machine Learning Repository [http://archive.ics.uci.edu/ml]. Irvine, CA: University of California, School of Information and Computer Science.

Listing 3-5. Creating GUI applications for visualizing data with PyQt5 and Matplotlib

```python
# pyqt_matplotlib.py
# Import necessary modules
import sys, csv
from PyQt5.QtWidgets import QApplication, QMainWindow, QWidget,
QVBoxLayout, QHBoxLayout

import numpy as np
import matplotlib
matplotlib.use('Qt5Agg') # Configure the backend to use Qt5
from matplotlib.backends.backend_qt5agg import FigureCanvasQTAgg,
NavigationToolbar2QT
from matplotlib.figure import Figure

class CreateCanvas(FigureCanvasQTAgg):

    def __init__(self, parent=None, nrow=1, ncol=1):
        # Create Matplotlib Figure object
        figure = Figure(figsize=(6, 5), dpi=100)
        # Reserve width and height space for subplots
        figure.subplots_adjust(wspace= 0.3, hspace=0.4)
        # Create the axes and set the number of rows/columns for the
        subplot(s)
        self.axes = figure.subplots(nrow, ncol)
        super(CreateCanvas, self).__init__(figure)

class DisplayGraph(QMainWindow):

    def __init__(self):
        super().__init__()
        self.initializeUI()

    def initializeUI(self):
        """Initialize the window and display its contents."""
        self.setMinimumSize(1000, 800)
        self.setWindowTitle("3.2 - PyQt5 + Matplotlib")
```

```python
        self.setupChart()
        self.show()

    def setupChart(self):
        """Set up the GUI's window and widgets that are embedded with
        Matplotlib figures."""
        # Load the iris dataset from the CSV file
        iris_data = self.loadCSVFile()

        # Create the different feature variables for each of the columns in
        the iris dataset
        sepal_length, sepal_width = iris_data[:, 0].astype(float), iris_
        data[:, 1].astype(float)
        petal_length, petal_width = iris_data[:, 2].astype(float), iris_
        data[:, 3].astype(float)
        labels = iris_data[:, 4].astype(str)

        # Convert target labels to encoded labels that will be used for
        color coding the points in the scatter plots
        encoded_labels = []

        for label in labels:
            if label == "Setosa":
                encoded_labels.append(0)
            elif label == "Versicolor":
                encoded_labels.append(1)
            elif label == "Virginica":
                encoded_labels.append(2)

        # Create a canvas object for the scatter plot that visualizes the
        relationship between sepal_length and sepal_width
        scatter_canvas = CreateCanvas(self)
        scatter_canvas.axes.set_title('Sepal Length vs. Sepal Width',
        fontsize=16)
        scatter_canvas.axes.scatter(sepal_length, sepal_width, s=100 *
        petal_width,
            c=encoded_labels, cmap='viridis', alpha=0.4)
        scatter_canvas.axes.set_xlabel("Sepal length (cm)", fontsize=12)
```

115

```
scatter_canvas.axes.set_ylabel("Sepal width (cm)", fontsize=12)
self.addToolBar(NavigationToolbar2QT(scatter_canvas, self))

# Regression line for petal length vs. petal width
reg_line = np.polyfit(petal_length, petal_width, 1)
poly_reg_line = np.poly1d(reg_line)

# Create a canvas object for the scatter plot and histogram that
visualize the relationship between petal_length and petal_width
mixed_canvas = CreateCanvas(self, nrow=2, ncol=1)
mixed_canvas.axes[0].scatter(petal_length, petal_width, alpha=0.5,
    c=encoded_labels, cmap='viridis')
mixed_canvas.axes[0].set_title("Regression Analysis for Iris
Petals", fontsize=14)
mixed_canvas.axes[0].plot(petal_length, poly_reg_line(petal_
length), c='black')
mixed_canvas.axes[0].set_xlabel("Petal length (cm)", fontsize=12)
mixed_canvas.axes[0].set_ylabel("Petal width (cm)", fontsize=12)
mixed_canvas.axes[0].grid(True)

# Create histogram for petal length
mixed_canvas.axes[1].hist(petal_length[:50], bins=15,
color='purple', alpha=0.6, label="Setosa")
mixed_canvas.axes[1].hist(petal_length[51:100], bins=15,
color='lightgreen', alpha=0.6, label="Versicolor")
mixed_canvas.axes[1].hist(petal_length[101:149], bins=15,
color='yellow', alpha=0.6, label="Virginica")

mixed_canvas.axes[1].set_title("Histogram for Iris Petals",
fontsize=14,)
mixed_canvas.axes[1].set_xlabel("Petal length (cm)", fontsize=12)
mixed_canvas.axes[1].set_ylabel("Petal width (cm)", fontsize=12)
mixed_canvas.axes[1].legend()
self.addToolBar(NavigationToolbar2QT(mixed_canvas, self))

charts_h_box = QHBoxLayout()
charts_h_box.addWidget(scatter_canvas)
charts_h_box.addWidget(mixed_canvas)
```

```
        main_v_box = QVBoxLayout()
        main_v_box.addLayout(charts_h_box)

        container = QWidget()
        container.setLayout(main_v_box)
        self.setCentralWidget(container)

    def loadCSVFile(self):
        """Load the iris dataset and store the data in a numpy array."""
        file_name = "files/iris.csv"

        with open(file_name, "r") as csv_f:
            reader = csv.reader(csv_f)
            header_labels = next(reader)
            data = np.array(list(reader))
        return data

if __name__ == '__main__':
    app = QApplication(sys.argv)
    window = DisplayGraph()
    sys.exit(app.exec_())
```

The PyQt GUI with embedded Matplotlib canvases can be seen in Figure 3-9.

Explanation

For this project, we will once again be using the csv module for working with data. We also need to import a few basic classes from QtWidgets to create the GUI's window. The numpy module is used for configuring the data from the Iris dataset into NumPy arrays, making it easier to work with our data in Matplotlib, and for calculating the line of best fit.

Next, let's take a look at the classes we need for embedding Matplotlib. We need to be sure to use the Qt5Aff backend for this project with the use() function. From backend_qt5aff, let's import

- FigureCanvasQTAgg – Creates the canvas object where the rendered figure is placed. The canvas, which is modified to import from the Qt5 backend, is also a Qt widget.

- NavigationToolbar2QT – The toolbar widget that gives a user access to interact with the plot.

Figure objects are the outmost container for a plot in Matplotlib and can contain one or more Axes. An Axes object in Matplotlib is actually the rectangular area for generating plots.

Embedding Matplotlib Canvases in PyQt

If you only want to quickly display a Matplotlib plot in a PyQt GUI, then the following short code in Listing 3-6 shows you how to get started creating a figure, canvas, and axes with little trouble.

Listing 3-6. Embedding a Matplotlib plot in a PyQt application

```python
# Import necessary PyQt5 and matplotlib modules
import sys
from PyQt5.QtWidgets import QApplication, QMainWindow
from matplotlib.backends.backend_qt5agg import FigureCanvasQTAgg
from matplotlib.figure import Figure

class MainWindow(QMainWindow):

    def __init__(self):
        super().__init__()

        # Create the figure that will be rendered in the canvas using the
        # Qt5 backend. figsize can be used to set the size of the figure in
        # inches.
        figure = Figure(figsize=(6, 5))
        canvas = FigureCanvasQTAgg(figure)
        # Create a single subplot in row 1, column 1 on subplot 1
        axes = figure.add_subplot(111)

        # Add a graph to axes instance using plot() or other functions
        axes.plot([1, 2, 1, 3, 0])
        axes.set_title("Creating a Basic Plot")
        axes.grid(True)
        axes.set_xlabel("Independent Variable")
        axes.set_ylabel("Dependent Variable")
```

```
        self.setCentralWidget(canvas)
        self.show()

app = QApplication(sys.argv)
window = MainWindow()
sys.exit(app.exec_())
```

The output of the code can be seen in Figure 3-10.

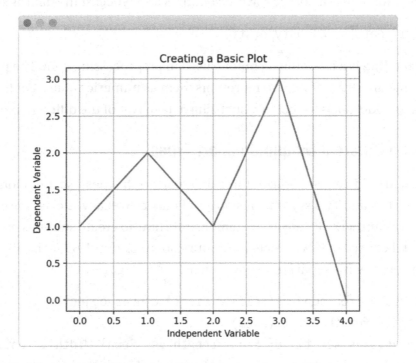

Figure 3-10. *A basic Matplotlib graph embedded in a PyQt GUI*

For this example, let's create the CreateCanvas class that inherits from FigureCanvasQTAgg. Here we construct the canvas, set up the figure, and set how many subplots there are in the canvas by specifying the number of rows, nrow, and columns, ncol, to create the axes. The dpi keyword specifies the resolution of the figure. The subplot() function in Listing 3-6 is used to create the axes based on rows and columns:

```
self.axes = figure.subplots(nrow, ncol)
```

Later in the program, we will use indexing to work with each of the different axes when there are multiple subplots. You can also add plots to a figure using add_subplot() or add_axes().

The DisplayGraph class sets up the GUI's main window. In setupChart(), we first load the Iris dataset and create a NumPy array, data, to hold the information. Next, we split up the data into separate arrays based on the iris features and label columns. An example for the labels array is seen in the following code from Listing 3-6, where [:, 4] states that we want to use all of the rows in column 4 and typecast the data as strings:

```
labels = iris_data[:, 4].astype(str)
```

Label encoding is a common technique used in preprocessing data. The process takes labels that are string types and represents them as numeric values. For this problem, we encode labels for better visualizing data in two of the different plots.

Working with Different Matplotlib Chart Types

The GUI created in Listing 3-4 utilizes three different graph types – scatter plots, a line chart, and a histogram. Two separate instances of the CreateCanvas class are created, scatter_canvas and mixed_canvas, to demonstrate how to create subplots on the same canvas object. Let's see how we create the scatter plot in Listing 3-6 for visualizing the relationship between iris sepal sizes shown on the left in Figure 3-9:

```
scatter_canvas = CreateCanvas(self) # Create canvas object
# Set the title for the plot (axes)
scatter_canvas.axes.set_title('Sepal Length vs. Sepal Width', fontsize=16)
# Create a scatterplot from the sepal_length and sepal_width data. s refers
# to marker size for each point; c is the color of each point; we use a
# built-in colormap (cmap); alpha refers the transparency of the points
scatter_canvas.axes.scatter(sepal_length, sepal_width, s=100 * petal_width,
c=encoded_labels, cmap='viridis', alpha=0.4)
# Set the labels for the x and y axes
scatter_canvas.axes.set_xlabel("Sepal length (cm)")
scatter_canvas.axes.set_ylabel("Sepal width (cm)")
```

Following the first plot, we create the mixed_canvas for visualizing data related to the iris petal lengths and widths. This canvas in Listing 3-6 has two rows and one column:

```
mixed_canvas = CreateCanvas(self, nrow=2, ncol=1)
```

The next scatter plot is produced in a similar manner as the first, except we use the index of axes for the `mixed_canvas` to generate the graph:

```
mixed_canvas.axes[0].scatter(petal_length, petal_width, alpha=0.5,
c=encoded_labels, cmap='viridis')
```

In Example 3.2, the function for calculating the regression line was written from scratch. NumPy already includes a function, `polyfit()`, for performing the same task. The `poly1d()` is used for working with one-dimensional polynomials. This is demonstrated in the following in code from Listing 3-6:

```
reg_line = np.polyfit(petal_length, petal_width, 1)
poly_reg_line = np.poly1d(reg_line)
```

The regression line, `poly_reg_line`, is then plotted on the same axes by

```
mixed_canvas.axes[0].plot(petal_length, poly_reg_line(petal_length),
c='black')
```

Finally, we can create a histogram with `hist()`. A histogram is similar to a bar chart, but shows how often an event occurs in the data. In order to display data for all three iris types in the same graph, we create three separate histogram instances. An example for the Setosa iris type is shown in the following snippet from Listing 3-6. The `bins` keyword refers to the number of bars used to visualize the data:

```
mixed_canvas.axes[1].hist(petal_length[:50], bins=15, color='purple',
alpha=0.6, label="Setosa")
```

A chart's legend can be created for each of the labels in an `axes` by

```
mixed_canvas.axes[1].legend()
```

A toolbar widget is also created and added to the main window for each of the canvas objects.

Creating a Navigation Toolbar

For the two canvases, a separate NavigationToolbar2QT object is created and added as a widget to the main window using `addToolBar()`:

```
self.addToolBar(NavigationToolbar2QT(scatter_canvas, self))
```

If you need to include Matplotlib's navigation toolbar, seen in Figure 3-11, the following buttons and functionality are already included (viewed from left to right):

- Home – When a user pans around or zooms in or out on a plot, its appearance is modified. Clicking Home will undo all actions performed on the plot.

- Back/Forward – Used to undo or redo the previous action performed on the plot.

- Pan/Zoom – This button has two modes: 1) With the left mouse button, the user can pan around the data in the chart. 2) Using the right mouse button, the user can zoom in and out of the selected region.

- Zoom-to-rectangle – User can define a rectangular area in the view and zoom into that region.

- Subplot-configuration – Configures the appearance of the plot.

- Figure-configuration – Configures the appearance of the figures. If multiple figures were created, the user will be able to select which axes they want to modify.

- Save – Opens a file dialog to save an image of the current figure.

Figure 3-11. *The NavigationToolbar2QT toolbar*

Toolbars can also be moved around and set in different locations within the GUI's window. For more information about Matplotlib's navigation toolbar, refer to https://matplotlib.org/3.1.1/users/navigation_toolbar.html.

Summary

Data science is a rapidly growing field, and the number of tools, with varying types, we use to understand and visualize data is also increasing. To build a project for identifying patterns in data, the data analysis process sets up some guidelines for collecting, processing and cleaning, visualizing, and deploying data models for public use.

There are an array of chart types, such as line graphs, bar graphs, or candlestick charts, for visualizing data and handling different analysis and statistics scenarios. An additional module, PyQtChart, can be installed for creating PyQt GUIs for 2D data visualization. Since PyQt charts are created on top of Qt's Graphics View Framework and the QPainter API, developers can not only integrate charts into their applications but also make them interactive, dynamic, and even stylized.

In this chapter, we saw how to set up basic line charts and create a user interface for generating and interacting with multiple line series and how to display different chart types on a single graph for regression analysis. We also walked through the process of using a popular plotting tool, Matplotlib, alongside PyQt for creating data-centric programs.

In Chapter 4, you will learn about creating GUIs for database handling using relational database management systems.

CHAPTER 4

Database Handling in PyQt

Let's continue exploring the possibilities of working with data with one of the most widely used tools for accessing and managing data – **Structured Query Language (SQL)**. Much of the world's data is collected and stored in the cloud or on **servers,** computers that store and provide data to **client** computers when the client makes requests for information from the server.

As you saw in Chapter 3, data can be visualized using various tools, such as charts and graphs. Tables and lists are also commonly used tools for visualizing and analyzing data. With only a few commands, SQL allows you to access information stored in a **database**, a collection of structured data, and edit only the data that you require.

Of course, the data that we collect isn't isolated. Data has relationships and is oftentimes associated with other information. The data collected from a store that sells shoes can be stored in databases to track information about their current inventory, the brands they sell, the current items on order, the customers' information, and so on. SQL allows you to manage those relationships in **relational databases**, where data is organized into tables that retain the connections between other tables.

This chapter will show you how to

- Use PyQt's `QtSql` module and classes to create and query small SQL databases.

- Work with JSON-formatted files for reading and writing data files.

- Utilize the `argparse` module to query databases from the command line.

© Joshua Willman 2021
J. Willman, *Modern PyQt*, https://doi.org/10.1007/978-1-4842-6603-8_4

- Build an application for managing SQL databases using model and view classes.

- Add splash screens to your PyQt applications with the `QSplashScreen` class.

The next section will introduce you to working with databases using PyQt.

Using SQL with PyQt

PyQt makes displaying the information in databases relatively straightforward using Qt's model/view architecture. PyQt has data model classes created specifically for handling SQL databases depending upon your needs. For example, **QSqlQueryModel** allows for easy access to databases in a read-only format, meaning you can only manipulate data with a **query** to the database. **QSqlTableModel** is handy for working with data in tables that have no relationships with other tables. Finally, **QSqlRelationalTableModel** is useful for handling databases where the tables do share relationships. Data in the table models can also be edited through a PyQt view class.

Other classes in the **QtSql** module allow connecting with and manipulating databases. Connections are made using the **QSqlDatabase** class, and interactions with the data are done with **QSqlQuery**. There are also other classes for accessing specific items in the database or for providing information about database errors.

In order to manage data, you will also need to select a **relational database management system** (**RDBMS**). An RDBMS is software that is used for creating and managing databases based on relational models. Commonly used RDBMS software includes PostgreSQL, MySQL, SQLite, and Open Database Connectivity (ODBC). These RDBMSs typically have slightly different purposes and syntax, but all of them rely on SQL as the main language for interacting with a database.

The QtSql module has different driver plugins related to the RDBMSs for communicating with the databases. QtSql and a few other drivers, including SQLite and ODBC, already come prebuilt when you install PyQt5. As of PyQt5 version 5.15, there is only support for a few of the SQL backends due to licensing arrangements with Qt and the various companies. If you want to use other drivers, such as MySQL, you can find more information about installing different drivers at `https://doc.qt.io/qt-5/sql-driver.html`. Another option is to roll back to a previous version if the driver that you want to use is currently not supported in your current version of PyQt5.

To find out which drivers you already have installed, open your Python 3 environment in the shell and run the following code:

```
>>> from PyQt5.QtSql import QSqlDatabase
>>> print(QSqlDatabase.drivers())
```

This will print out a list of the different plugins you have installed. Be aware that this does not necessarily mean that just because you have the driver, you can immediately use it. You may still need to build the plugin. Refer to the Qt documentation for assistance.

In this chapter, we will be working with SQLite3 (the QSQLITE driver). This is done for two reasons, the first being that SQLite3 in PyQt is supported on Mac, Windows, and Linux. SQLite3 ships with both Python and PyQt5, so there should not be any complications if you simply want to get the code in this chapter up and running. Second, SQLite3 is perfect for creating small- to medium-sized applications where your database is a single file and can be stored locally and not on a remote server.

When accessing databases on a server through a network, different clients are able to request different information from the same database at the same time. This is one of the benefits of using RDBMSs such as MySQL. If you choose to use the drivers, you will also need to specify other information such as the server name and the database name. The following code illustrates how this may be achieved with PyQt:

```
# Specify the information needed for connecting to the database
server = 'localhost' # 127.0.0.1
database = 'DB_NAME'
user_name = 'josh'
password = 'safe_password'
```

With PyQt, we could then use these settings specified by the user and pass them along to QSqlDatabase to connect to the database:

```
# Specify the driver type, such as QMYSQL, QSQLITE, or QPSQL
database = QSqlDatabase.addDatabase("QODBC3")
database.setHostName(server)
database.setDatabaseName(database)
database.setUserName(user_name)
database.setPassword(password)
```

In the first program, we will see how to create a database using the SQL classes in PyQt.

Example 4.1: Creating the Database

For this first example, we are going to find out how to use PyQt's QtSql module for creating and querying a small SQL database. The schematic displayed in Figure 4-1 shows the tables and the relationships between the data. Information in a database is stored in tabular format, where the rows are referred to as **records** and the columns as **fields**. The fields store information such as first_name, store_id, or model_year.

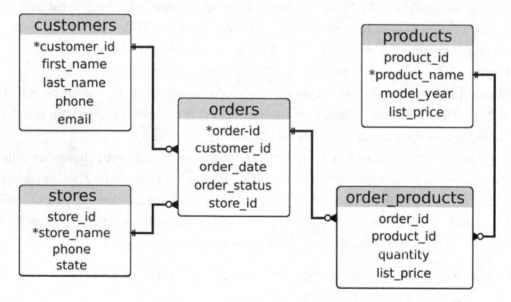

Figure 4-1. *The tables, items, and relationships in the FishingStores database*

The following lists information about the various tables that comprise the FishingStores database:

- customers – Information about the different customers, including their first and last names, phone number, and email.

- stores – Contains information about the different stores. Each record contains the store's name, phone number, and state.

- orders – Includes information about orders placed at the various stores and from which customers. Records contain the customer's ID, the order date, the status of the order, and the ID of the store where the sale occurred.

- products – Holds information about the different products that the different stores sell. Information includes the product's name, model year, and listing price.

- order_products – Consists of items purchased in an order. Items are connected to the order's ID and the product's ID. The table also includes the number of items ordered and the listing price.

Before jumping into the code, let's take a moment to get familiar with some common SQL commands.

Brief Introduction to SQL Commands

SQL statements are used to instruct the server to perform certain operations on the data. When creating items in a table, a developer can specify their data type using SQL keywords, such as INTEGER, DATE, TIME, CHAR, and VARCHAR, the last of which is useful for creating strings of variable length. There are also keywords that are used for creating and manipulating records, performing mathematical calculations, comparing data using set theory, and even deleting tables and records.

Let's look at a few example query statements for working with the database that you will create in Listing 4-1. First, we create a table called products that contains its own unique product_id:

```
CREATE TABLE products (
    product_id INTEGER PRIMARY KEY AUTOINCREMENT UNIQUE NOT NULL)
```

Foreign keys are specified by FOREIGN KEY and which table the key REFERENCES. Here we can see how the foreign key store_id references the store_name in a different table, stores:

```
FOREIGN KEY (store_id) REFERENCES stores (store_name))
```

SELECT statements are used to select data from a database. An asterisk, *, means that you wish to see all the information in a table:

```
SELECT * FROM orders
```

You can also SELECT specific fields or records:

```
SELECT first_name, last_name FROM customers WHERE customer_id > 20
```

INSERT is useful for adding new records into a table:

```
INSERT INTO products (product_name, model_year, list_price) VALUES
('Topwater Lure, 7 1/2"', 27.99, 2019)
```

To erase a record from a table, use DELETE. To delete an entire table, you can use DROP:

```
DROP TABLE IF EXISTS customers
```

SQL commands are generally followed by a semicolon, ;. However, we won't need to use them since the query commands are passed as arguments to PyQt functions. For a full list of keywords used in SQLite3, check out www.sqlite.org/lang_keywords.html.

In Listing 4-1, you will see how to use some of these commands to create and insert data into a database.

Note   Be sure to run Listing 4-1 to create the database before running any of the other programs.

Listing 4-1. Creates the FishingStores database used throughout this chapter

```python
# create_database.py
# Import necessary modules
import sys, os
from PyQt5.QtCore import QCoreApplication
from PyQt5.QtSql import QSqlDatabase, QSqlQuery

# Uncomment to load all relevant information about the different plugins,
# in this case SQL Drivers, that PyQt is trying to load. Useful if you want
# to use plugins other than SQLite and are getting errors
#os.environ['QT_DEBUG_PLUGINS'] = "1"

class CreateDatabaseObjects():
    """Select the SQL driver and set up the database tables."""
    # Create connection to the database. If .sql file does not exist, a new
    .sql file will be created.
    database = QSqlDatabase.addDatabase("QSQLITE") # SQLite version 3
    database.setDatabaseName("databases/FishingStores.sql")
```

```
if not database.open():
    print("Unable to open data source file.")
    print("Connection failed: ", database.lastError().text())
    sys.exit(1) # Error code 1 - signifies error in opening file

query = QSqlQuery()

# Erase tables if they already exist (avoids having duplicate data)
query.exec_("DROP TABLE IF EXISTS customers")
query.exec_("DROP TABLE IF EXISTS stores")
query.exec_("DROP TABLE IF EXISTS orders")
query.exec_("DROP TABLE IF EXISTS products")
query.exec_("DROP TABLE IF EXISTS order_products")

# Create customers table
query.exec_("""CREATE TABLE customers (
        customer_id INTEGER PRIMARY KEY AUTOINCREMENT UNIQUE NOT NULL,
        first_name VARCHAR (100) NOT NULL,
        last_name VARCHAR (100) NOT NULL,
        phone VARCHAR (25),
        email VARCHAR (255) NOT NULL)""")

# Create stores table
query.exec_("""CREATE TABLE stores (
        store_id INTEGER PRIMARY KEY AUTOINCREMENT UNIQUE NOT NULL,
        store_name VARCHAR (100) NOT NULL,
        phone VARCHAR (25),
        state VARCHAR (5))""")

# Create orders table
# order_status: Pending = 1, Processing = 2, Completed = 3, Rejected = 4
query.exec_("""CREATE TABLE orders (
        order_id INTEGER PRIMARY KEY AUTOINCREMENT UNIQUE NOT NULL,
        customer_id INTEGER,
        order_date TEXT NOT NULL,
        order_status TINYINT NOT NULL,
        store_id INTEGER NOT NULL,
        FOREIGN KEY (customer_id) REFERENCES customers (customer_id),
        FOREIGN KEY (store_id) REFERENCES stores (store_name))""")
```

131

```python
    # Create products table
    query.exec_("""CREATE TABLE products (
            product_id INTEGER PRIMARY KEY AUTOINCREMENT UNIQUE NOT NULL,
            product_name VARCHAR (100) NOT NULL,
            model_year VARCHAR (100) NOT NULL,
            list_price DECIMAL (10, 2) NOT NULL)""")

    # Create order_products table
    query.exec_("""CREATE TABLE order_products (
            order_id INTEGER,
            product_id INTEGER,
            quantity INTEGER NOT NULL,
            list_price DECIMAL (10, 2) NOT NULL,
            FOREIGN KEY (order_id) REFERENCES orders (order_id),
            FOREIGN KEY (product_id) REFERENCES products (product_name))""")

class InsertDataIntoTables():
    """Create data and populate the tables."""
    customers = [["James", "Smith", 'NULL'], ["Mary", "Johnson", 'NULL'],
                 ["John", "Williams", 'NULL'], ["Patricia", "Brown",
                  '(716) 472-1234'],
                 ["Lijing", "Ye", 'NULL'], ["Andrea", "Cotman", 'NULL'],
                 ["Aaron", "Rountree", 'NULL'], ["Malik", "Ranger", 'NULL'],
                 ["Helen", "Rodriguez", 'NULL'], ["Linda", "Martinez",
                  'NULL'],
                 ["William", "Hernandez", '(757) 408-1121'], ["Elizabeth",
                  "Lopez", '(804) 543-9876'],
                 ["David", "Gonzalez", 'NULL'], ["Barbara", "Wilson",
                  'NULL'],
                 ["Richard", "Anderson", 'NULL'], ["Susan", "Thomas",
                  '(213) 854-7771'],
                 ["Joseph", "Taylor", '(609) 341-9801'], ["Jessica",
                  "Moore", '(707) 121-0909'],
                 ["Thomas", "Jackson", 'NULL'], ["Sarah", "Martin", 'NULL'],
                 ["Ryan", "Lee", 'NULL'], ["Cynthia", "Perez", '(754)
                  908-5432'],
```

```
        ["Jacob", "Thompson", '(763) 765-1023'], ["Kathleen",
        "White", 'NULL'],
        ["Gary", "Harris", 'NULL'], ["Amy", "Sanchez", '(213)
        198-4510'],
        ["Nicholas", "Clark", 'NULL'], ["Shirley", "Ramirez",
        '(231) 480-1567'],
        ["Eric", "Lewis", 'NULL'], ["Angela", "Miller", 'NULL']]

stores = [['Boston Fish Supplies', '(617) 987-6543', 'MA'],
          ['Miami Fish Supplies', '(786) 123-4567', 'FL']]

orders = [[2, '2020-01-04', 1, 1], [18, '2020-01-05', 2, 1], [30,
'2020-01-08', 1, 2], [6, '2020-01-10', 3, 2],
          [21, '2020-01-11', 1, 2], [19, '2020-01-11', 3, 1], [27,
          '2020-01-12', 3, 1], [1, '2020-01-14', 2, 2],
          [5, '2020-01-15', 1, 2], [29, '2020-01-15', 2, 1], [28,
          '2020-01-16', 1, 2], [9, '2020-01-17', 1, 1],
          [26, '2020-01-17', 2, 2], [10, '2020-01-18', 3, 1], [3,
          '2020-01-18', 3, 2], [11, '2020-01-19', 4, 2],
          [14, '2020-01-20', 1, 1], [20, '2020-01-20', 2, 1], [8,
          '2020-01-20', 3, 1], [12, '2020-01-20', 2, 2],
          [15, '2020-01-21', 4, 1], [4, '2020-01-23', 1, 1], [22,
          '2020-01-24', 3, 2], [13, '2020-01-26', 2, 2],
          [7, '2020-01-26', 1, 2], [16, '2020-01-27', 3, 2], [17,
          '2020-01-29', 2, 1], [23, '2020-01-30', 3, 1],
          [24, '2020-02-01', 1, 2], [25, '2020-02-03',2, 2]]

products = [['Orca Topwater Lure, 7 1/2"', 27.99, 2019], ['Feather
Lure, 6"', 12.99, 2019],
          ['Sailure Fishing Lure, 5 1/2"', 24.99, 2020], ['Waxwing
          Saltwater Jig, 1/2 oz.', 13.99, 2020],
          ['7\'3" Bait-Stik Spinning Rod', 59.99, 2018], ['6\'6"
          Handcrafted Spinning Rod', 119.95, 2019],
          ['7\' Lite Spinning Rod', 169.99, 2020], ['7\' Boat
          Spinning Rod', 79.99, 2020],
          ['6\'6" Conventional Rod', 69.99, 2020], ['165 qt. Maxcold
          Cooler', 129.99, 2018],
```

```
            ['120 qt. Premium Marine Cooler', 399.99, 2019], ['5.3
            Lever Drag Casting Reel', 199.99, 2018],
            ['4.6 Lever Drag Casting Reel', 249.99, 2020], ['Offshore
            Tackle Bag', 159.99, 2017]]

order_products = [[1, 2, 1, 24.99], [2, 14, 2, 159.99], [3, 11, 1,
399.99], [4, 1, 8, 27.99], [5, 1, 2, 12.99],
                  [6, 4, 4, 13.99], [7, 1, 1, 27.99], [8, 8, 2, 79.99],
                  [9, 8, 1, 79.99], [10, 13, 1, 249.99],
                  [11, 1, 1, 27.99], [12, 11, 3, 399.99], [13, 12, 2,
                  199.99], [14, 7, 1, 169.99], [15, 3, 3, 24.99],
                  [16, 10, 1, 129.99], [17, 13, 1, 249.99], [18, 6, 2,
                  119.95], [19, 5, 1, 59.99], [20, 8, 1, 79.99],
                  [21, 6, 1, 119.95], [22, 5, 2, 59.99], [23, 14, 1,
                  159.99], [24, 2, 2, 12.99], [25, 1, 1, 27.99],
                  [26, 10, 1, 129.99], [27, 2, 3, 12.99], [28, 9, 1,
                  69.99], [29, 13, 1, 249.99], [30, 6, 1, 119.95]]

# Create the QSqlQuery instance
query = QSqlQuery()

# Positional binding to insert records into the customers table
query.prepare("INSERT INTO customers (first_name, last_name, phone,
email) VALUES (?, ?, ?, ?)")
# Add the values to the query to be inserted into the customers table
for i in range(len(customers)):
    first_name = customers[i][0]
    last_name = customers[i][1]
    phone = customers[i][2]
    email = (last_name).lower() + "." + (first_name).lower() +
    "@email.com"
    query.addBindValue(first_name)
    query.addBindValue(last_name)
    query.addBindValue(phone)
    query.addBindValue(email)
    query.exec_()
```

```
# Positional binding to insert records into the stores table
query.prepare("INSERT INTO stores (store_name, phone, state) VALUES (?,
?, ?)")
# Add the values to the query to be inserted into the stores table
for i in range(len(stores)):
    store_name = stores[i][0]
    phone = stores[i][1]
    state = stores[i][2]
    query.addBindValue(store_name)
    query.addBindValue(phone)
    query.addBindValue(state)
    query.exec_()

# Positional binding to insert records into the orders table
query.prepare("INSERT INTO orders (customer_id, order_date, order_
status, store_id) VALUES (?, ?, ?, ?)")
# Add the values to the query to be inserted into the orders table
for i in range(len(orders)):
    customer_id = orders[i][0]
    order_date = orders[i][1]
    order_status = orders[i][2]
    store_id = orders[i][3]
    query.addBindValue(customer_id)
    query.addBindValue(order_date)
    query.addBindValue(order_status)
    query.addBindValue(store_id)
    query.exec_()

# Positional binding to insert records into the products table
query.prepare("INSERT INTO products (product_name, model_year, list_
price) VALUES (?, ?, ?)")
# Add the values to the query to be inserted into the products table
for i in range(len(products)):
    product_name = products[i][0]
    model_year = products[i][1]
    list_price = products[i][2]
```

```
        query.addBindValue(product_name)
        query.addBindValue(model_year)
        query.addBindValue(list_price)
        query.exec_()

    # Positional binding to insert records into the order_products table
    query.prepare("INSERT INTO order_products (order_id, product_id,
    quantity, list_price) VALUES (?, ?, ?, ?)")
    # Add the values to the query to be inserted into the order_products table
    for i in range(len(order_products)):
        order_id = order_products[i][0]
        product_id = order_products[i][1]
        quantity = order_products[i][2]
        list_price = order_products[i][3]
        query.addBindValue(order_id)
        query.addBindValue(product_id)
        query.addBindValue(quantity)
        query.addBindValue(list_price)
        query.exec_()

    print("[INFO] Database successfully created.")
    sys.exit(0) # Exit the program after creating the database

if __name__ == "__main__":
    app = QCoreApplication(sys.argv)
    CreateDatabaseObjects()
    InsertDataIntoTables()
    sys.exit(app.exec_())
```

This program creates the FishingStores database that we will visualize and manipulate in Listings 4-2 and 4-3.

Explanation

Unlike previous applications in this book, no GUI will appear when the user runs the program. Instead, we use QCoreApplication to create a PyQt application that can be run using the command line. After executing the program, the following line will be printed in the command window:

```
$ [INFO] Database successfully created.
```

The first time you run this program, you will create the `FishingStores.sql` file in the `databases/` directory.

Tip Rerunning this script will recreate the database. This is useful if you have made changes to the data and want to start over again.

We only need to import two classes from `QtSql` – `QSqlDatabase` for creating the connection to a database and `QSqlQuery` for executing queries and manipulating SQL databases. The program is separated into two classes:

- `CreateDatabaseObjects` – Connect to the database, drop existing tables, and create new tables.

- `InsertDataIntoTables` – Populate the various tables.

When using PyQt SQL classes, the first thing you must do is connect to the database using `QSqlDatabase`. For SQLite3, that merely means specifying the `QSQLITE` driver using `addDatabase()` and stating the file name of the database with `setDatabaseName()`. It is possible to use more than one database in the same application. If the database file does not already exist, then it will be created. The `open()` function must be called to establish the connection.

To begin executing queries in Listing 4-1, make an instance of `QSqlQuery`:

```
query = QSqlQuery()
```

Next, let's use the SQL command `DROP` to delete any tables that already exist. This is useful if you are rerunning the Python script. If you do not drop the table first, then you will append the new information to the existing tables:

```
query.exec_("DROP TABLE IF EXISTS orders")
```

The `exec_()` function is used to execute the `query` statement.

Since the process used in Listing 4-1 for creating each table is similar, we will only discuss how to set up the `orders` table in the following section of code. Use `CREATE TABLE orders` to generate the new table. Each entry in `orders` will have a unique `order_id` using `AUTOINCREMENT` and `UNIQUE`. The `orders` table will include information about an order's ID, a link to a customer who purchased the product, the date of purchase, the current status of the order, and the ID of the store where it was purchased. Using FOREIGN KEY and REFERENCES, you can establish the relationships between different tables. All of the database's connections are illustrated in Figure 4-1:

```
# Create orders table
query.exec_("""CREATE TABLE orders (
        order_id INTEGER PRIMARY KEY AUTOINCREMENT UNIQUE NOT NULL,
        customer_id INTEGER,
        order_date TEXT NOT NULL,
        order_status TINYINT NOT NULL,
        store_id INTEGER NOT NULL,
        FOREIGN KEY (customer_id) REFERENCES customers (customer_id),
        FOREIGN KEY (store_id) REFERENCES stores (store_name))""")
```

Since we know that the store_id will only consist of value 1 or 2, we use a TINYINT to conserve disk space since they only use 1 byte compared to the 4 bytes that INTEGERS use.

Now we can begin inserting records into the tables we created. The records in Listing 4-1 are stored in a Python list that is used to populate the table. For example, the first record in the orders table is shown in the following in the orders list:

```
orders = [[2, '2020-01-04', 1, 1], ...]
```

The first value in the list, 2, corresponds to customer_id, '2020-01-04' refers to order_date, 1 to order_status, and finally 1 to store_id. The other items in the orders list are set up in the same fashion. The exec_() function is very useful for performing queries, such as retrieving tables and even inserting a new record into a table. However, if you have a large database and need to insert a lot of information, you can use placeholders, ?, and the prepare() function. The question mark acts as a temporary variable, allowing you to insert multiple records using the same query instance. Let's take a look at how to insert data into the orders table in Listing 4-1:

```
# Positional binding to insert records into the orders table
query.prepare("INSERT INTO orders (customer_id, order_date, order_status,
store_id) VALUES (?, ?, ?, ?)")
```

Each of the values, such as customer_id or store_id, corresponds to one of the placeholders. The order_id is not included in the following section of code from Listing 4-1 since AUTOINCREMENT is used to update its value:

```
# i refers to item at the ith index in the orders list
for i in range(len(orders)):
    customer_id = orders[i][0]
    order_date = orders[i][1]
    order_status = orders[i][2]
    store_id = orders[i][3]
    query.addBindValue(customer_id)
    query.addBindValue(order_date)
    query.addBindValue(order_status)
    query.addBindValue(store_id)
    query.exec_()
```

The prepare() function gets the query ready for execution. Next, we need to cycle through all the values in the orders list and bind them to their placeholders using addBindValue(). Call exec_() at the end of each iteration to insert the values into the orders table.

Of course, you can also add a single record to any table using exec_():

```
query.exec_("INSERT INTO orders(customer_id, order_date, order_status,
store_id) VALUES(12, '1990-04-20', 3, 1")
```

With your database built, you are now ready to use PyQt's SQL classes and the QTableView widget to visualize the data.

Example 4.2: Displaying Data with QTableView

Tables, lists, charts, and other types of visual tools are helpful for humans to visualize, organize, understand, and find meaning in data. In this next example seen in Figure 4-2, you will use two different QtSql models, QSqlQueryModel and QSqlTableModel, for displaying a SQL database using PyQt's QTableView class.

	first_name	last_name	phone	email
		Ex 4.2 - Display SQL Data in PyQt Tables		
1	James	Smith	NULL	smith.james@email.com
2	Mary	Johnson	NULL	johnson.mary@email.com
3	John	Williams	NULL	williams.john@email.com
4	Patricia	Brown	(716) 472-1234	brown.patricia@email.com
5	Lijing	Ye	NULL	ye.lijing@email.com
6	Andrea	Cotman	NULL	cotman.andrea@email.com
7	Aaron	Rountree	NULL	rountree.aaron@email.com
8	Malik	Ranger	NULL	ranger.malik@email.com
9	Helen	Rodriguez	NULL	rodriguez.helen@email.com
10	Linda	Martinez	NULL	martinez.linda@email.com
11	William	Hernandez	(757) 408-1121	hernandez.william@email.com
12	Elizabeth	Lopez	(804) 543-9876	lopez.elizabeth@email.com
13	David	Gonzalez	NULL	gonzalez.david@email.com
14	Barbara	Wilson	NULL	wilson.barbara@email.com
15	Richard	Anderson	NULL	anderson.richard@email.com
16	Susan	Thomas	(213) 854-7771	thomas.susan@email.com

Figure 4-2. *The customers table from the FishingStores database*

In order to specify which model class we want to use for handling the data in Listing 4-2, we will also take advantage of Python's `argparse` module for passing arguments to our application using the command line.

Listing 4-2. Code for interacting with the FishingStores database using different QtSql model classes and the command line

```
# view_database.py
# Import necessary modules
import sys, argparse
from PyQt5.QtWidgets import (QApplication, QMainWindow, QTableView,
QHeaderView, QMessageBox)
from PyQt5.QtSql import QSqlDatabase, QSqlQuery, QSqlQueryModel,
QSqlTableModel

def parseCommandLine():
    """Use argparse to parse the command line for the SQL data model and
    any queries to the database. Users can enter multiple queries in the
    command line."""
    parser = argparse.ArgumentParser()
    parser.add_argument("-d", "--data-model", type=str,
```

```
        choices=['read-only', 'read-write'], default="read-only",
        help="Select the type of data model for viewing SQL data: \
            read-only = QSqlQueryModel; read-write = QSqlTableModel")
    parser.add_argument("-q", "--query", type=str, default=["SELECT * FROM
    customers"],
        nargs="*", help="Pass a query in the command line")
    args = vars(parser.parse_args())
    return args

class DisplayDatabase(QMainWindow):

    def __init__(self):
        super().__init__()
        self.initializeUI()

    def initializeUI(self):
        """Initialize the window and its contents."""
        self.setMinimumSize(1000, 500)
        self.setWindowTitle("Ex 4.2 - Display SQL Data in PyQt Tables")

        self.createConnection()
        self.setupTable(args["data_model"], args["query"])
        self.show()

    def createConnection(self):
        """Set up connection to the database. Check if the tables needed
        exist."""
        self.database = QSqlDatabase.addDatabase("QSQLITE")
        self.database.setDatabaseName("databases/FishingStores.sql")

        if not self.database.open():
            print("Unable to open data source file.")
            print("Connection failed: ", self.database.lastError().text())
            sys.exit(1) # Error code 1 - signifies error in opening file

        # Check if the tables we want to use exist in the database
        tables_needed = {'customers', 'stores', 'orders', 'products',
        'order_products'}
        tables_not_found = tables_needed - set(self.database.tables())
```

141

```
        if tables_not_found:
            QMessageBox.critical(None, 'Error',
                'The following tables are missing from the database: {}'.
                format(tables_not_found))
            sys.exit(1) # Error code 1 - signifies error

    def setupTable(self, data_model, query_cmdline):
        """Set up the main window. The SQL model used is based on data_
        model; The query_cmdline argument is a list of queries from the
        command line."""
        if data_model == "read-write":
            # Create the model instance
            self.model = QSqlTableModel()
            # Populate the model with data. Example of using setQuery()
            to display data in the table view; you would typically use
            setTable() to populate the model
            for qry in query_cmdline:
                query = QSqlQuery(qry)
                self.model.setQuery(query)

        elif data_model == "read-only":
            self.model = QSqlQueryModel()
            # Populate the model with data
            for qry in query_cmdline:
                self.model.setQuery(qry)

        table_view = QTableView()
        table_view.setModel(self.model)
        table_view.hideColumn(0) # Useful if you don't want to view the id
        values
        table_view.horizontalHeader().setSectionResizeMode(QHeaderView.
        Stretch)

        self.setCentralWidget(table_view)
```

```
if __name__ -- "__main__":
    args = parseCommandLine() # Return any command line arguments
    app = QApplication(sys.argv)
    window = DisplayDatabase()
    sys.exit(app.exec_())
```

The database created in Listing 4-1 can be viewed using different PyQt model classes and a table view object. An example of this is shown in Figure 4-2.

Explanation

On top of the QtWidgets needed for creating the QTableView object and tampering with its headers using QHeaderView and the SQL classes, we also need to import the Python module argparse.

For the purposes of this project, argparse will allow the user to pass arguments in the command line for choosing a SQL data model, QSqlTableModel or QSqlQueryModel, and for managing data and one or more query statements.

First, let's create the parser instance to parse the command line. The add_argument() method is used to fill the parser with information about the arguments to be passed. The parse_args() function returns an object with two attributes, --data-model and --query. The user is able to pass more than one query argument as we shall see soon.

The DisplayDatabase class creates the parameters and functions for setting up the GUI's main window. createConnection() is used to establish and test the connection to the database similar to Listing 4-1. However, this time we already know the contents of the database we want to check out. Let's also take a moment to make sure that the tables we want to interact with also exist. If a table we request is not present, then a QMessageBox.critical() dialog will appear to inform us of the missing table. The program will then exit using sys.exit(1).

If no errors occur, we can begin setting up the data model and table view instances in setupTable() using the following line from Listing 4-2:

```
self.setupTable(args["data_model"], args["query"])
```

The two parameters in setupTable() correspond to the --data-model and --query arguments passed using argparse. If neither argument was specified, then the default model arguments will be passed. The command is shown in the following, and the results are shown in Figure 4-2:

```
$ python3 view_database.py
```

Otherwise, the user can specify the type of data model and any number of queries. Make sure the last statement in --query is a SELECT statement. Otherwise, no data will appear in the table. The following lines of code show example commands for you to try out and see the results in the GUI window. You should also definitely try out your own.

The following selects the QSqlTableModel with read-write, creates a new stores record, and displays the stores table. The result can be seen in Figure 4-3. Also, notice how each query is a string specified with "" and a space between each one.

```
$ python3 view_database.py --data-model read-write --query "INSERT INTO
stores (store_name, phone, state) VALUES ('Hampton Fish Supplies', '(757)
987-6543', 'VA')" "SELECT * FROM stores"
```

Note   Any changes you make using queries or in the QSqlTableModel will also alter the actual data. To recreate the original database, rerun Listing 4-1.

---

	store_name	phone	state
1	Boston Fish Supplies	(617) 987-6543	MA
2	Miami Fish Supplies	(786) 123-4567	FL
3	Hampton Fish Supplies	(757) 987-6|	VA

Ex 4.2 - Display SQL Data in PyQt Tables

Figure 4-3. *The stores table with a new record added. Using QSqlTableModel, data can also be edited in the table as shown in the image*

Use QSqlQueryModel and delete customers with customer_ids less than 20.

```
$ python3 view_database.py --data-model read-only --query "DELETE FROM
customers WHERE customer_id <= 20" "SELECT * FROM customers" "SELECT * FROM
customers"
```

Only display product_id and product_name columns from the products table:

```
$ python3 view_database.py --query "SELECT product_id, product_name FROM
products"
```

Update the email for the customer with customer_id = 3:

```
$ python3 view_database.py -q "UPDATE customers SET email = 'hahaha@email.
com' WHERE customer_id = 3" "SELECT * from customers"
```

QSqlTableModel inherits from the QSqlQueryModel class, and therefore you can use setQuery() to update the data shown in the table view. It is generally a better practice to use other functions such as setTable() or setSort() if you already know which tables you want to view and edit. This is mostly due to how QSqlTableModel manages data shown in tabular form.

Project 4.1: SQL Manager GUI

Now that we have seen how to create SQL databases, modify the data using SQL commands, and display the records with PyQt classes, we can move on to this chapter's final project – a graphical user interface for managing SQL databases in a single application.

SQL Manager GUI Solution

For the general user who needs to interact with data, manipulating SQL databases using the command line isn't very convenient or user-friendly. The purpose of this application is to create the foundation for a light and user-friendly GUI that makes accessing and editing data faster and easier. Creating a GUI can speed up the process for creating databases, writing SQL code, comparing relationships, modifying data, and more.

This application is broken into two scripts:

1. `Login.py` – Creates the login UI

2. `sql_manager.py` – The GUI for interacting with the FishingStores database

Part 1: The Login Script

Software systems that manage relational databases often allow for multiple users to handle the data at any given time. Accessing a database often requires a user to connect to a secure server or to the cloud by entering their username and password into the application's login screen. The login window you will create for this project is shown in Figure 4-4.

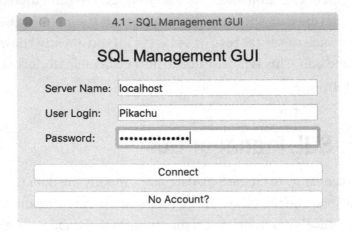

Figure 4-4. *The login window for the SQL Manager application*

The application in Listing 4-3 has two main purposes. If the user already has an account, then they simply enter their username and password and log in. Otherwise, they will need to click the No Account? button seen in Figure 4-4 to register as a new user.

Listing 4-3. Code for the login GUI. Imported in the sql_manager script (Listing 4-4)

```
# Login.py
# Import necessary modules
import sys, time, json
from PyQt5.QtWidgets import (QWidget, QDialog, QLabel, QPushButton,
QLineEdit, QMessageBox, QFormLayout, QVBoxLayout)
```

```python
from PyQt5.QtCore import Qt
from PyQt5.QtGui import QFont

class LoginGUI(QWidget):

    def __init__(self, parent=None):
        super().__init__()
        self.parent = parent
        self.initializeUI()

    def initializeUI(self):
        """Initialize the Login GUI window."""
        self.setFixedSize(400, 240)
        self.setWindowTitle("4.1 - SQL Management GUI")
        self.setupWindow()

    def setupWindow(self):
        """Set up the widgets for the login GUI."""
        header_label = QLabel("SQL Management GUI")
        header_label.setFont(QFont('Arial', 20))
        header_label.setAlignment(Qt.AlignCenter)

        server_name_entry = QLineEdit()
        server_name_entry.setMinimumWidth(250)
        server_name_entry.setText("localhost")

        self.user_entry = QLineEdit()
        self.user_entry.setMinimumWidth(250)

        self.password_entry = QLineEdit()
        self.password_entry.setMinimumWidth(250)
        self.password_entry.setEchoMode(QLineEdit.Password)

        # Arrange the QLineEdit widgets into a QFormLayout
        login_form = QFormLayout()
        login_form.setLabelAlignment(Qt.AlignLeft)
        login_form.addRow("Server Name:", server_name_entry)
        login_form.addRow("User Login:", self.user_entry)
        login_form.addRow("Password:", self.password_entry)
```

```python
        connect_button = QPushButton("Connect")
        connect_button.clicked.connect(self.connectToDatabase)

        new_user_button = QPushButton("No Account?")
        new_user_button.clicked.connect(self.createNewUser)

        main_v_box = QVBoxLayout()
        main_v_box.setAlignment(Qt.AlignTop)
        main_v_box.addWidget(header_label)
        main_v_box.addSpacing(10)
        main_v_box.addLayout(login_form)
        main_v_box.addWidget(connect_button)
        main_v_box.addWidget(new_user_button)
        self.setLayout(main_v_box)

    def connectToDatabase(self):
        """Check the user's information. Close the login window if a match
        is found, and open the SQL manager window."""
        users = {} # Create an empty dictionary to store user information

        with open('files/login.json') as json_f:
            login_data = json.load(json_f)

        # Load information from json file into a dictionary
        for login in login_data['loginList']:
            user, pswd = login['username'], login['password']
            users[user] = pswd # Set the dict's key and value pair

        # Collect information that the user entered
        user_name = self.user_entry.text()
        password = self.password_entry.text()
        if (user_name, password) in users.items():
            self.close()
            # Open the SQL management application
            time.sleep(0.5) # Pause slightly before showing the parent
            window
            self.parent.show()
```

```
        else:
            QMessageBox.warning(self, "Information Incorrect",
                "The user name or password is incorrect.", QMessageBox.Close)

def createNewUser(self):
    """Set up the dialog box for the user to create a new user account."""
    self.hide() # Hide the login window
    self.new_user_dialog = QDialog(self)
    self.new_user_dialog.setWindowTitle("Create New User")

    header_label = QLabel("Create New User Account")
    self.new_user_entry = QLineEdit()

    self.new_password = QLineEdit()
    self.new_password.setEchoMode(QLineEdit.Password)

    self.confirm_password = QLineEdit()
    self.confirm_password.setEchoMode(QLineEdit.Password)

    # Arrange QLineEdit widgets in a QFormLayout
    dialog_form = QFormLayout()
    dialog_form.addRow("New User Login:", self.new_user_entry)
    dialog_form.addRow("New Password", self.new_password)
    dialog_form.addRow("Confirm Password", self.confirm_password)

    # Create sign up button
    create_acct_button = QPushButton("Create New Account")
    create_acct_button.clicked.connect(self.acceptUserInfo)

    dialog_v_box = QVBoxLayout()
    dialog_v_box.setAlignment(Qt.AlignTop)
    dialog_v_box.addWidget(header_label)
    dialog_v_box.addSpacing(10)
    dialog_v_box.addLayout(dialog_form, 1)
    dialog_v_box.addWidget(create_acct_button)
    self.new_user_dialog.setLayout(dialog_v_box)

    self.new_user_dialog.show()
```

```python
    def acceptUserInfo(self):
        """Verify that the user's passwords match. If so, save them user's
        info to the json file and display the login window."""
        user_name_text = self.new_user_entry.text()
        pswd_text = self.new_password.text()
        confirm_text = self.confirm_password.text()

        if pswd_text != confirm_text:
            QMessageBox.warning(self, "Error Message",
                "The passwords you entered do not match. Please try again.",
                QMessageBox.Close)
        else:
            # If the passwords match, save the passwords to the json file
            and return to the login screen.
            user_info = {}

            with open('files/login.json', "r+") as json_f:
                login_data = json.load(json_f)
                login_data['loginList'].append({
                    "username": user_name_text,
                    "password": pswd_text})

                login_data.update(user_info)
                json_f.seek(0) # Reset the file pointer to position 0
                json.dump(login_data, json_f, indent=2)
        self.new_user_dialog.close()
        self.show()
```

The login interface is displayed in Figure 4-4.

Explanation

This part of the application is a simple GUI, composed of widgets from the QtWidgets
module. Since we will also be working with files formatted using JavaScript Object
Notation (JSON), the json module is also imported. More information about working
with JSON files can be found at https://docs.python.org/3/library/json.
html#module-json.tool.

The LoginGUI class in Listing 4-3 creates the interface for logging into the SQL Manager application in Listing 4-4. When the user starts the application, they will first be greeted by a splash screen, which is then followed by the login window. We will discuss creating splash screens with PyQt a little later in this chapter.

The window is composed of a few labels, line edit widgets, and buttons that are arranged using QFormLayout. Since we are using SQLite3, we don't need to worry about our server name, which is specified as localhost. It is included in the application as an example. If you were using other RDBMSs, you would need to collect other information from the user, such as the server or database name. You could definitely modify this window should you choose to use different drivers.

If the user already has an account, they can input their username and password in the current fields and click the connect_button. This sends a signal that is connected to the connectToDatabase() slot. In the following snippet of code from Listing 4-3, we collect the user_name and password text and look for a match in the login.json file. If one is found, we close() the login window and open the parent window, created in Listing 4-4:

```
if (user_name, password) in users.items():
    self.close() # Close login window
    # Open the SQL management application
    self.parent.show()
```

If the user does not have an account, they can create a new one by clicking the new_user_button. This emits a signal that calls createNewUser(), which displays the new_user_dialog shown in Figure 4-5. After the user successfully enters their login information and clicks the create_acct_button, they can then log into the SQL Manager application.

Figure 4-5. *The dialog box to create a new user*

There are numerous ways to improve this system for logging into an application. For example, you could validate the type of characters a user inputs to meet certain formatting standards, use hashing to create secure passwords, or even check if a username already exists in the database of users.

Working with JSON Files

Whether the user is logging in or creating a new account, we need a way to manage their username and password. If the user is logging in, we need to read from the login. json file shown in Figure 4-6 and look for a username and password combination that matches what the user entered.

We first need to read from the file and use load() to return the information in the file as a dictionary. This is demonstrated in the following bit of code from Listing 4-3:

```
with open('files/login.json') as json_f:
    login_data = json.load(json_f)
```

Then we load the information and store the key and value pairs in the users dictionary:

```
# Load information from json file into a dictionary
for login in login_data['loginList']:
    user, pswd = login['username'], login['password']
    users[user] = pswd # Set the dict's key and value
```

We'll use those values and compare them to the user's entries.

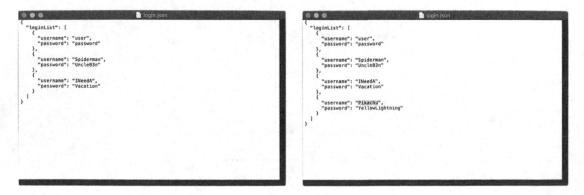

Figure 4-6. *The login.json file before creating a new user account (left) and with the new user's information stored in the file (right)*

To write to a file in Listing 4-3, we first need to open the file and use json's load() function to create a dictionary object:

```
with open('files/login.json', "r+") as json_f:
    login_data = json.load(json_f)
```

Next, let's add our new information to the loginList:

```
login_data['loginList'].append({
    "username": user_name_text,
    "password": pswd_text})
```

We then update the dictionary item with the user_info using update(), return the pointer back to the beginning of the file, and overwrite the previous information using dump():

```
login_data.update(user_info)
json_f.seek(0) # Reset the file pointer to position 0
json.dump(login_data, json_f, indent=2)
```

Now that the user has logged in, they can begin interacting with the SQL Manager GUI.

Part 2: The SQL Manager Script

The QSqlQueryModel class gives us the high-level functionality we need to quickly and easily query databases and display the results using QTableView. The following program displayed in Figure 4-7 has four main components:

- A QTreeView widget for displaying the available database files

- A QTextEdit widget for entering queries

- A QToolbar widget for executing queries or clearing the text edit widget

- A QTableView widget for displaying query results

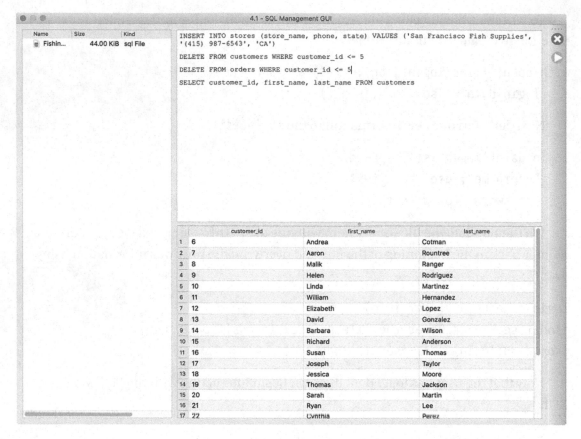

Figure 4-7. *The SQL Manager GUI. The image showcases the available directories in the tree view, a few example queries, and their results visualized in the table view*

Let's have a look at the SQL Manager GUI found in Listing 4-4.

Listing 4-4. The code for the SQL Manager application

```
# sql_manager.py
# Import necessary modules
import sys
from PyQt5.QtWidgets import (QApplication, QMainWindow, QWidget, QTextEdit,
QTableView, QTreeView, QHeaderView, QSplitter, QToolBar, QAction,
QFileSystemModel, QMessageBox, QHBoxLayout, QSplashScreen)
from PyQt5.QtSql import QSqlDatabase, QSqlQuery, QSqlQueryModel
from PyQt5.QtGui import QFont, QIcon, QPixmap
from PyQt5.QtCore import Qt, QSize, QDir
from Login import LoginGUI # Import the login script
```

```python
class SQLManager(QMainWindow):

    def __init__(self):
        super().__init__()
        self.initializeUI()

    def initializeUI(self):
        """Initialize the window and its contents."""
        self.setMinimumSize(1100, 800)
        self.move(QApplication.desktop().screen().rect().center() - self.
        rect().center())
        self.setWindowTitle("4.1 - SQL Management GUI")

        self.login = LoginGUI(self)
        self.login.show()

        self.createConnection()
        self.setupWindow()
        self.setupToolbar()

    def createConnection(self):
        """Set up connection to the database. Check if the tables needed
        exist."""
        self.database = QSqlDatabase.addDatabase("QSQLITE")
        self.database.setDatabaseName("databases/FishingStores.sql")

        if not self.database.open():
            print("Unable to open data source file.")
            sys.exit(1) # Error code 1 - signifies error in opening file

        # Check if the tables we want to use exist in the database
        tables_needed = {'customers', 'stores', 'orders', 'products',
        'order_products'}
        tables_not_found = tables_needed - set(self.database.tables())
        if tables_not_found:
            QMessageBox.critical(None, 'Error',
                'The following tables are missing from the database: {}'.
                format(tables_not_found))
            sys.exit(1) # Error code 1 - signifies error
```

```python
    def setupWindow(self):
        """Set up the directory model/view instances, SQL model/view
        instances, and other widgets to be displayed in the main window."""
        # Create tree model/view for displaying databases in the directory
        directory = QDir.currentPath() + "/databases"

        system_model = QFileSystemModel()
        system_model.setRootPath(directory)
        index = system_model.index(directory)

        tree_view = QTreeView()
        tree_view.setIndentation(15) # Indentation of items in view
        tree_view.setMaximumWidth(300)
        tree_view.setModel(system_model)
        tree_view.setRootIndex(index)

        self.query_entry_field = QTextEdit()
        self.query_entry_field.setFont(QFont("Courier", 14))
        self.query_entry_field.setPlaceholderText("Enter your queries
        here...")

        # Create the model/view instances
        self.sql_model = QSqlQueryModel()

        # Create the table view instance and set its parameters and its
        delegate
        table_view = QTableView()
        table_view.setAlternatingRowColors(True)
        table_view.setModel(self.sql_model)
        table_view.horizontalHeader().setSectionResizeMode(QHeaderView.
        Stretch)
        table_view.verticalHeader().setSectionResizeMode(QHeaderView.
        Stretch)

        # Create splitter that contains the text edit and table view objects
        splitter = QSplitter()
        splitter.setOrientation(Qt.Vertical)
        splitter.addWidget(self.query_entry_field)
        splitter.addWidget(table_view)
```

```python
    main_h_box = QHBoxLayout()
    main_h_box.addWidget(tree_view)
    main_h_box.addWidget(splitter)

    main_container = QWidget()
    main_container.setLayout(main_h_box)
    self.setCentralWidget(main_container)

def setupToolbar(self):
    """Create the toolbar for running queries and clearing the text
    edit widget."""
    toolbar = QToolBar(self)
    toolbar.setIconSize(QSize(24, 24))
    self.addToolBar(Qt.RightToolBarArea, toolbar)

    # Create actions
    clear_text_act = QAction(QIcon("icons/clear.png"), "Clear Query",
    toolbar)
    clear_text_act.setToolTip("Clear the queries in the text field.")
    clear_text_act.triggered.connect(self.clearText)

    run_query_act = QAction(QIcon("icons/run.png"), "Run Query",
    toolbar)
    run_query_act.setToolTip("Run the queries in the text field.")
    run_query_act.triggered.connect(self.runQuery)

    # Add actions to the toolbar
    toolbar.addAction(clear_text_act)
    toolbar.addAction(run_query_act)

def runQuery(self):
    """Run the query/queries entered in the QTextEdit widget."""
    query_text = self.query_entry_field.toPlainText()
    queries = query_text.split('\n')

    if query_text != "":
        for qry in queries:
            if qry == "":
```

```
                        # Pass over empty lines
                        pass
                   else:
                        query = QSqlQuery(qry)
                        self.sql_model.setQuery(query)

     def clearText(self):
          """Clear the QTextEdit widget's text."""
          self.query_entry_field.clear()

if __name__ == '__main__':
     app = QApplication(sys.argv)

     # Display splash screen
     splash = QSplashScreen(QPixmap("images/sql_splashscreen.png"))
     splash.show()
     app.processEvents()

     window = SQLManager()
     splash.finish(window)

     sys.exit(app.exec_())
```

The GUI for the SQL Manager can be seen in Figure 4-7.

Explanation

For this application, we will need to import quite a few classes. QMainWindow is needed for easily setting up the toolbar. QFileSystemModel, QDir, and QTreeView are used for accessing the local file system, accessing paths and files, and displaying the contents of the path, respectively. The text edit and table widgets are arranged in a QSplitter widget. QSplashScreen is used to add a splash screen to the application. The last import is the LoginGUI class from Listing 4-3.

The class SQLManager creates the main window and is centered in the computer's screen in Listing 4-4 using

```
self.move(QApplication.desktop().screen().rect().center() - self.rect().
center())
```

We begin by connecting to the database just like in Listing 4-2. In the `setupWindow()` function, the three main widgets are created and arranged in the main window using a `QSplitter` container for the text edit and table widgets and a `QHBoxLayout` to arrange all of the objects.

First, we create the directory for displaying database files using model/view programming in Listing 4-4. The `QFileSystemModel` class provides the model for accessing data on the computer's local system:

```
system_model = QFileSystemModel() # Create system model
# Set the root path the the current file path
system_model.setRootPath(directory)
# Get the index of the system model
index = system_model.index(directory)
```

Then set the model for the `tree_view` and set its root index to the `system_model`'s index:

```
tree_view = QTreeView()
tree_view.setModel(system_model)
tree_view.setRootIndex(index)
```

Second, the `QTextEdit` object, `query_entry_field`, is used for entering query statements. Each statement is placed on a new line by pressing the Return key. The user can run queries or clear the `query_entry_field` using the `toolbar` on the right of the window. The `toolbar` and its actions are created in the `setupToolbar()` function.

Since this application uses `QSqlQueryModel`, the FishingStores database can only be interacted with using the `query_entry_field`. You could use QSqlTableModel or QSqlRelationalTableModel for creating an editable table. The `table_view` has alternating row colors by setting `setAlternatingRowColors()` to `True`; its horizontal and vertical headers will also stretch to fill available space.

If the user has entered a query into the `query_entry_field`, they can execute the statements by triggering the `run_query_act` button in the `toolbar`. The signal emitted triggers `runQuery()`. All of the lines in the text edit widget are converted into a `queries` list, and then, if there are no errors, each `qry` in `queries` is executed using `setQuery()`:

```
query = QSqlQuery(qry)
self.sql_model.setQuery(query)
```

An example of how to query the database can be seen in Figure 4-7.

Example SQL Queries

This section includes a few example queries that you can try out yourself in the SQL Manager GUI built in Listing 4-4. These queries can be entered into `query_entry_field` and run using the `run_query_act` button in the `toolbar`.

For example, if you would like to display all of the rows from a specific table, use the following command:

```
SELECT * FROM products
```

If you have specific columns of data that you would like to visualize, be sure to specify the column names rather than using the asterisk:

```
SELECT product_name, model_year FROM products
```

The SQL Manager GUI also allows you to create and insert new records. The next example shows how to create a new row and insert it into the `orders` table:

```
INSERT INTO orders (customer_id, order_date, order_status, store_id) VALUES
(31, "2020-02-16", 2, 1)
select * from orders
```

Using the application, you can enter multiple queries at one time. You can also drop existing tables and even create new ones in the FishingStores database. The following code demonstrates how to create a new table, `brands`, add a few records into the table, and view the items in the table view:

```
DROP TABLE IF EXISTS brands
CREATE TABLE brands (brand_id INTEGER PRIMARY KEY UNIQUE NOT NULL, brand_
name VARCHAR (100))
INSERT INTO brands (brand_name) VALUES ("Hardy")
INSERT INTO brands (brand_name) VALUES ("Greys")
Select * FROM brands
```

Feel free to experiment with other types of queries and create new tables and records. Be sure to use the correct punctuation, such as parentheses and apostrophes for strings, when adding new entries into the database.

Creating a Splash Screen

A **splash screen** is a graphical element used in many programs for displaying a logo and/or textual information about the application. They are typically seen when an application is launched and can be useful if your application needs some time to load the main window. The SQL Manager application introduces how to set up a simple splash screen, shown in Figure 4-8.

Figure 4-8. *The SQL Manager application's splash screen. Image used for the splash screen is from www.flaticon.com*

The general process for displaying a simple splash screen in Listing 4-4 is as follows:

```
app = QApplication(sys.argv) # QApplication instance

# Create and display splash screen
splash = QSplashScreen(QPixmap("images/sql_splashscreen.png"))
splash.show()
app.processEvents() # The splash screen is displayed before the main event
loop starts. We need to use processEvents() to receive mouse clicks
window = SQLManager() # The main window instance
```

```
splash.finish(window) # Closes the splash screen once the main window is
displayed
sys.exit(app.exec_()) # Begin the main loop
```

You can also display messages in the splash screen to inform the user about packages that are being loaded or other useful information. Clicking the splash screen will hide it and display the login window for the application.

Summary

SQL is a very important tool used by data scientists for creating databases and manipulating and retrieving data stored in databases. In a world influenced greatly by data, working with databases is another way that we can better understand the underlying relationships of the world we live in. Creating tools and applications that streamline the process for handling data is very important, whether for small companies that work with single-file databases or for large companies that unify data and machine learning techniques to create competitive products while reducing cost.

In this chapter, we have explored how to use PyQt and SQLite3 to create a small database, edit and retrieve information from the database, and create an interactive application for making the process of visualizing data easier using PyQt widgets and model/view programming.

In Chapter 5, you will see how to work with image and video data to create GUIs for computer vision.

CHAPTER 5

GUIs for Computer Vision

When you look at the following image in Figure 5-1, what do you see? You will probably notice the people walking, the street signs, the buildings, and even the lights and the storefronts. From the image, you might recall memories of similar bustling streets that you yourself have walked on or times spent with your family and friends in the city. Smaller details in the picture, such as the sign for the "Restricted parking ZONE," will probably stand out to you, and other information, such as the national flag of the United Kingdom, will give you clues and details about where the image was taken. Moreover, you can also visually distinguish all the different people and clothes in the foreground as they begin to move and blur together into the background.

Figure 5-1. *What information can you infer by looking at the image? Image is from https://unsplash.com*

These concepts of memories and visual cues that we can easily gather from a single image are generally trivial to a human. However, to a computer, the image in Figure 5-1 is merely an array of pixels, a bunch of numbers organized together that represent the colors of red, green, and blue. Similar to how humans have trouble obtaining meaning from rows and columns filled with numerical values without any context, a computer has difficulty understanding meaning from the objects and colors in an image.

© Joshua Willman 2021
J. Willman, *Modern PyQt*, https://doi.org/10.1007/978-1-4842-6603-8_5

Let's look at a few more examples of images that are easy for us to understand, but have proven difficult for machines. Take a look at the images in Figure 5-2. All of the images display the same famous landmark, the Sydney Opera House, and even though the building is viewed from different viewpoints and under different lighting conditions, we are still able to recognize the structure. What may appear as subtle changes to us, visual changes in view or lighting, can also pose problems for a computer. The ability to correctly match key features that make an object or a person identifiable is important for computers, especially for object recognition and image registration.

Figure 5-2. *The Sydney Opera House in Sydney, New South Wales, Australia, seen from different viewpoints. Images are from* `https://pixabay.com`

Another complication for computers can be seen in Figure 5-3. **Occlusion** occurs when two or more objects move close together causing the objects to appear to merge together or when one object covers part or all of another object from view in an image. This can cause problems, especially when creating a computer system for tracking objects.

Fortunately, recent decades have witnessed a new field of study, computer vision, emerge in the hopes that computers will be able to make sense of not only photos but also videos, as well as humans do.

Figure 5-3. *How many sheep do you see? Occlusion can even prove difficult for humans. Image is from* `https://unsplash.com`

Computer vision is used in a number of different industries and fields of research. This chapter focuses primarily on introducing some of the fundamental ideas for creating graphical user interfaces to solve computer vision problems using PyQt and Python. Since visual data can be visualized using images and thus videos, this chapter is also broken into two parts to cover both digital media.

In this chapter, you will

- Be introduced to the field of computer vision.

- Learn about and install the OpenCV library.

- Create GUIs for working with either images or video data.

- Discover OpenCV functions used in computer vision applications for

  - Image processing

  - Human detection and tracking

- Briefly learn about threading in PyQt applications using QThread.

In the next sections, you will learn a little about computer vision, digital images, and the OpenCV library.

What Is Computer Vision?

Computer vision[1] is a field of computer science aimed at creating computer systems that can interpret and react accordingly to visual information acquired from digital data. Using 2D or 3D digital media, computer vision seeks to recover three-dimensional structure and understanding about the world to gain better insight about a visual scene. The domain combines engineering, scientific, and statistical methods to solve complex problems that are easy for the human visual system.

The implementation of computer vision systems has been used to improve the capabilities of many industries, including computer graphics, retail, medicine, surveillance, facial and object recognition, and more. We are surrounded by applications that use computer vision techniques to unlock our phones using facial recognition, organize and recommend images to us, and even manage and moderate image content in online message boards.

Machines have also benefited greatly from computer vision techniques. Applied to the fields of artificial intelligence, machine learning, and deep learning, robots are beginning to better understand and interact with the visual world. Repetitive tasks can be automated using machines, and autonomous vehicles can analyze video feeds in real time to accurately navigate and detect other cars, pedestrians, and the road. The large amounts of visual content we upload to the Internet every day, along with increased computational processing power in recent years, only help to improve the potential of intelligent computer systems.

Before jumping into the code, let's have a look at the basic structure of a digital image to help create GUI applications in PyQt.

Brief Overview of Digital Images

Digital images are visual representations of our environments. As humans, we are able to visually perceive and identify objects, people, or locations in images. However, to a computer, an image is an array of integer values. This concept is represented in Figure 5-4.

---

[1]Some great resources to learn more about computer vision, OpenCV, and other related topics are
    Szeliski, R. (2010). Computer vision: Algorithms and applications. Springer Science & Business Media.
    Adrian Rosebrock. *Practical Python and OpenCV*. PyImageSearch. https://www.pyimages-earch.com/practical-python-opencv/, accessed in August 2020.

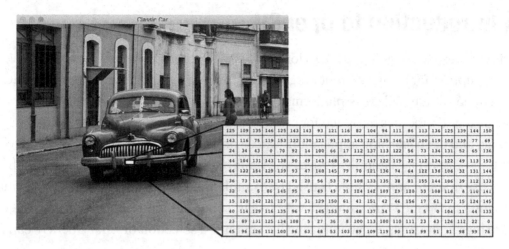

Figure 5-4. *Representation of how a computer sees only numbers in a grayscale image. Values of 0 and 255 represent black pixels and white pixels, respectively, and values in between stand for varying shades of gray. Modified image is originally from* https://pixabay.com

The visual information stored in digital images is actually encoded as numerical values. Each integer represents the intensity value for a given color, from 0 to 255, and is assigned to a pixel, the smallest element in an image. By combining and organizing pixels as a two-dimensional matrix of pixels, we can create an image. The rows and columns in the matrix correspond to the height and width of the image, respectively. The **resolution** of an image refers to the size of, or number of pixels in, an image.

Since images can be defined with matrices, individual pixels can also be accessed and manipulated using the specific coordinates of a pixel, which we will denote as x for row values and y for column values. With the top-left corner of the image starting at (0, 0), x values increase as you move down the rows, and y values increase as you move to the right across the columns.

For grayscale images, like the one shown in Figure 5-4, pixel values represent the brightness of a pixel as an 8-bit integer expressing the possible range of 0–255 values. Color images have a third dimension, **channels**, that is commonly specified using three colors, red, green, and blue (RGB). Each color denotes one channel, meaning that RGB images have three channels. Mixing different RGB values will produce new colors. PyQt and OpenCV both have methods for working with RGB as well as other color spaces, such as BGR (blue, green, red); hue, saturation, value (HSV); and grayscale.

Working with videos is also straightforward, as they are simply comprised of a sequence of images played together at a very fast rate to produce the impression of motion.

An Introduction to OpenCV

In this chapter, we are going to take a look at a very popular software library, **OpenCV**, that has support for a few different programming languages, including Python. OpenCV is both open source and cross-platform and contains an extensive list of optimized algorithms and modules designed for creating real-time computer vision, machine learning, and deep learning applications whose processes can be accelerated using OpenCV's support for Graphics Processing Units (GPUs). The library is designed with ease of use in mind and is publicly used by a number of companies, both large and small.

Images in OpenCV are stored as `Mat` objects, container matrices that contain the pixel values in the image. The following list contains a selection of what OpenCV can be used for:

- Functions for image processing, such as image filtering, transformations, and color space conversions

- Camera calibration and 3D reconstruction to gain 3D information from 2D images and videos

- Analyzing videos for motion extraction and feature tracking

- Object detection, which also includes facial and person recognition

- Machine learning and deep learning for classification and regression analysis

- Image stitching for creating panoramas from multiple images

More information about OpenCV can be found at `https://opencv.org`.

Next, let's see how to install OpenCV using the `pip` package manager and then get started creating our first GUI for displaying images.

Installing OpenCV

There are a couple of options for downloading OpenCV. One way is to download and install OpenCV from source from the OpenCV website or from GitHub at `https://github.com/opencv/opencv`. There is also support for installing OpenCV using the Anaconda package manager.

Thankfully, there is also an unofficial PyPI wheel that makes it simple to download OpenCV using the pip3 command on your desktop computer. Depending upon your needs, there are a few different options. If you only need OpenCV's main modules, which include image processing, video analysis, and machine learning, open your computer's command-line interface and run

```
$ pip3 install opencv-python
```

This command is sufficient for the examples found in this chapter. If you want access to extra modules, including modules for working with GPUs, enter

```
$ pip3 install opencv-contrib-python
```

The current version of OpenCV as of publication is version 4.4.0. After the installation is complete, open up the Python 3 shell and check to make sure OpenCV works properly. Enter

```
>>> import cv2
```

If no errors appear, then you are ready to get started using OpenCV.

Tip   While you will receive no error now, there is a possibility that after you run the first GUI program, you may receive errors about how PyQt and OpenCV need to use shared Qt resources. The version of Qt used to compile PyQt5 is different from the version used by OpenCV. If this occurs, first, uninstall OpenCV using `pip3 uninstall <opencv-package-name>`. Then, install the headless environment using `pip3 install opencv-python-headless` or `opencv-contrib-python-headless` depending upon your requirements. These packages do not contain any GUI functionality.

For Linux users (specifically Ubuntu) running into issues using OpenCV and PyQt, you can also try to use the APT package manager. Try running the following code to install OpenCV if the previous installation options are still giving you trouble:

```
$ sudo apt install python3-opencv
```

More information about installation can be found in the OpenCV documentation, specifically in the "OpenCV Tutorials" section of the website, at https://docs.opencv.org/master/.

Note   Before moving on, make sure you also have the NumPy library installed for handling image data in OpenCV. Installing NumPy is covered back in Chapter 3.

Example 5.1: Display Images from OpenCV in PyQt

For this first example, you are going to see how to use both PyQt image classes and OpenCV functions for reading and displaying images. You will create a simple GUI that also demonstrates how to use the different color spaces and how to convert OpenCV images so they can be viewed using PyQt widgets. Figure 5-5 illustrates how the images will look in the application's window.

Figure 5-5. *Both images are displayed on a QLabel widget using Qt classes. The image on the left displays the original image. The image on the right shows the same image, but in the BGR color space used by OpenCV*

The GUI window depicted in Figure 5-5, created in Listing 5-1, is comprised of a menu bar with options for the user to select images from their computer and a few QLabel widgets for displaying images and textual information.

Listing 5-1. Demonstrates how to convert and display images loaded from OpenCV onto QLabel widgets

```python
display_images.py
# Import necessary modules
import sys, os, cv2
from PyQt5.QtWidgets import (QApplication, QMainWindow, QWidget, QLabel,
QFileDialog, QMessageBox, QHBoxLayout, QVBoxLayout, QAction)
from PyQt5.QtGui import QPixmap, QImage
from PyQt5.QtCore import Qt

style_sheet = """
    QLabel#ImageLabel{
        color: darkgrey;
        border: 2px dashed darkgrey
    }

    QLabel{
        qproperty-alignment: AlignCenter
    }"""

class DisplayImage(QMainWindow):

    def __init__(self):
        super().__init__()
        self.initializeUI()

    def initializeUI(self):
        """Initialize the window and display its contents to the screen."""
        self.setMinimumSize(800, 500)
        self.setWindowTitle('Ex 5.1 - Displaying Images')

        self.setupWindow()
        self.setupMenu()
        self.show()

    def setupWindow(self):
        """Set up widgets in the main window."""
```

```python
        # Create two QLabels, one for original image and one for displaying
        # example from OpenCV
        original_img_header = QLabel("Original Image")
        self.original_label = QLabel()
        self.original_label.setObjectName("ImageLabel")

        opencv_img_header = QLabel("OpenCV Image")
        self.opencv_label = QLabel()
        self.opencv_label.setObjectName("ImageLabel")

        # Create horizontal and vertical layouts
        original_v_box = QVBoxLayout()
        original_v_box.addWidget(original_img_header)
        original_v_box.addWidget(self.original_label, 1)

        opencv_v_box = QVBoxLayout()
        opencv_v_box.addWidget(opencv_img_header)
        opencv_v_box.addWidget(self.opencv_label, 1)

        main_h_box = QHBoxLayout()
        main_h_box.addLayout(original_v_box, Qt.AlignCenter)
        main_h_box.addLayout(opencv_v_box, Qt.AlignCenter)

        # Create container widget and set main window's widget
        container = QWidget()
        container.setLayout(main_h_box)
        self.setCentralWidget(container)

    def setupMenu(self):
        """Simple menu bar to select local images."""
        # Create actions for file menu
        open_act = QAction('Open...', self)
        open_act.setShortcut('Ctrl+O')
        open_act.triggered.connect(self.openImageFile)

        # Create menu bar
        menu_bar = self.menuBar()
        menu_bar.setNativeMenuBar(False)
```

```python
        # Create file menu and add actions
        file_menu = menu_bar.addMenu('File')
        file_menu.addAction(open_act)

    def openImageFile(self):
        """Open an image file and display the contents in the two label
        widgets."""
        image_file, _ = QFileDialog.getOpenFileName(self, "Open Image",
        os.getenv('HOME'), "Images (*.png *.jpeg *.jpg *.bmp)")

        if image_file:
            image = QImage() # Create QImage instance
            image.load(image_file)
            # Set the pixmap for the original_label using the QImage instance
            self.original_label.setPixmap(QPixmap.fromImage(image).scaled(
                    self.original_label.width(), self.original_label.
                    height(), Qt.KeepAspectRatioByExpanding))

            # Display the image that has been converted from the OpenCV Mat
            # object to a Qt QImage
            converted_image = self.convertCVToQImage(image_file)
            self.opencv_label.setPixmap(QPixmap.fromImage(converted_image).
            scaled(
                self.opencv_label.width(), self.opencv_label.height(),
                Qt.KeepAspectRatioByExpanding))
            self.adjustSize() # Adjust the size of the main window to
            better fit its contents
        else:
            QMessageBox.information(self, "Error",
                "No image was loaded.", QMessageBox.Ok)

    def convertCVToQImage(self, image_file):
        """Demonstrates how to load a cv image and convert the image to a
        Qt QImage. Displays the OpenCV image for comparison. Returns the
        converted Qimage."""
        cv_image = cv2.imread(image_file)
```

```
        # Demonstrate what the cv_image looks like using imshow()
        cv2.imshow('OpenCV Image', cv_image)
        cv2.waitKey(0) # waits for user to press any key
        cv2.destroyAllWindows() # Close the cv window

        # Get the shape of the image, height * width * channels. BGR/RGB/
        HSV images have 3 channels
        height, width, channels = cv_image.shape # Format: (rows, columns,
        channels)
        # Number of bytes required by the image pixels in a row; dependency
        on the number of channels
        bytes_per_line = width * channels
        # Create instance of QImage using data from cv_image
        converted_Qt_image = QImage(cv_image, width, height, bytes_per_
        line, QImage.Format_RGB888)
        return converted_Qt_image

if __name__ == '__main__':
    app = QApplication(sys.argv)
    app.setStyleSheet(style_sheet)
    window = DisplayImage()
    sys.exit(app.exec_())
```

The GUI window can be seen in Figure 5-5.

Explanation

Let's begin by importing a few libraries, including sys, os, and OpenCV with cv2. From QtWidgets, we need classes for creating the main window, widgets, layouts, dialog boxes, and actions in the menu bar. QPixmap and QImage will be used for handling image data.

Next, we create a simple Qt Style Sheet for creating dashed borders around the QLabel widgets that use the ImageLabel tag. When the application is first started, the label widgets will be empty, as seen in Figure 5-6, and the user can then use the menu bar to select an image for viewing. Note that drag and drop functionality from Chapter 2 could also be added to this application for loading images.

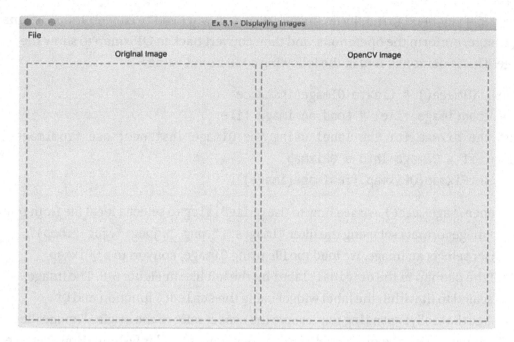

Figure 5-6. *The initial window for Listing 5-1. The label widgets are empty and outlined using Qt Style Sheets*

The setup for this GUI is very straightforward. After initializing the main window's minimum size and title in setupWindow(), we create four QLabel objects, two for displaying the headers above the images and two for displaying the images, original_label and opencv_label. All of the labels are organized into a nested layout using a combination of QHBoxLayout and QVBoxLayouts.

This GUI also includes a menu bar created in setupMenu(). Image files are loaded using open_act. When selected, open_act emits a signal that calls the openImageFile() slot for loading and displaying images in the window.

Displaying Images Using PyQt Widgets

PyQt has a few different classes for managing image data. For the purposes of this chapter, we will focus on two of them – QPixmap and QImage. **QPixmap** is the main class you will be using in your applications for displaying 2D images. If you only need to read or write an image without manipulating the file, then create a QPixmap object and call QLabel's setPixmap() function to set the pixmap and show the image on the screen.

However, if you need to modify an image's data, you will need to convert from QPixmap to **QImage**, perform the operations, and then convert back to QPixmap to show the image. This is demonstrated in the following code from Listing 5-1:

```
image = QImage() # Create QImage instance
image.load(image_file) # Load an image file
# Set the pixmap for the label using the QImage instance; use fromImage()
to convert a QImage into a QPixmap
label.setPixmap(QPixmap.fromImage(image))
```

In openImageFile(), we see how to use QFileDialog to select a local file from one of four image formats set using the filter "Images (*.png *.jpeg *.jpg *.bmp)". If the user selects an image, we load the file using QImage, convert to a QPixmap, and set the pixmap in the original_label on the left like in Figure 5-6. The image is also scaled to fit within the label widget using the scaled() function and Qt. KeepAspectRatioByExpanding to preserve the aspect ratio of the original image file.

The image displayed on the right is also created in a similar fashion. However, the image is loaded using OpenCV's imshow() function. The general process for reading and displaying an image in OpenCV is shown in Listing 5-2.

Listing 5-2. Demonstrates how to show an image using OpenCV

```
cv_image = cv2.imread(image_file) # Load file
cv2.imshow('OpenCV Image', cv_image)
cv2.waitKey(0) # Waits for user to press any key
cv2.destroyAllWindows() # Close the cv2 window
```

This is also included in the convertCVToQImage() function for comparison. The output from imshow() is shown in Figure 5-7. After the OpenCV window appears, press any key to close it.

Figure 5-7. *An image displayed using OpenCV. Image displayed in the window is from https://pixabay.com*

In order to convert the OpenCV Mat object into a QImage instance, we need the image's height, width, and number of channels. These values are then passed to the QImage instance along with the number of bytes_per_line. The converted_Qt_Image is returned, converted to a QPixmap, and finally displayed in the GUI window.

You will notice that the fox in the OpenCV image in Figure 5-6 is blue, but in Figure 5-7 the animal's colors are normal. This is because of the way OpenCV represents image data. Pixel values are stored using the BGR color space, rather than the more commonly used RGB. To display Mat objects using libraries other than OpenCV, you will need to change the color space. Converting the colors can be handled in one of two ways.

- After an image is loaded using imread(), use cv2.cvtColor(image, cv2.COLOR_BGR2RGB) on the Mat object to convert the image pixel values to RGB or other color spaces.

- When creating a QImage object, pass QImage.Format_BGR888 as an argument to reverse the colors from BGR to RGB.

In the following project, we are going to take what we learned in Example 5.1 and see how to create an interface for image processing.

Project 5.1: Image Processing GUI

As we discussed back in Chapter 3, the process for cleaning and organizing data is a necessary step for data visualization, even when working with images and videos. In a computer vision system, cleaning up images can help to remove noise or distortion or better help to extract useful information from the image data. The process for image processing generally involves importing an image, analyzing and applying operations, and outputting the resulting image or information from the analysis.

Some common image processing techniques include

- Geometric transformations such as rotations, scaling, translations, and shearing

- Point operators for pixel and color transformations

- Finding edges, corners, lines, and other shapes using feature detection

- Image filtering for smoothing or sharpening edges and removing noise

- Histogram equalization for improving an image's quality

Image processing can become more costly with images that have higher resolutions and on large image datasets.

For this project, we are going to create a GUI, shown in Figure 5-8, that displays an image loaded using OpenCV, performs a few basic image processing techniques, and then outputs the image for viewing on a QLabel widget in the GUI window.

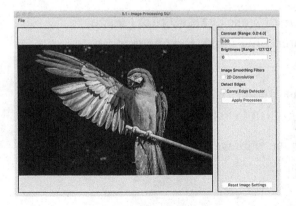

Figure 5-8. *The original image (left). The altered image with brightness, contrast, and smoothing techniques applied (right). Image displayed in the window is from* `https://pixabay.com`

Image Processing GUI Solution

This GUI, created in Listing 5-3, builds on the ideas learned in Example 5.1. After the application opens, the user can still select an image to view in the window using the menu bar. Also included is the ability to save an altered image.

The side panel on the right of the window in Figure 5-8 utilizes a few of the many image processing functions that are included in OpenCV. The user can use the two spin boxes for selecting values that change the contrast and brightness; the two checkboxes are used for applying either smoothing filter or edge detection algorithms. One or multiple operations can be applied at a time using the Apply Processes button. Finally, a button is included at the bottom of the side panel to reset the image settings.

Listing 5-3. Code for image processing GUI

```
image_processing.py
# Import necessary modules
import sys, os, cv2
import numpy as np
from PyQt5.QtWidgets import (QApplication, QMainWindow, QWidget, QLabel,
QPushButton, QCheckBox, QSpinBox, QDoubleSpinBox, QFrame, QFileDialog,
QMessageBox, QHBoxLayout, QVBoxLayout, QAction)
from PyQt5.QtGui import QPixmap, QImage
from PyQt5.QtCore import Qt

style_sheet = """
    QLabel#ImageLabel{
        color: darkgrey;
        border: 2px solid #000000;
        qproperty-alignment: AlignCenter
    }"""

class ImageProcessingGUI(QMainWindow):

    def __init__(self):
        super().__init__()
        self.initializeUI()
```

```python
def initializeUI(self):
    """Initialize the window and display its contents to the screen."""
    self.setMinimumSize(900, 600)
    self.setWindowTitle('5.1 - Image Processing GUI')

    self.contrast_adjusted = False
    self.brightness_adjusted = False
    self.image_smoothing_checked = False
    self.edge_detection_checked = False

    self.setupWindow()
    self.setupMenu()
    self.show()

def setupWindow(self):
    """Set up widgets in the main window."""
    self.image_label = QLabel()
    self.image_label.setObjectName("ImageLabel")

    # Create various widgets for image processing in the side panel
    contrast_label = QLabel("Contrast [Range: 0.0:4.0]")
    self.contrast_spinbox = QDoubleSpinBox()
    self.contrast_spinbox.setMinimumWidth(100)
    self.contrast_spinbox.setRange(0.0, 4.0)
    self.contrast_spinbox.setValue(1.0)
    self.contrast_spinbox.setSingleStep(.10)
    self.contrast_spinbox.valueChanged.connect(self.adjustContrast)

    brightness_label = QLabel("Brightness [Range: -127:127]")
    self.brightness_spinbox = QSpinBox()
    self.brightness_spinbox.setMinimumWidth(100)
    self.brightness_spinbox.setRange(-127, 127)
    self.brightness_spinbox.setValue(0)
    self.brightness_spinbox.setSingleStep(1)
    self.brightness_spinbox.valueChanged.connect(self.adjustBrightness)

    smoothing_label = QLabel("Image Smoothing Filters")
    self.filter_2D_cb = QCheckBox("2D Convolution")
    self.filter_2D_cb.stateChanged.connect(self.imageSmoothingFilter)
```

```
edges_label = QLabel("Detect Edges")
self.canny_cb = QCheckBox("Canny Edge Detector")
self.canny_cb.stateChanged.connect(self.edgeDetection)

self.apply_process_button = QPushButton("Apply Processes")
self.apply_process_button.setEnabled(False)
self.apply_process_button.clicked.connect(self.
applyImageProcessing)

reset_button = QPushButton("Reset Image Settings")
reset_button.clicked.connect(self.resetImageAndSettings)

# Create horizontal and vertical layouts for the side panel and
main window
side_panel_v_box = QVBoxLayout()
side_panel_v_box.setAlignment(Qt.AlignTop)
side_panel_v_box.addWidget(contrast_label)
side_panel_v_box.addWidget(self.contrast_spinbox)
side_panel_v_box.addWidget(brightness_label)
side_panel_v_box.addWidget(self.brightness_spinbox)
side_panel_v_box.addSpacing(15)
side_panel_v_box.addWidget(smoothing_label)
side_panel_v_box.addWidget(self.filter_2D_cb)
side_panel_v_box.addWidget(edges_label)
side_panel_v_box.addWidget(self.canny_cb)
side_panel_v_box.addWidget(self.apply_process_button)
side_panel_v_box.addStretch(1)
side_panel_v_box.addWidget(reset_button)

side_panel_frame = QFrame()
side_panel_frame.setMinimumWidth(200)
side_panel_frame.setFrameStyle(QFrame.WinPanel)
side_panel_frame.setLayout(side_panel_v_box)

main_h_box = QHBoxLayout()
main_h_box.addWidget(self.image_label, 1)
main_h_box.addWidget(side_panel_frame)
```

```
        # Create container widget and set main window's widget
        container = QWidget()
        container.setLayout(main_h_box)
        self.setCentralWidget(container)

    def setupMenu(self):
        """Simple menu bar to select and save local images."""
        # Create actions for file menu
        open_act = QAction('Open...', self)
        open_act.setShortcut('Ctrl+O')
        open_act.triggered.connect(self.openImageFile)

        save_act = QAction('Save...', self)
        save_act.setShortcut('Ctrl+S')
        save_act.triggered.connect(self.saveImageFile)

        # Create menu bar
        menu_bar = self.menuBar()
        menu_bar.setNativeMenuBar(False)

        # Create file menu and add actions
        file_menu = menu_bar.addMenu('File')
        file_menu.addAction(open_act)
        file_menu.addAction(save_act)

    def adjustContrast(self):
        """The slot corresponding to adjusting image contrast."""
        if self.image_label.pixmap() != None:
            self.contrast_adjusted = True

    def adjustBrightness(self):
        """The slot corresponding to adjusting image brightness."""
        if self.image_label.pixmap() != None:
            self.brightness_adjusted = True

    def imageSmoothingFilter(self, state):
        """The slot corresponding to applying 2D Convolution for smoothing
        the image."""
```

```python
        if state == Qt.Checked and self.image_label.pixmap() != None:
            self.image_smoothing_checked = True
        elif state != Qt.Checked and self.image_label.pixmap() != None:
            self.image_smoothing_checked = False

    def edgeDetection(self, state):
        """The slot corresponding to applying edge detection."""
        if state == Qt.Checked and self.image_label.pixmap() != None:
            self.edge_detection_checked = True
        elif state != Qt.Checked and self.image_label.pixmap() != None:
            self.edge_detection_checked = False

    def applyImageProcessing(self):
        """For the boolean variables related to the image processing
        techniques, if True, apply the corresponding process to the image
        and display the changes in the QLabel, image_label."""
        if self.contrast_adjusted == True or self.brightness_adjusted ==
        True:
            contrast = self.contrast_spinbox.value()
            brightness = self.brightness_spinbox.value()
            self.cv_image = cv2.convertScaleAbs(self.cv_image, self.
            processed_cv_image, contrast, brightness)
        if self.image_smoothing_checked == True:
            kernel = np.ones((5, 5), np.float32) / 25
            self.cv_image = cv2.filter2D(self.cv_image, -1, kernel)
        if self.edge_detection_checked == True:
            self.cv_image = cv2.Canny(self.cv_image, 100, 200)
        self.convertCVToQImage(self.cv_image)

        self.image_label.repaint() # Repaint the updated image on the label

    def resetImageAndSettings(self):
        """Reset the displayed image and widgets used for image
        processing."""
        answer = QMessageBox.information(self, "Reset Image",
                "Are you sure you want to reset the image settings?",
                QMessageBox.Yes | QMessageBox.No, QMessageBox.No)
```

```
        if answer == QMessageBox.No:
            pass
        elif answer == QMessageBox.Yes and self.image_label.pixmap() != None:
            self.resetWidgetValues()
            self.cv_image = self.copy_cv_image
            self.convertCVToQImage(self.copy_cv_image)

    def resetWidgetValues(self):
        """Reset the spinbox and checkbox values to their beginning
        values."""
        self.contrast_spinbox.setValue(1.0)
        self.brightness_spinbox.setValue(0)
        self.filter_2D_cb.setChecked(False)
        self.canny_cb.setChecked(False)

    def openImageFile(self):
        """Open an image file and display the contents in the label
        widget."""
        image_file, _ = QFileDialog.getOpenFileName(self, "Open Image",
            os.getenv('HOME'), "Images (*.png *.jpeg *.jpg *.bmp)")

        if image_file:
            self.resetWidgetValues() # Reset the states of the widgets
            self.apply_process_button.setEnabled(True)

            self.cv_image = cv2.imread(image_file) # Original image
            self.copy_cv_image = self.cv_image # A copy of the original
            image
            # Create a destination image for the contrast and brightness
            processes
            self.processed_cv_image = np.zeros(self.cv_image.shape, self.
            cv_image.dtype)
            self.convertCVToQImage(self.cv_image) # Convert the OpenCV
            image to a Qt Image
```

```python
        else:
            QMessageBox.information(self, "Error",
                "No image was loaded.", QMessageBox.Ok)

    def saveImageFile(self):
        """Save the contents of the image_label to file."""
        image_file, _ = QFileDialog.getSaveFileName(self, "Save Image",
        os.getenv('HOME'),
            "JPEG (*.jpeg);;JPG (*.jpg);;PNG (*.png);;Bitmap (*.bmp)")

        if image_file and self.image_label.pixmap() != None:
            # Save the file using OpenCV's imwrite() function
            cv2.imwrite(image_file, self.cv_image)
        else:
            QMessageBox.information(self, "Error",
                "Unable to save image.", QMessageBox.Ok)

    def convertCVToQImage(self, image):
        """Load a cv image and convert the image to a Qt QImage. Display
        the image in image_label."""
        cv_image = cv2.cvtColor(image, cv2.COLOR_BGR2RGB)

        # Get the shape of the image, height * width * channels. BGR/RGB/
        HSV images have 3 channels
        height, width, channels = cv_image.shape # Format: (rows, columns,
        channels)
        # Number of bytes required by the image pixels in a row; dependency
        on the number of channels
        bytes_per_line = width * channels
        # Create instance of QImage using data from cv_image
        converted_Qt_image = QImage(cv_image, width, height, bytes_per_
        line, QImage.Format_RGB888)

        self.image_label.setPixmap(QPixmap.fromImage(converted_Qt_image).
        scaled(
            self.image_label.width(), self.image_label.height(),
            Qt.KeepAspectRatio))
```

```
if __name__ == '__main__':
    app = QApplication(sys.argv)
    app.setStyleSheet(style_sheet)
    window = ImageProcessingGUI()
    sys.exit(app.exec_())
```

The image processing application can be seen in Figure 5-8.

Explanation

Begin by importing many of the same modules and classes used in Example 5.1. This time, be sure to import numpy and a few extra widget classes – QCheckbox, QSpinBox, QDoubleSpinBox, and QFrame.

The ImageProcessingGUI class is where we set up the main window seen in Figure 5-9. You can see the empty image label on the left and a couple of widgets for applying image processing operations on the right.

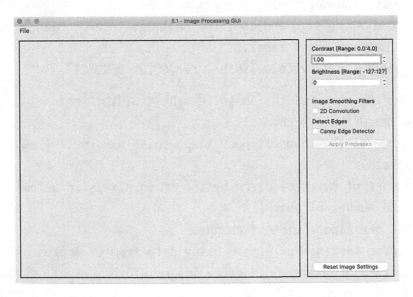

Figure 5-9. *The initial window for Listing 5-3*

- contrast_spinbox – A QDoubleSpinBox for selecting float values that modify the image's contrast. The widget's range is from 0.0 to 4.0. Connected to the adjustContrast() slot. Used in conjunction with brightness_spinbox.

186

- brightness_spinbox – A QSpinBox for selecting int values that adjust the image's brightness. The widget's range is from –127 to 127. Connected to the adjustBrightness() slot. Used together with contrast_spinbox.

- filter_2D_cb – A QCheckBox that applies smoothing using 2D convolution, if checked. Connected to the imageSmoothingFilter() slot.

- canny_cb – A QCheckBox that applies the Canny edge detection algorithm, if checked. Connected to the edgeDetection() slot.

Corresponding Boolean variables are created for each of the widgets and are set to True in each of the slots. We check if the user has selected an image by checking if the label has a pixmap set in Listing 5-3:

```
if self.image_label.pixmap() != None:
    self.contrast_adjusted = True
```

If an image has been loaded, then the user can apply any of the different operations by clicking the apply_process_button. The reset_button resets the widgets and the image back to their original settings. These widgets are all arranged in the side_panel_v_box layout. A QFrame object, side_panel_frame, acts as a container for the different widgets. The menu bar contains two actions, open_act and save_act:

- open_act – Emits a signal that calls openImageFile(). Loads an image using OpenCV's imread(), creating the Mat object, cv_image, on which operations will be performed. copy_cv_image is used when resetting the image. processed_cv_image is a NumPy array filled with zeros with the same dimensions as cv_image and is used as the destination image for contrast and brightness processes.

- save_act – Saves the current cv_image using OpenCV's imwrite() function.

While OpenCV has many different functions for manipulating images, this GUI only employs a few of them to demonstrate how to integrate OpenCV into your own projects.

A Few Image Processing Techniques

Depending upon which widgets the user has interacted with in the side panel, the selected operations will be applied in `applyImageProcessing()`. Once the operations are complete, the output will be displayed on the `image_label` using `convertCVToQImage()`. Refer back to Example 5.1 for information about using PyQt image classes.

Now, let's take a moment to talk about the image processing techniques used in this application.

Point Operators

Point operators are operations performed on the pixels in an image to produce a modified output image. For Project 5.1, we are specifically looking at the equation for changing the contrast and brightness in an image:

$$g(\mathbf{X}) = af(\mathbf{X}) + b$$

where matrix $\mathbf{X}$ refers to an image comprised of pixel locations, a is the contrast parameter and $a > 0$, b is the brightness term, $f(\mathbf{X})$ refers to the operation over some finite range (the input image), and $g(\mathbf{X})$ is the output image.

Since the terms are correlated, we check if either `contrast_spinbox` or `brightness_spinbox` values have changed in the following code from Listing 5-3. If at least one has changed, then we can apply the `convertScaleAbs()` function to the image to change the contrast or brightness. If only one spin box value was changed, we still need to get the other value using `value()` to perform the calculations:

```
if self.contrast_adjusted == True or self.brightness_adjusted == True:
    contrast = self.contrast_spinbox.value()
    brightness = self.brightness_spinbox.value()
    self.cv_image = cv2.convertScaleAbs(self.cv_image, self.processed_cv_
image, contrast, brightness)
```

Image Filters

Image filtering is a very useful technique for editing the properties of an image. Filters are useful for enhancing some features in an image to make them sharper or removing other features, such as noise, by smoothing the image.

If `filter_2D_cb` is checked, we create a 5 × 5 filter, or **kernel**, filled with ones and divide all of the values by 25. Each entry in the matrix is therefore equal to 1/25. The `filter2D()` function performs 2D matrix convolution using the provided kernel and `cv_image`. This is shown in the following code from Listing 5-3:

```
if self.image_smoothing_checked == True:
    kernel = np.ones((5, 5), np.float32) / 25
    self.cv_image = cv2.filter2D(self.cv_image, -1, kernel)
```

Using this specific kernel means that for every pixel in the image, the 5 × 5 matrix is centered on the pixel, and for every pixel that falls under the kernel, the values are summed and then divided by 25. Using this kernel will make the features in the image smoother. You can also modify the kernel to see how different sizes and values will affect the output.

OpenCV also has other techniques provided for image filtering, including Gaussian and median filtering.

Edge Detection

Finally, let's take a look at **edge detection**, which is useful for gathering information about edges, boundaries, and structures of objects in an image. For this project, we will be specifically using Canny edge detection. What is important to note is that this method reduces the amount of noise in an image, making the accuracy of detecting edges greater. If you are interested in learning more about Canny edge detection, more information can be found on the OpenCV documentation website.

If the `canny_cb` is checked, we use the `Canny()` function, passing the `cv_image` and minimum and maximum threshold values to determine if a detected edge is really an edge or not in the following snippet from Listing 5-3:

```
if self.edge_detection_checked == True:
    self.cv_image = cv2.Canny(self.cv_image, 100, 200)
    self.convertCVToQImage(self.cv_image)
```

Figure 5-10 displays the results of using edge detection on an image.

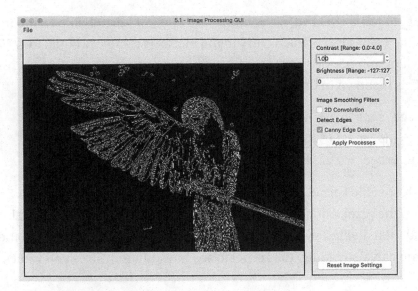

Figure 5-10. *Output from Canny edge detection algorithm displayed in the window*

The previous two examples have demonstrated methods for visualizing images using OpenCV in PyQt GUIs. Next, let's see how to work with video data.

Example 5.2: Display Videos from OpenCV in PyQt

Now that we have taken a look at how to create GUIs for handling images, this next example, shown in Figure 5-11, explains how to load video files using OpenCV and play the videos on PyQt widgets. Users are able to use the application to either view video files or use their computer's built-in camera.

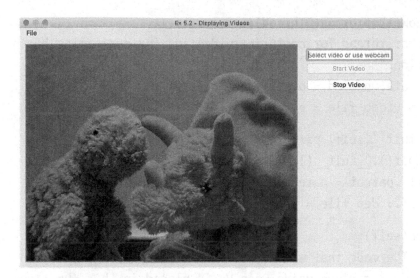

Figure 5-11. *Displays a video in the window using the computer's web cam*

The program created in Listing 5-4 shows how to display videos loaded using OpenCV and introduces concepts about threading and demonstrates how to implement threading into your applications.

Listing 5-4. Demonstrates how to display videos loaded using OpenCV in PyQt

```
display_video.py
# Import necessary modules
import sys, os, cv2
from numpy import ndarray
from PyQt5.QtWidgets import (QApplication, QMainWindow, QWidget, QLabel,
QPushButton, QLineEdit, QFrame, QFileDialog, QMessageBox, QHBoxLayout,
QVBoxLayout, QAction)
from PyQt5.QtGui import QPixmap, QImage
from PyQt5.QtCore import Qt, QThread, pyqtSignal

style_sheet = """
    QLabel#VideoLabel{
        color: darkgrey;
        border: 2px solid darkgrey;
        qproperty-alignment: AlignCenter
    }"""
```

```python
class VideoWorkerThread(QThread):
    """Worker thread for capturing video and for performing human
    detection."""
    frame_data_updated = pyqtSignal(ndarray)
    invalid_video_file = pyqtSignal()

    def __init__(self, parent, video_file=None):
        super().__init__()
        self.parent = parent
        self.video_file = video_file

    def run(self):
        """The code that we want to run in a separate thread, in this case
        capturing video using OpenCV, is placed in this function. run() is
        called after start()."""
        capture = cv2.VideoCapture(self.video_file) # 0 opens the default
        camera

        if not capture.isOpened():
            self.invalid_video_file.emit()
        else:
            while self.parent.thread_is_running:
                # Read frames from the camera
                ret_val, frame = capture.read()
                if not ret_val:
                    break # Error or reached the end of the video
                else:
                    frame = cv2.cvtColor(frame, cv2.COLOR_BGR2RGB)
                    self.frame_data_updated.emit(frame)
                    # waitKey() displays the image for specified time, in
                    this case 30 ms
                    cv2.waitKey(30)

    def stopThread(self):
        """Process all pending events before stopping the thread."""
        self.wait()
        QApplication.processEvents()
```

```python
class DisplayVideo(QMainWindow):

    def __init__(self):
        super().__init__()
        self.initializeUI()

    def initializeUI(self):
        """Initialize the window and display its contents to the screen."""
        self.setMinimumSize(800, 500)
        self.setWindowTitle('Ex 5.2 - Displaying Videos')

        self.thread_is_running = False

        self.setupWindow()
        self.setupMenu()
        self.show()

    def setupWindow(self):
        """Set up widgets in the main window."""
        self.video_display_label = QLabel()
        self.video_display_label.setObjectName("VideoLabel")

        self.display_video_path_line = QLineEdit()
        self.display_video_path_line.setClearButtonEnabled(True)
        self.display_video_path_line.setPlaceholderText("Select video or
        use webcam")

        self.start_button = QPushButton("Start Video")
        self.start_button.clicked.connect(self.startVideo)

        stop_button = QPushButton("Stop Video")
        stop_button.clicked.connect(self.stopCurrentVideo)

        # Create horizontal and vertical layouts
        side_panel_v_box = QVBoxLayout()
        side_panel_v_box.setAlignment(Qt.AlignTop)
        side_panel_v_box.addWidget(self.display_video_path_line)
        side_panel_v_box.addWidget(self.start_button)
        side_panel_v_box.addWidget(stop_button)
```

```python
        side_panel_frame = QFrame()
        side_panel_frame.setMinimumWidth(200)
        side_panel_frame.setLayout(side_panel_v_box)

        main_h_box = QHBoxLayout()
        main_h_box.addWidget(self.video_display_label, 1)
        main_h_box.addWidget(side_panel_frame)

        # Create container widget and set main window's widget
        container = QWidget()
        container.setLayout(main_h_box)
        self.setCentralWidget(container)

    def setupMenu(self):
        """Simple menu bar to select local videos."""
        # Create actions for file menu
        open_act = QAction('Open...', self)
        open_act.setShortcut('Ctrl+O')
        open_act.triggered.connect(self.openVideoFile)

        # Create menu bar
        menu_bar = self.menuBar()
        menu_bar.setNativeMenuBar(False)

        # Create file menu and add actions
        file_menu = menu_bar.addMenu('File')
        file_menu.addAction(open_act)

    def startVideo(self):
        """Create and begin running the worker thread to play the video."""
        self.thread_is_running = True
        self.start_button.setEnabled(False)
        self.start_button.repaint()

        # Create an instance of the worker thread if a user has chosen a
        local file
        if self.display_video_path_line.text() != "":
            video_file = self.display_video_path_line.text()
            self.video_thread_worker = VideoWorkerThread(self, video_file)
```

```
    else:
        # Use the webcam
        self.video_thread_worker = VideoWorkerThread(self, 0)

    # Connect to the thread's signal to update the frames in the video_
    display_label
    self.video_thread_worker.frame_data_updated.connect(self.
    updateVideoFrames)
    self.video_thread_worker.invalid_video_file.connect(self.
    invalidVideoFile)
    self.video_thread_worker.start() # Start the thread

def stopCurrentVideo(self):
    """Stop the current video, process events, and clear the video_
    display_label."""
    if self.thread_is_running == True:
        self.thread_is_running = False
        self.video_thread_worker.stopThread()

        self.video_display_label.clear()
        self.start_button.setEnabled(True)

def openVideoFile(self):
    """Open a video file and display the file's path in the line edit
    widget."""
    video_file, _ = QFileDialog.getOpenFileName(self, "Open Video",
    os.getenv('HOME'), "Videos (*.mp4 *.avi)")

    if video_file:
        self.display_video_path_line.setText(video_file) # Use selected
        file's path
    else:
        QMessageBox.information(self, "Error", "No video was loaded.",
        QMessageBox.Ok)

def updateVideoFrames(self, video_frame):
    """A video is a collection of images played together in quick
    succession. For each frame (image) in the video, convert it to a
    QImage object to be displayed in the QLabel widget."""
```

195

```
            # Get the shape of the frame, height * width * channels. BGR/RGB/
            HSV images have 3 channels
            height, width, channels = video_frame.shape # Format: (rows,
            columns, channels)
            # Number of bytes required by the image pixels in a row; dependency
            on the number of channels
            bytes_per_line = width * channels
            # Create instance of QImage using data from the video file
            converted_Qt_image = QImage(video_frame, width, height, bytes_per_
            line, QImage.Format_RGB888)

            # Set the video_display_label's pixmap
            self.video_display_label.setPixmap(QPixmap.fromImage(converted_Qt_
            image).scaled(
                    self.video_display_label.width(), self.video_display_label.
                    height(), Qt.KeepAspectRatioByExpanding))

    def invalidVideoFile(self):
        """Display a dialog box to inform the user that an error occurred
        while loading the video."""
        QMessageBox.warning(self, "Error", "No video was loaded.",
        QMessageBox.Ok)
        self.start_button.setEnabled(True)

    def closeEvent(self, event):
        """Reimplement the closing event to ensure that the thread
        closes."""
        if self.thread_is_running == True:
            self.video_thread_worker.quit()

if __name__ == '__main__':
    app = QApplication(sys.argv)
    app.setStyleSheet(style_sheet)
    window = DisplayVideo()
    sys.exit(app.exec_())
```

The completed application for playing videos can be seen in Figure 5-11.

Explanation

Creating a GUI for displaying videos with OpenCV and PyQt takes a little bit more work because of the way that applications are created in PyQt. We will still need many of the same packages that we imported in other examples, along with a few additional ones.

From numpy, we import the ndarray class that we will use to create arrays that hold the data for each of the separate frames in a video. QThread is used to create a separate thread from the application's main thread. pyqtSignal is used in PyQt for creating custom signals.

The application's main window consists of a QLabel for displaying the videos and a side panel composed of a QLineEdit widget for displaying a video file's path if one is selected and two QPushButton widgets for playing and stopping the video. Figure 5-12 shows the window when the application is first opened.

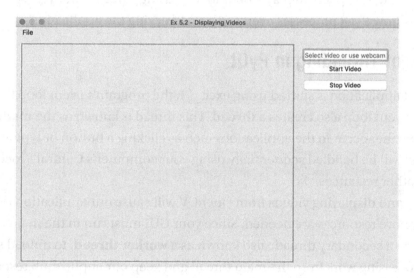

Figure 5-12. *The initial application created in Listing 5-4*

Running a video is similar to displaying an image with OpenCV. The key difference is that we need to create a loop to read in every frame in succession. This is shown in Listing 5-5.

Listing 5-5. Example code for displaying a video in OpenCV

```
capture = cv2.VideoCapture(0) # Video capture object

while (True):
    ret_val, frame = capture.read() # Read frames
    # Display resulting frames in the video
    cv2.imshow('Frame', frame)
    # Display frames at speed of 1 ms; press q to quit
    if cv2.waitKey(1) & 0xFF == ord('q'):
        break
capture.release() # Release the capture object
cv2.destroyAllWindows() # Destroy all of the windows
```

However, if we are going to play videos loaded using OpenCV in PyQt, we need to consider first how PyQt processes events to avoid freezing the application.

Overview of Threading in PyQt

When a PyQt application is started using exec_(), the program's event loop begins. Starting the event loop also creates a **thread**. This thread is known as the **main thread**, and all events that occur in the application, such as clicking a button or typing text in line edit widgets, will be handled sequentially using your computer's Central Processing Unit (CPU) and other resources.

Opening and displaying videos from OpenCV will cause our application to become hung up as more resources are needed. Since your GUI must run in the main thread, we need to create a secondary thread, also known as a **worker thread**, to unload some of the extra processing work from the main thread and keep our application responsive. The communication between the main thread and any secondary threads in PyQt is managed with signals and slots.

The process for creating a secondary thread involves

1. Subclassing QThread and reimplementing the run() function

2. Creating an instance of the worker thread in the main thread and calling start() to begin running the thread

VideoWorkerThread will serve as the worker thread for this application and handles opening the video file and updating the frames. While all widget classes have their own built-in signals, you can also create custom signals for classes that inherit from QObject using pyqtSignal. The two custom signals created in the VideoWorkerThread class in Listing 5-4 are shown in the following code:

```
frame_data_updated = pyqtSignal(ndarray)
invalid_video_file = pyqtSignal()
```

The signal frame_data_updated is emitted whenever we need to update the video frames. There are many PyQt classes, including all widgets, that cannot be run in a secondary thread. In order to display an error message using QMessageBox to the user if the video_file path is incorrect, invalid_video_file is used to emit a signal in the main thread.

Any processes that we want to perform in the secondary thread need to be added to run(). Create the videoCapture instance and pass video_file as an argument. Use the isOpened() function to check if the capture is valid; if not, we emit the invalid_video_file signal and call the invalidVideoFile() slot in the main thread to inform the user of the error.

Otherwise, as long as thread_is_running is True, use read() to load the image data for that frame, convert from the BGR color space to RGB, and emit the frame_data_updated signal to update the frames in the updateVideoFrames() slot.

If the user clicks the start_button, we create an instance of VideoWorkerThread, connect the custom pyqtSignals to their corresponding slots, and run the worker thread by calling start() in the main thread of Listing 5-4:

```
self.video_thread_worker.start() # Start the thread
```

Finally, if the stop_button is pressed, the stopThread() function is called, blocking the main thread until run() is complete using wait(). QApplication.processEvents() is then called to process all pending events in the main thread. Playing a video in the GUI can be seen in Figure 5-13. In Project 5.2, we will see how to apply object recognition techniques to detect humans in videos.

Figure 5-13. *Displaying a selected video file in the GUI window*

Project 5.2: Human Detection and Tracking GUI

Detecting objects, specifically faces and people, in images and videos has a number of practical applications, especially in visual surveillance systems, photography, and the detection of pedestrians by autonomous vehicles. Detection and tracking of people in image and video data are two slightly different tasks. **Human detection** involves finding all instances of people that exist in an image. With a person located, **human tracking** can use the detections in a video sequence to follow the path of an individual. This can be particularly useful in tracking pedestrians walking in environments that are cluttered with other moving objects and people.

Figure 5-14. *The HOG (Histogram of Oriented Gradients) descriptor integrated into a PyQt application. The right image shows an instance where the descriptor incorrectly predicts detecting a human*

In this project, you will create a simple human detection and tracking application using a combination of common tools – a Histogram of Oriented Gradients (HOG) descriptor and a Linear Support Vector Machine (SVM)[2] – used for detecting human beings in videos. These algorithms go beyond the scope of this book. For more information, check out the OpenCV documentation or the references mentioned in the footnotes of this chapter.

Human Detection and Tracking GUI Solution

Listing 5-6 has a similar structure to the application you built in Example 5.2 with a few features removed, the most notable being the deletion of the menu bar. This will allow us to focus more on implementing the functionality for human detection. QThread is used this time to create a secondary thread for playing the video and for detecting humans using the HOG descriptor.

Note   Refer to the GitHub link found in the "Introduction" to download the video file used in the code, or edit the `video_file` path in Listing 5-6 to use your own video.

Listing 5-6. Code for human detection and tracking GUI

```
human_detection.py
# Import necessary modules
import sys, cv2
from numpy import ndarray, array
from PyQt5.QtWidgets import (QApplication, QMainWindow, QWidget, QLabel,
QPushButton, QFrame, QHBoxLayout, QVBoxLayout)
from PyQt5.QtGui import QPixmap, QImage
from PyQt5.QtCore import Qt, QThread, pyqtSignal
```

---

[2]This method was used as a pedestrian detector in the following research paper: Dalal, N., & Triggs, B. (2005, June). Histograms of oriented gradients for human detection. In *2005 IEEE computer society conference on computer vision and pattern recognition (CVPR'05)* (Vol. 1, pp. 886-893). IEEE.

```python
style_sheet = """
    QLabel#VideoLabel{
        color: darkgrey;
        border: 2px solid darkgrey;
        qproperty-alignment: AlignCenter
    }"""

class VideoWorkerThread(QThread):
    """Worker thread for capturing video."""
    frame_data_updated = pyqtSignal(ndarray)

    def __init__(self, parent, video_file=None):
        super().__init__()
        self.parent = parent
        self.video_file = video_file

    def run(self):
        """The code that we want to run in a separate thread, in this case
        capturing video using OpenCV, is placed in this function. run() is
        called after start()."""
        self.capture = cv2.VideoCapture(self.video_file) # 0 opens the
        default camera

        while self.parent.thread_is_running:
            # Read frames from the camera
            ret_val, frame = self.capture.read()

            if not ret_val:
                break # Error or reached the end of the video
            else:
                frame = cv2.cvtColor(frame, cv2.COLOR_BGR2RGB)
                # Resize an image for faster detection
                frame = cv2.resize(frame, (600, 400))
                rects = self.createHOGDescriptor(frame)

                # Draw the detections (rects) in the frame; tr and br refer
                # to the top-left and bottom-left corners of the detected
                # rects, respectively.
```

```python
        for (x_tr, y_tr, x_br, y_br) in rects:
            frame = cv2.rectangle(frame, (x_tr, y_tr), (x_br, y_
            br), (0, 0, 255), 2)
        self.frame_data_updated.emit(frame)

    def createHOGDescriptor(self, frame):
        """Function creates the HOG Descriptor for human detection and
        returns the detections (rects)."""
        # Initialize OpenCV's HOG Descriptor and SVM classifier
        hog = cv2.HOGDescriptor()
        hog.setSVMDetector(cv2.HOGDescriptor_getDefaultPeopleDetector())

        # Detect people in the image and return the bounding rectangles.
        # Altering the parameters in detectMultiScale() can affect the
        # accuracy of detections. winStride refers to the number of steps the
        # sliding window moves in the x and y directions; the sliding window
        # is padded to improve accuracy; a smaller scale value will increase
        # detection accuracy, but also increase processing time
        rects, weights = hog.detectMultiScale(frame, winStride=(4, 4),
            padding=(8, 8), scale=1.1)
        # For each of the rects detected in an image, add the values for
        # the corners of the rect to an array
        rects = array([[x, y, x + width, y + height] for (x, y, width,
        height) in rects])
        return rects

    def stopThread(self):
        """Process all pending events before stopping the thread."""
        self.wait()
        QApplication.processEvents()

class DisplayVideo(QMainWindow):

    def __init__(self):
        super().__init__()
        self.initializeUI()
```

```python
def initializeUI(self):
    """Initialize the window and display its contents to the screen."""
    self.setMinimumSize(800, 500)
    self.setWindowTitle('5.2 - Human Detection GUI')

    self.thread_is_running = False

    self.setupWindow()
    self.show()

def setupWindow(self):
    """Set up widgets in the main window."""
    self.video_display_label = QLabel()
    self.video_display_label.setObjectName("VideoLabel")

    self.start_button = QPushButton("Start Video")
    self.start_button.clicked.connect(self.startVideo)

    stop_button = QPushButton("Stop Video")
    stop_button.clicked.connect(self.stopCurrentVideo)

    # Create horizontal and vertical layouts
    side_panel_v_box = QVBoxLayout()
    side_panel_v_box.setAlignment(Qt.AlignTop)
    side_panel_v_box.addWidget(self.start_button)
    side_panel_v_box.addWidget(stop_button)

    side_panel_frame = QFrame()
    side_panel_frame.setMinimumWidth(200)
    side_panel_frame.setLayout(side_panel_v_box)

    main_h_box = QHBoxLayout()
    main_h_box.addWidget(self.video_display_label, 1)
    main_h_box.addWidget(side_panel_frame)

    # Create container widget and set main window's widget
    container = QWidget()
    container.setLayout(main_h_box)
    self.setCentralWidget(container)
```

```python
def startVideo(self):
    """Create and begin running the worker thread to play the video."""
    self.thread_is_running = True
    self.start_button.setEnabled(False)
    self.start_button.repaint()

    # Create an instance of the worker thread using a local video file
    video_file = "media/people_mall.mp4"
    self.video_thread_worker = VideoWorkerThread(self, video_file)

    # Connect to the thread's signal to update the frames in the video_
    display_label
    self.video_thread_worker.frame_data_updated.connect(self.
    updateVideoFrames)
    self.video_thread_worker.start() # Start the thread

def stopCurrentVideo(self):
    """Stop the current video, process events, and clear the video_
    display_label."""
    if self.thread_is_running == True:
        self.thread_is_running = False
        self.video_thread_worker.stopThread()

        self.video_display_label.clear()
        self.start_button.setEnabled(True)

def updateVideoFrames(self, video_frame):
    """A video is a collection of images played together in quick
    succession. For each frame (image) in the video, convert it to a
    QImage object to be displayed in the QLabel widget."""
    # Get the shape of the frame, height * width * channels. BGR/RGB/
    HSV images have 3 channels
    height, width, channels = video_frame.shape # Format: (rows,
    columns, channels)
    # Number of bytes required by the image pixels in a row; dependency
    on the number of channels
    bytes_per_line = width * channels
```

```
        # Create instance of QImage using data from the video file
        converted_Qt_image = QImage(video_frame, width, height, bytes_per_
        line, QImage.Format_RGB888)

        # Set the video_display_label's pixmap
        self.video_display_label.setPixmap(QPixmap.fromImage(converted_Qt_
        image).scaled(
                self.video_display_label.width(), self.video_display_label.
                height(), Qt.KeepAspectRatioByExpanding))

    def closeEvent(self, event):
        """Reimplement the closing event to ensure that the thread
        closes."""
        if self.thread_is_running == True:
            self.video_thread_worker.quit()

if __name__ == '__main__':
    app = QApplication(sys.argv)
    app.setStyleSheet(style_sheet)
    window = DisplayVideo()
    sys.exit(app.exec_())
```

Figure 5-14 shows the completed GUI with examples of accurate and false predictions of human detection.

Explanation

Refer to Example 5.2 for more information about threading or setting up this application's main window. After the application is opened, which is depicted in Figure 5-15, the user can click the start_button to begin playing the video. Doing so will create the video_thread_worker instance and start the secondary thread where updating the frames and detecting pedestrians occurs.

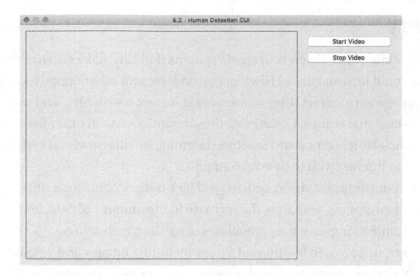

Figure 5-15. *The human detection and tracking GUI created in Listing 5-6*

In the secondary thread's `run()` method, we create the `videoCapture` object and use the `read()` function to load the frames in the video. Depending upon your computer's CPU, running a video and detecting objects can considerably impact the playback speed. Resizing the images to a smaller size with `resize()` can have an effect on your application's performance, but can also result in a loss of information in the image.

Next, we call the `createHOGDescriptor()` function where an instance of the `HOGDescriptor()` is created and then fed into the SVM detector. The `detectMultiScale()` function detects humans in the frame and produces the values for the rectangular boundaries around the different detections seen in Figure 5-14. All of the different detections for that single frame are appended to the `rects` list using list comprehension, returned, and drawn on the image using

```
for (x_tr, y_tr, x_br, y_br) in rects:
    frame = cv2.rectangle(frame, (x_tr, y_tr), (x_br, y_br), (0, 0, 255), 2)
```

The process is repeated until either the user clicks the `stop_button` or the end of the video file is reached.

207

Summary

The purpose of computer vision is to create systems that can make sense of the information found in visual data. Using images, videos, and other digital formats, we can use computer vision to extract three-dimensional features, structure, and understanding from two-dimensional scenes. Combining these techniques with other fields of study, including artificial intelligence and machine learning, intelligent visual systems can be created that can interact with their environments.

While current computer vision systems still lack deeper contextual understanding and situational awareness, research, the increase in the amount of data, and faster hardware continue to improve the capabilities of modern technology.

Visual data can be stored in different forms, including images and videos. With that in mind, PyQt GUIs were created in this chapter to cover aspects of both formats and integrated with the OpenCV library. The main projects in this chapter focused on image processing and human detection, introducing some of the common methods used in computer vision. The programs created could be used as foundations for larger GUI applications. It is also worth noting that PyQt has its own modules for handling images, video, and even audio. We will take a look at PyQt's media classes briefly in Chapter 9.

In Chapter 6, you will see how to build GUIs for visualizing 3D data using PyQt5.

CHAPTER 6

Visualizing 3D Data

Humans are creatures living in a three-dimensional world with eyes that only see two dimensions. The brain uses the visual information received from both of our eyes to perceive depth, allowing humans to have stereoscopic vision. Visual cues such as shading, shadows, and perspective also help give us the perception of depth. Our eyes are even able to understand three dimensions when shown an image or video.

The data that researchers collect exists within a three-dimensional world, and 3D data visualizations are great for creating models and maps, developing virtual environments for games, building simulations, localization in robotics, and more. Adding a third dimension to the 2D charts that we created back in Chapter 3 can also help to see data from a different perspective. When data is no longer restricted to a flat image, the user is able to freely move around and manipulate the items in a scene, visualizing depth, size, and other complex relationships that two-dimensional graphs sometimes lack.

With PyQt, you are able to build your own 3D graphical user interfaces. The tools you need to design and conceptualize three-dimensional data are provided to you. Choosing the right method for visualizing your data can be a crucial step for effectively communicating with others the results of your data.

This chapter will show you how to

- Install and get started in using the `PyQtDataVisualization` module for visualizing 3D data.

- Create interactive 3D bar graphs using public datasets.

- Build 3D graphs that visualize the information from multiple datasets.

- Work with built-in functions for controlling various parameters about the data displayed in a graph.

Before we see how to create an application, let's find out a little more about the module we'll be using in this chapter.

J. Willman, *Modern PyQt*, https://doi.org/10.1007/978-1-4842-6603-8_6

The PyQtDataVisualization Module

In Chapter 3, we saw how to work with two-dimensional data to create interactive GUIs. PyQt also includes a module, **PyQtDataVisualization**, for visualizing three-dimensional data. The module is a Python binding for the Qt Data Visualization library and allows you to create fluid and responsive 3D applications by utilizing the various features that are already built into the library.

With PyQtDataVisualization, you can create scatter, bar, and surface graphs or even make dynamic applications that receive data from digital sensors. More information about the PyQtDataVisualization module can be found at the Riverbank Computing's website, `www.riverbankcomputing.com/software/pyqtdatavisualization/intro`.

If you are also interested in finding out more about The Qt Company's Qt Data Visualization library, have a look at `https://doc.qt.io/qt-5/qtdatavisualization-index.html`. There, you will find more information about the different classes and see a few examples of other applications that you can build.

Installing PyQtDataVisualization

To download the wheel from PyPI for PyQtDataVisualization, open up your command-line application and enter

```
$ pip3 install PyQtDataVisualization
```

Once the installation is complete, run the command `python3` to enter the Python 3 shell environment. Enter the following line of code to check that the module was installed correctly:

```
>>> import PyQt5.QtDataVisualization
```

If there are no errors, then you are ready to get started visualizing 3D data with PyQt.

Example 6.1: Creating a 3D Bar Graph

Bar graphs are an effective tool for comparing different groups of data or for showing changes over time. They are great for visually conveying patterns or trends quickly to consumers. In many cases, using two variables is enough to capture the meaning in your data, but sometimes adding an additional axis to a graph is key to better understand the depth or volume that can only be visualized by including a third dimension.

The GUI you will make in Figure 6-1 illustrates how to create a 3D bar graph using the Q3DBars class. Interaction with the data is performed by rotating the scene or zooming into the graph or by clicking individual bars to access further information about a particular item. PyQt allows a user to intuitively perform these actions using the mouse. Additional features can be implemented to create more informative and responsive graphs, such as allowing users to select entire rows or columns of data at a single time.

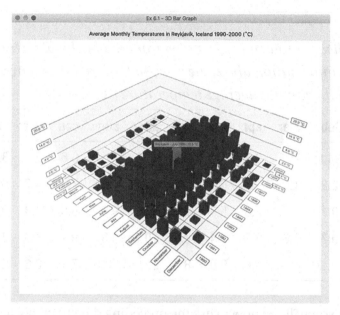

Figure 6-1. *Bar graph representing the average temperature per month in Reykjavík, Iceland, from 1990 to 2000. Clicking a bar will reveal information specific to that item*

Just as we did in Chapter 3, this chapter will also take advantage of public datasets to demonstrate how to create graphs using PyQt.

Quick Glance at the Dataset

Understanding climate data is important for creating daily weather forecasts and, on a long-term scale, showing how the climate is changing globally or in a particular country or city. Using data that has been collected over decades can help to provide important clues about what the future may hold as the climate changes. Graphs, charts, and maps are useful and assist scientists and researchers in planning for extreme weather conditions or future energy needs.

For this example, we are going to visualize and compare the data for the annual and monthly climate in Reykjavík, Iceland,[1] over an 11-year period (1990–2000). A sample of the Reykjavík climate dataset is shown in Table 6-1.

Note   The datasets for this chapter can be found on GitHub at the link in the "Introduction."

Table 6-1.   *The header row and select rows from the Reykjavik_temp.csv file. The dataset includes information about the year (ar), the average temperature per month (°C), and the annual average temperature (arid)*

nr	ar	jan	feb	mar	apr	mai	jun	jul	aug	sep	oct	nov	des	arid
1	1990	0.4	-1.6	-1.5	0.4	7.2	9.8	11.6	11.1	6.6	5	3.7	-0.3	4.4
1	1991	1.1	2.2	1.8	1.3	6.8	9.5	13	11	7.7	4.7	0.2	1.3	5
1	1992	2.5	0.1	0.5	2.6	5.8	7.8	9.9	9.9	6.8	4.3	0.8	-0.5	4.2
1	1993	-2.3	0.7	1.3	3.7	5.4	9.1	10.1	9.3	9.1	4.8	3.5	-1.6	4.4
1	1994	-1.7	-1.7	-1.4	1.6	6.9	8	12	10.6	7	3.6	2.4	-1	4.1

In Listing 6-1, you will see how to use the preceding data to create a 3D bar graph using PyQtDataVisualization.

Listing 6-1. The code for creating a basic bar graph with the PyQtDataVisualization module

```
# bar_graph_3D.py
# Import necessary modules
import sys, csv
import numpy as np
from PyQt5.QtWidgets import QApplication, QWidget, QLabel, QVBoxLayout
from PyQt5.QtDataVisualization import (Q3DBars, QBarDataItem, QBar3DSeries,
QValue3DAxis, Q3DCamera)
```

---

[1]Data from the Icelandic Meteorological Office website, Climatology, Climatological data, published in May 2012. Retrieved on September 1, 2020, from `https://en.vedur.is`.

```python
from PyQt5.QtCore import Qt
from PyQt5.QtGui import QColor

class SimpleBarGraph(QWidget):

    def __init__(self):
        super().__init__()
        self.initializeUI()

    def initializeUI(self):
        """Initialize the window and display its contents."""
        self.setMinimumSize(800, 700)
        self.setWindowTitle('6.1 - 3D Bar Graph')

        self.setupGraph()
        self.show()

    def setupGraph(self):
        """Load data and set up the window for the bar graph."""
        header_label = QLabel("Average Monthly Temperatures in Reykjavík,
        Iceland 1990-2000 (°C)")
        header_label.setAlignment(Qt.AlignCenter)

        # Load the data about average temperatures in Reykjavík from the
        CSV file
        temperature_data = self.loadCSVFile()
        # Select 11 sample years: 1990-2000. Don't select the first and
        last columns
        rows, columns = temperature_data.shape
        years = temperature_data[rows - 11:rows, 1]
        monthly_temps = temperature_data[rows - 11:rows, 2:columns -
        1].astype(float)

        bar_graph = Q3DBars() # Create instance for bar graph
        bar_graph.scene().activeCamera().setCameraPreset(Q3DCamera.
        CameraPresetFront)
```

```
# Create a list of QBarDataItem objects
data_items = []
for row in monthly_temps:
    data_items.append([QBarDataItem(value) for value in row])

months = ["January", "February", "March", "April", "May", "June",
"July", "August", "September", "October", "November", "December"]

# Create instance of QBar3DSeries, change the base color and color
of selected items, and add data and labels to the series
series = QBar3DSeries()
series.setBaseColor(QColor("#17A4D9"))
series.setSingleHighlightColor(QColor("#F8A307"))
series.dataProxy().addRows(data_items)
series.dataProxy().setRowLabels(years) # rowLabel
series.dataProxy().setColumnLabels(months) # colLabel

# Create the valueLabel. Use QValue3dAxis so we can format the
axis's label
temperature_axis = QValue3DAxis()
temperature_axis.setRange(-10, 20)
temperature_axis.setLabelFormat(u"%.1f \N{degree sign}C")
bar_graph.setValueAxis(temperature_axis)

# When items in the graph are selected, a label appears overhead
with information about that item. Set the format of information in
the label
series.setItemLabelFormat("Reykjavík - @colLabel @rowLabel:
@valueLabel")

bar_graph.addSeries(series)# Add the series to the bar graph

# 3D graph classes inherit QWindow, so we must use
createWindowContainer() to create a holder for the 3D graph in our
window since they can't be used as a normal widget
container = self.createWindowContainer(bar_graph)
v_box = QVBoxLayout()
v_box.addWidget(header_label)
```

214

```
        v_box.addWidget(container, 1)
        self.setLayout(v_box)

    def loadCSVFile(self):
        """Load the data from a CSV-formatted file using csv and numpy."""
        file_name = "files/Reykjavik_temp.csv"

        with open(file_name, "r") as csv_f:
            reader = csv.reader(csv_f)
            header_labels = next(reader)
            data = np.array(list(reader))
        return data

if __name__ == '__main__':
    app = QApplication(sys.argv)
    window = SimpleBarGraph()
    sys.exit(app.exec_())
```

Figure 6-1 displays the 3D bar graph representing the monthly and annual temperature data for Reykjavík, Iceland, from 1990 to 2000.

Explanation

To begin, we need to import the modules we need. The data we want to use is saved in CSV-formatted files, so we need to include csv. We will use numpy to make loading and working with the data easier. Information about installing NumPy can be found in Chapter 3.

Next, we import the classes we need from QtWidgets for the GUI's window. To visualize 3D data in PyQt, we need to import a few classes from QtDataVisualization, including

- Q3DBars – Class for creating 3D bar graphs

- QBarDataItem – Class that holds the data for a single bar in the graph

- QBar3DSeries – Represents the data series for 3D bar graphs

- QValue3DAxis – Class for manipulating a graph's axis

- Q3DCamera – Creates a camera in 3D space, used for rotating and zooming in and out

215

The `SimpleBarGraph` class inherits from `QWidget` and will serve as the application's main window. To begin setting up the graph, we need to first load the CSV data from `Reykjavik_temp.csv` using `loadCSVFile()`. This returns a NumPy array that contains the `temperature_data`. The following code found in Listing 6-1 illustrates how to select the years and the months from the data shown in Table 6-1:

```
# Get the shape of the array (rows * columns)
rows, columns = temperature_data.shape
# Select the last 11 rows and the second column (index starts at 0, so we
use 1 select the second column)
years = temperature_data[rows - 11:rows, 1]
# Select the last 11 rows and all of the month columns
monthly_temps = temperature_data[rows - 11:rows, 2:columns -
1].astype(float)
```

The next step is to instantiate `Q3DBars` and the scene's camera. The camera will allow the user to rotate and zoom into the scene. An example of this is shown in Figure 6-2.

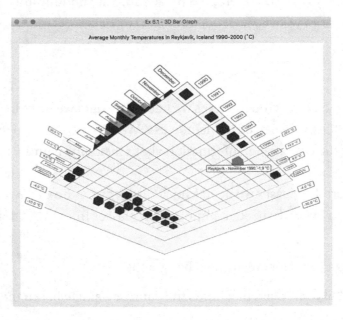

Figure 6-2. *Rotating the graph in the window will show the underside of the figure*

The Q3DCamera class has a number of preset views, including `CameraPresetLeft`, `CameraPresetRight`, and `CameraPresetBehind`, which we can set using `setCameraPreset()`, shown in the following line from Listing 6-1. There are a total of 25 presets. We'll explore these in Project 6.1:

```
bar_graph.scene().activeCamera().setCameraPreset(Q3DCamera.
CameraPresetFront)
```

Each of the bars in the bar graph in Listing 6-1 is represented as a `QBarDataItem`. To insert a row of data items, use a Python for loop and append `QBarDataItem` objects to the `data_items` list:

```
for row in monthly_temps:
    data_items.append([QBarDataItem(value) for value in row])
```

There are 12 items in each row, one for each month. The data displayed in PyQt graphs is represented using series classes. For Q3DBars, we use `QBar3DSeries`. You can set the base color of the bars and the color when they are selected in Listing 6-1 with

```
series.setBaseColor(QColor("#17A4D9"))
series.setSingleHighlightColor(QColor("#F8A307"))
```

A PyQt data proxy class is used to add, insert, change, or remove rows of data for PyQtDataVisualization classes. For this example, we would use QBarDataProxy. However, the data proxy in Listing 6-1 can also be accessed by calling `dataProxy()`:

```
# Add data to the series, and set the row labels
series.dataProxy().addRows(data_items)
series.dataProxy().setRowLabels(years) # Row labels
series.dataProxy().setColumnLabels(months) # Column labels
```

To manipulate the third axis's range and label in Listing 6-1, create an instance of `QValue3DAxis` and use `setRange()` and `setLabelFormat()`:

```
temperature_axis = QValue3DAxis()
temperature_axis.setRange(-10, 20)
temperature_axis.setLabelFormat(u"%.1f \N{degree sign}C")
bar_graph.setValueAxis(temperature_axis) # Set the axis
```

217

When a bar is clicked in the graph, textual information is displayed to the user above the selected item. The text displayed can be modified using setItemLabelFormat(). The following code from Listing 6-1 displays information about the column, row, and value of the clicked item:

```
series.setItemLabelFormat("Reykjavík - @colLabel @rowLabel: @valueLabel")
```

The different labels, axes, and item labels can be seen in Figures 6-1 and 6-2. The last step in Listing 6-1 is to add the series to the bar_graph so the user can see the data:

```
bar_graph.addSeries(series)
```

Since Q3DBars inherits from the QWindow class, if you only want to display a graph as a top-level window, you don't need to create a QApplication instance. Instead, you could use QGuiApplication since you don't need the support for widgets that QApplication has. If you want to display a 3D graph in a QApplication, create a container widget, and pass the graph object as an argument to createWindowContainer(). Then add the container to a layout.

The next application demonstrates how to display multiple series in Q3DBars and how to tinker around with the different graph and series properties.

Project 6.1: 3D Data Visualization GUI

Example 6.1 demonstrated how to visualize a single country's climate data. However, what happens if you want to compare the data for multiple countries or cities in the same graph? Thankfully, Q3DBars also allows you to graph multiple series concurrently, even if the series have different row and column sizes.

The GUI[2] created in the project in Figure 6-3 shows how you can use the climate data collected from multiple cities in the United States and graph them in the same Q3DBars instance.

---

[2]This application was influenced by the example found in the Qt documentation: https://doc.qt.io/qt-5/qtdatavisualization-bars-example.html.

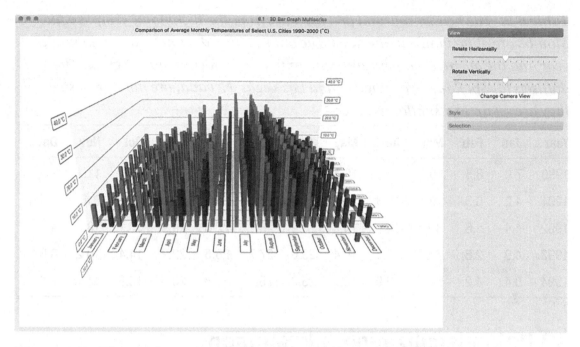

Figure 6-3. *The 3D data visualization GUI displaying data related to the average monthly temperatures for three different US cities from 1990 to 2000*

Quick Glance at the Dataset

The climatological data[3] used in this example pertains to different cities in the United States. The cities – Spokane, Washington; Las Vegas, Nevada; and Richmond, Virginia – pertain to different regions of the United States with varying seasonal climates.

The original dataset uses temperatures in degrees Fahrenheit; data has been converted to degrees Celsius for this project. Table 6-2 lists a few rows from the Richmond dataset.

---

[3]Source: NOAA National Centers for Environmental information, Climate at a Glance: City Time Series, published in September 2020, retrieved on September 1, 2020, from www.ncdc.noaa.gov/cag/.

Table 6-2. *The header row and first five rows from the Richmond_temp.csv file. Months are abbreviated in the table. The dataset includes information about the year and the average temperature per month (°C) in Richmond, Virginia. The datasets for Spokane, Washington, and Las Vegas, Nevada, are not shown since they are set up in a similar manner*

Year	Jan	Feb	Mar	Apr	May	Jun	Jul	Aug	Sep	Oct	Nov	Dec
1990	7.6	8.5	10.8	14.1	18.4	23.6	26.3	24.2	20.5	16.9	11.1	7.6
1991	4.2	6.3	10.1	15.3	21.9	23.7	26.7	25.5	21.6	15.2	9.4	6.4
1992	4.4	5.6	8.1	14	16.2	21.2	26	22.8	20.9	13.1	10	4.7
1993	4.9	2.8	7.3	12.9	19.4	23.6	27.7	25.5	22.2	14.4	10.2	3.6
1994	0.4	4.2	9.1	16.9	16.9	25.2	26.9	23.8	20.3	13.9	11.1	7.2

3D Data Visualization GUI Solution

The program in Listing 6-2 builds upon the previous concepts learned in this chapter. There are many noticeable differences, including the use of new datasets, adding multiple series in the same Q3DBars graph, and using several widgets in a QToolBox object for adjusting and controlling the properties of the graph and different series.

Listing 6-2. Code for the 3D data visualization GUI

```python
# bar_3D_multiseries.py
# Import necessary modules
import sys, csv
import numpy as np
from PyQt5.QtWidgets import (QApplication, QMainWindow, QWidget, QLabel,
QSlider, QComboBox, QPushButton, QCheckBox, QToolBox, QHBoxLayout,
QVBoxLayout)
from PyQt5.QtDataVisualization import (Q3DBars, QBarDataItem, QBar3DSeries,
QValue3DAxis, QAbstract3DSeries, QAbstract3DGraph, Q3DCamera, Q3DTheme)
from PyQt5.QtCore import Qt, QObject, pyqtSignal
```

```python
style_sheet = """
    QToolBox:tab { /* Style for tabs in QToolBox */
        background: qlineargradient(x1: 0, y1: 0, x2: 0, y2: 1,
                            stop: 0 #E1E1E1, stop: 0.4 #DDDDDD,
                            stop: 0.5 #D8D8D8, stop: 1.0 #D3D3D3);
        border-radius: 5px;
        color: #777C80
    }

    QToolBox:tab:selected { /* Style for tabs when selected */
        background: qlineargradient(x1: 0, y1: 0, x2: 0, y2: 1,
                            stop: 0 #6FC7E8, stop: 0.4 #6CC6E8,
                            stop: 0.5 #66BBDA, stop: 1.0 #60B9DA);
        color: #FFFFFF
    }"""

class GraphModifier(QObject):
    # Create pyqtSignals for keeping track of the state of the background
    and grid when the theme is changed
    background_selected = pyqtSignal(bool)
    grid_selected = pyqtSignal(bool)

    def __init__(self, parent, bar_graph):
        super().__init__()
        self.graph = bar_graph
        self.parent = parent

        # Set up rotation and visual variables
        self.horizontal_rotation = 0
        self.vertical_rotation = 0
        self.camera_preset = Q3DCamera.CameraPresetFront
        self.bar_style = QAbstract3DSeries.MeshBar
        self.bars_are_smooth = False

    def rotateHorizontal(self, rotation):
        self.graph.scene().activeCamera().setCameraPosition(
            rotation, self.vertical_rotation)
```

```python
    def rotateVertical(self, rotation):
        self.graph.scene().activeCamera().setCameraPosition(
            self.horizontal_rotation, rotation)

    def changeCameraView(self):
        """Change the camera's preset (the angle from which we view the
        camera) by cycling through Qt's different preset camera views."""
        self.graph.scene().activeCamera().setCameraPreset(self.camera_
        preset + 1)
        preset = int(self.camera_preset) + 1

        if preset > Q3DCamera.CameraPresetDirectlyBelow:
            # Reset predefined position for camera to 0
            (CameraPresetFrontLow)
            self.camera_preset = Q3DCamera.CameraPresetFrontLow
        else:
            self.camera_preset = Q3DCamera.CameraPreset(preset)

    def showOrHideBackground(self, state):
        self.graph.activeTheme().setBackgroundEnabled(state)

    def showOrHideGrid(self, state):
        self.graph.activeTheme().setGridEnabled(state)

    def smoothenBars(self, state):
        """Smoothen the edges of the items in all series."""
        self.bars_are_smooth = state
        for series in self.graph.seriesList():
            series.setMeshSmooth(self.bars_are_smooth)

    def changeTheme(self, theme):
        """Change the theme and appearance of the graph. Update the
        QCheckbox widgets."""
        active_theme = self.graph.activeTheme()
        active_theme.setType(Q3DTheme.Theme(theme))
        self.background_selected.emit(active_theme.isBackgroundEnabled())
        self.grid_selected.emit(active_theme.isGridEnabled())
```

```python
def changeBarStyle(self, style):
    """Change the visual style of the bars."""
    combo_box = self.sender()
    if isinstance(combo_box, QComboBox):
        self.bar_style = QAbstract3DSeries.Mesh(combo_box.
        itemData(style))
        for series in self.graph.seriesList():
            series.setMesh(self.bar_style)

def showOrHideSeries(self, state):
    """Show or hide the secondary series. seriesList()[1] refers to
    Spokane; seriesList()[2] refers to Richmond."""
    checkbox = self.sender()
    if state == Qt.Checked and checkbox.text() == "Show Second Series":
        self.graph.seriesList()[1].setVisible(True)
    elif state != Qt.Checked and checkbox.text() == "Show Second Series":
        self.graph.seriesList()[1].setVisible(False)

    if state == Qt.Checked and checkbox.text() == "Show Third Series":
        self.graph.seriesList()[2].setVisible(True)
    elif state != Qt.Checked and checkbox.text() == "Show Third Series":
        self.graph.seriesList()[2].setVisible(False)

def changeSelectionStyle(self, style):
    """Choose the style used to select data, by rows, columns or other
    options."""
    combo_box = self.sender()
    if isinstance(combo_box, QComboBox):
        selection_style = combo_box.itemData(style)
        self.graph.setSelectionMode(QAbstract3DGraph.
        SelectionFlags(selection_style))

def selectYears(self, year):
    """Select a specific year to view."""
    if year >= len(self.parent.years):
        self.graph.axes()[1].setRange(0, len(self.parent.years) - 1)
    else:
        self.graph.axes()[1].setRange(year, year)
```

```python
    def selectMonths(self, month):
        """Select a specific month to view."""
        if month >= len(self.parent.months):
            self.graph.axes()[0].setRange(0, len(self.parent.months) - 1)
        else:
            self.graph.axes()[0].setRange(month, month)

class SimpleBarGraph(QMainWindow):

    def __init__(self):
        super().__init__()
        self.initializeUI()

    def initializeUI(self):
        """Initialize the window and display its contents."""
        self.showMaximized()
        self.setMinimumSize(1000, 800)
        self.setWindowTitle('6.1 - 3D Bar Graph Multiseries')

        self.setupWindow()
        self.show()

    def setupWindow(self):
        """The window is comprised of two main parts: A Q3DBars graph on
        the left, and QToolBox on the right containing different widgets
        for tweaking different settings in the Q3DBars graph."""
        header_label = QLabel("Comparison of Average Monthly Temperatures
        of Select U.S. Cities 1990-2000 (°C)")
        header_label.setAlignment(Qt.AlignCenter)

        # Load and prepare the data for the three datasets
        data_files = ["LasVegas_temp.csv", "Spokane_temp.csv", "Richmond_
        temp.csv"]
        temperature_data = {}
        # Create a dictionary with key, value pairs pertaining to each city
        and dataset
        for f in data_files:
```

```
    data_name = f.split("_")[0] + "_data" # Create a dictionary key
    for each city
    data = self.loadCSVFile("files/" + f)

    # Select 11 years: 1990-2000; the first column in each file is
    the years
    rows, columns = data.shape
    self.years = data[:, 0]
    monthly_temps = data[:, 1:columns].astype(float)
    temperature_data[data_name] = monthly_temps

bar_graph = Q3DBars() # Create instance for bar graph
bar_graph.setMultiSeriesUniform(True) # Bars are scaled
proportionately
bar_graph.scene().activeCamera().setCameraPreset(Q3DCamera.
CameraPresetFront)

# Create lists of QBarDataItem objects for each city
vegas_data_items = []
for row in temperature_data["LasVegas_data"]:
    vegas_data_items.append([QBarDataItem(value) for value in row])

spokane_data_items = []
for row in temperature_data["Spokane_data"]:
    spokane_data_items.append([QBarDataItem(value) for value in row])

richmond_data_items = []
for row in temperature_data["Richmond_data"]:
    richmond_data_items.append([QBarDataItem(value) for value in
    row])

self.months = ["January", "February", "March", "April", "May",
"June",
"July", "August", "September", "October", "November", "December"]

# Create instances of QBar3DSeries for each set of data;
dataProxy() handles modifying data in the series
vegas_series = QBar3DSeries()
vegas_series.dataProxy().addRows(vegas_data_items)
```

```python
vegas_series.dataProxy().setRowLabels(self.years) # rowLabel
vegas_series.dataProxy().setColumnLabels(self.months) # colLabel

spokane_series = QBar3DSeries()
spokane_series.dataProxy().addRows(spokane_data_items)

richmond_series = QBar3DSeries()
richmond_series.dataProxy().addRows(richmond_data_items)

# Create the valueLabel
temperature_axis = QValue3DAxis()
temperature_axis.setRange(-10, 40)
temperature_axis.setLabelFormat(u"%.1f \N{degree sign}C")
bar_graph.setValueAxis(temperature_axis)

# Set the format for the labels that appear when items are
clicked on
vegas_series.setItemLabelFormat("LasVegas - @colLabel @rowLabel:
@valueLabel")
spokane_series.setItemLabelFormat("Spokane - @colLabel @rowLabel:
@valueLabel")
richmond_series.setItemLabelFormat("Richmond - @colLabel @rowLabel:
@valueLabel")

# Add the three series to the bar graph
bar_graph.setPrimarySeries(vegas_series)
bar_graph.addSeries(spokane_series)
bar_graph.addSeries(richmond_series)

# Create a QWidget to hold only the graph
graph_container = QWidget.createWindowContainer(bar_graph)
main_h_box = QHBoxLayout() # Main layout for the entire window
graph_v_box = QVBoxLayout() # Layout that holds the graph
graph_v_box.addWidget(header_label)
graph_v_box.addWidget(graph_container, 1)
```

```
####################################################################
# The following section creates the QToolBox that appears on the
right of the window and contains widgets for interacting with the
graph
self.modifier = GraphModifier(self, bar_graph) # Create modifier
instance

settings_toolbox = QToolBox()
settings_toolbox.setFixedWidth(300)
settings_toolbox.setCurrentIndex(0) # Show the first tab

# The first tab - Widgets for rotating the bar graph and changing
the camera
horizontal_rotation_slider = QSlider(Qt.Horizontal)
horizontal_rotation_slider.setTickInterval(20)
horizontal_rotation_slider.setRange(-180, 180)
horizontal_rotation_slider.setValue(0)
horizontal_rotation_slider.setTickPosition(QSlider.TicksBelow)
horizontal_rotation_slider.valueChanged.connect(self.modifier.
rotateHorizontal)

vertical_rotation_slider = QSlider(Qt.Horizontal)
vertical_rotation_slider.setTickInterval(20)
vertical_rotation_slider.setRange(-180, 180)
vertical_rotation_slider.setValue(0)
vertical_rotation_slider.setTickPosition(QSlider.TicksBelow)
vertical_rotation_slider.valueChanged.connect(self.modifier.
rotateVertical)

# QPushButton for changing the camera's view point
camera_view_button = QPushButton("Change Camera View")
camera_view_button.clicked.connect(self.modifier.changeCameraView)

# Layout for the View tab (first tab)
view_tab_container = QWidget()
view_tab_v_box = QVBoxLayout()
view_tab_v_box.setAlignment(Qt.AlignTop)
view_tab_v_box.addWidget(QLabel("Rotate Horizontally"))
```

```
view_tab_v_box.addWidget(horizontal_rotation_slider)
view_tab_v_box.addWidget(QLabel("Rotate Vertically"))
view_tab_v_box.addWidget(vertical_rotation_slider)
view_tab_v_box.addWidget(camera_view_button)
view_tab_container.setLayout(view_tab_v_box)

settings_toolbox.addItem(view_tab_container, "View")

# The second tab - Widgets for changing the appearance of the graph.
Recheck the background and grid checkboxes if the theme has changed
show_background_cb = QCheckBox("Show Background")
show_background_cb.setChecked(True)
show_background_cb.stateChanged.connect(self.modifier.
showOrHideBackground)
self.modifier.background_selected.connect(show_background_
cb.setChecked)

show_grid_cb = QCheckBox("Show Grid")
show_grid_cb.setChecked(True)
show_grid_cb.stateChanged.connect(self.modifier.showOrHideGrid)
self.modifier.grid_selected.connect(show_grid_cb.setChecked)

smooth_bars_cb = QCheckBox("Smoothen Bars")
smooth_bars_cb.stateChanged.connect(self.modifier.smoothenBars)

# QComboBox for selecting the Qt theme
themes = ["Qt", "Primary Colors", "Digia", "Stone Moss", "Army Blue",
"Retro", "Ebony", "Isabelle"]
select_theme_combo = QComboBox()
select_theme_combo.addItems(themes)
select_theme_combo.setCurrentIndex(0)
select_theme_combo.currentIndexChanged.connect(self.modifier.
changeTheme)

# QComboBox for selecting the visual style of the bars
bar_style_combo = QComboBox()
bar_style_combo.addItem("Bar", QAbstract3DSeries.MeshBar)
bar_style_combo.addItem("Pyramid", QAbstract3DSeries.MeshPyramid)
```

```python
bar_style_combo.addItem("Cylinder", QAbstract3DSeries.MeshCylinder)
bar_style_combo.addItem("Sphere", QAbstract3DSeries.MeshSphere)
bar_style_combo.setCurrentIndex(0)
bar_style_combo.currentIndexChanged.connect(self.modifier.
changeBarStyle)

# Layout for the Style tab (second tab)
style_tab_container = QWidget()
style_tab_v_box = QVBoxLayout()
style_tab_v_box.setAlignment(Qt.AlignTop)
style_tab_v_box.addWidget(show_background_cb)
style_tab_v_box.addWidget(show_grid_cb)
style_tab_v_box.addWidget(smooth_bars_cb)
style_tab_v_box.addWidget(QLabel("Select Qt Theme"))
style_tab_v_box.addWidget(select_theme_combo)
style_tab_v_box.addWidget(QLabel("Select Bar Style"))
style_tab_v_box.addWidget(bar_style_combo)
style_tab_container.setLayout(style_tab_v_box)

settings_toolbox.addItem(style_tab_container, "Style")

# The third tab - Widgets for hiding/showing different series and
changing how items are viewed and selected
second_series_cb = QCheckBox("Show Second Series")
second_series_cb.setChecked(True)
second_series_cb.stateChanged.connect(self.modifier.
showOrHideSeries)

third_series_cb = QCheckBox("Show Third Series")
third_series_cb.setChecked(True)
third_series_cb.stateChanged.connect(self.modifier.
showOrHideSeries)

# QComboBox for changing how items in the bar graph are selected
selection_mode_combo = QComboBox()
selection_mode_combo.addItem("None", QAbstract3DGraph.
SelectionNone)
selection_mode_combo.addItem("Bar", QAbstract3DGraph.SelectionItem)
```

```python
selection_mode_combo.addItem("Row", QAbstract3DGraph.SelectionRow)
selection_mode_combo.addItem("Column", QAbstract3DGraph.
SelectionColumn)
selection_mode_combo.addItem("Item, Row, Column", QAbstract3DGraph.
SelectionItemRowAndColumn)
selection_mode_combo.setCurrentIndex(1)
selection_mode_combo.currentIndexChanged.connect(self.modifier.
changeSelectionStyle)

# QComboBox for selecting which years to view
select_year_combo = QComboBox()
select_year_combo.addItems(self.years)
select_year_combo.addItem("All Years")
select_year_combo.setCurrentIndex(len(self.years))
select_year_combo.currentIndexChanged.connect(self.modifier.
selectYears)

# QComboBox for selecting which months to view
select_month_combo = QComboBox()
select_month_combo.addItems(self.months)
select_month_combo.addItem("All Months")
select_month_combo.setCurrentIndex(len(self.months))
select_month_combo.currentIndexChanged.connect(self.modifier.
selectMonths)

# Layout for the Selection tab (third tab)
selection_tab_container = QWidget()
selection_tab_v_box = QVBoxLayout()
selection_tab_v_box.addWidget(second_series_cb)
selection_tab_v_box.addWidget(third_series_cb)
selection_tab_v_box.addWidget(QLabel("Choose Selection Mode"))
selection_tab_v_box.addWidget(selection_mode_combo)
selection_tab_v_box.addWidget(QLabel("Select Year"))
selection_tab_v_box.addWidget(select_year_combo)
selection_tab_v_box.addWidget(QLabel("Select Month"))
selection_tab_v_box.addWidget(select_month_combo)
```

```
        selection_tab_container.setLayout(selection_tab_v_box)

        settings_toolbox.addItem(selection_tab_container, "Selection")

        # Set up the layout for the settings toolbox
        settings_v_box = QVBoxLayout()
        settings_v_box.addWidget(settings_toolbox, 0, Qt.AlignTop)

        main_h_box.addLayout(graph_v_box)
        main_h_box.addLayout(settings_v_box)

        main_widget = QWidget()
        main_widget.setLayout(main_h_box)
        self.setCentralWidget(main_widget)

    def loadCSVFile(self, file_name):
        """Load CSV files. Return data as numpy arrays."""
        with open(file_name, "r") as csv_f:
            reader = csv.reader(csv_f)
            header_labels = next(reader)
            data = np.array(list(reader))
        return data

if __name__ == '__main__':
    app = QApplication(sys.argv)
    app.setStyleSheet(style_sheet)
    window = SimpleBarGraph()
    sys.exit(app.exec_())
```

The 3D data visualization application's interface can be seen in Figure 6-3.

Explanation

For this project, we also need to include a few widget classes for adjusting the
parameters of the graph, including QSlider, QComboBox, QPushButton, and QCheckBox;
QToolBox is used for creating a container to hold and arrange those widgets on the side
of the window.

The classes associated with creating a Q3DBars graph are included along with some new ones. QAbstract3DSeries is the base class for all 3D series types, and QAbstract3DGraph provides the window and rendering process for the graph. Q3DTheme provides the visual appearance and parameters for the graph.

The style_sheet is used to change the appearance of the QToolBox widget's tabs when they are selected or not selected.

Creating Multiple Series

Let's start by looking at the setupWindow() function. Just like in Example 6.1, we begin by loading the CSV data, but this time for each of the three file paths in the data_files list. Each file contains the temperature data for a different city in the United States from 1990 to 2000. An example of the data can be seen in Table 6-2.

For each of the files in Listing 6-2, a name is created from the file path and used as the key in the temperature_data dictionary:

```
for f in data_files:
    # Dictionary key for each city stored in data_name
    data_name = f.split("_")[0] + "_data"
    data = self.loadCSVFile("files/" + f)
```

Data for the years and monthly_temps is selected from the NumPy array, data, for each city. years is used for the labels in the graph; monthly_temps contains the values for the current city while iterating through the for loop. Those values are assigned to the current city, data_name, in the temperature_date dictionary in Listing 6-2 by

```
temperature_data[data_name] = monthly_temps
```

After iterating through the for loop, temperature_data will contain three keys – LasVegas_data, Spokane_data, and Richmond_data. Each key will also have the values for monthly_temps as its corresponding value, 12 items for each row (months), and 11 rows (years, 1990–2000).

We can now create the Q3DBars instance and set the scene's camera preset. For each of the cities, we also need to create a list of QBarDataItem objects. The following code from Listing 6-2 creates the data items from the LasVegas_data:

```
vegas_data_items = []
for row in temperature_data["LasVegas_data"]:
    vegas_data_items.append([QBarDataItem(value) for value in row])
```

A QBar3DSeries object is also created for each of the cities. Let's take a look at the series for Las Vegas, vegas_series, in Listing 6-2. The other series are set up in a similar fashion:

```
vegas_series = QBar3DSeries()
vegas_series.dataProxy().addRows(vegas_data_items)
# Set the row and column labels
vegas_series.dataProxy().setRowLabels(self.years)
vegas_series.dataProxy().setColumnLabels(self.months)
```

The data proxy is used to add the rows of QBarDataItems to the series. Since we do not explicitly define the row and column axes for the richmond_series and spokane_series, row and column values are taken from the first added series. The temperature_axis is set up just like in Example 6.1. Item labels are also created in Listing 6-2 for each series using the setItemLabelFormat() function. The three series are then added to bar_graph:

```
bar_graph.setPrimarySeries(vegas_series)
bar_graph.addSeries(spokane_series)
bar_graph.addSeries(richmond_series)
```
Notice how setPrimarySeries() is used for the vegas_series. The primary series of the graph determines the row and column axis labels.

Also, in order to place a 3D graph in the window, we need to use createWindowContainer() to create a QWidget wrapper for Q3DBars (since it inherits QWindow), allowing it to be placed inside a QWidget-based application.

Setting Up the QToolBox

This application is made up of two major parts: the graph and the toolbox that houses the widgets for interacting with the items in the graph. The QToolBox instance, settings_toolbox, is a column of three tabs used to sort the different widgets for modifying the graph and series properties. Each tab has an index position that can be set with setCurrentIndex().

When the application begins, the user will see the View tab (seen in Figure 6-4 on the left). Here they can use the two sliders to rotate the graph horizontally or vertically or click the camera_view_button to cycle through many camera presets. Widgets in the tab are arranged into a QVBoxLayout and placed inside a container QWidget. This step is shown in the following code from Listing 6-2:

```
view_tab_container.setLayout(view_tab_v_box)
settings_toolbox.addItem(view_tab_container, "View")
```

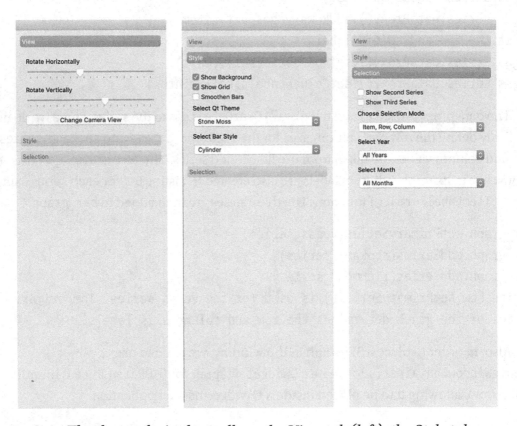

Figure 6-4. *The three tabs in the toolbox: the View tab (left), the Style tab (middle), and the Selection tab (right)*

The next tab, Style, is seen in the middle image of Figure 6-4. The tab is comprised of QCheckBox widgets for showing the graph's background or grid and for smoothing the bars. The QComboBox widgets are used for selecting the different built-in visual themes or for choosing a different shape to depict the data items (bar, pyramid, cylinder, or sphere). There are also other shapes that are not included in this project.

Lastly, the image on the right in Figure 6-4 shows the Selection tab. Here the user can hide or display the secondary series, the Richmond and Spokane datasets, with QCheckboxes. The three QComboBox widgets allow for choosing how to select data items in the graph and for displaying specific years or months. Items selected in the bar graph will appear highlighted with a different color. In this application, users can select a single item or an entire row, column, or both. There are also many other selection options that are not included.

All of these widgets are connected to different signals that we will examine in the next section.

Adjusting Properties with Widgets

The GraphModifier class inherits from QObject and is used to update the bar graph and the different series and create a few custom signals with pyqtSignal. The instance of the class, modifier, is instantiated in the SimpleBarGraph's setupWindow() function.

The following lists the 13 different widgets in the settings_toolbox, the signals they emit, and information about the slots they are connected to in the GraphModifier class:

- horizontal_rotation_slider – Emits a signal when the user moves the slider and changes the values. Connected to rotateHorizontal(). Uses the setCameraPosition() function to rotate the scene's camera horizontally.

- vertical_rotation_slider – Similar to horizontal_rotation_slider. Calls rotateVertical() and rotates the camera vertically.

- camera_view_button – When clicked, connects to the changeCameraView() slot. Cycles through the different camera presets. Each preset is associated with an integer value, 1 for CameraPresetFrontLow to 23 for CameraPresetDirectlyBelow.

- show_background_cb – When checked, sets setBackgroundEnabled() to True in the showOrHideBackground() slot.

- show_grid_cb – When checked, sets setGridEnabled() to True in the showOrHideGrid() slot.

- smooth_bars_cb – When checked, connects to smoothenBars(). For all of the series in the graph, smooths the shapes for the bars using setMeshSmooth().

- select_theme_combo – Emits a signal when a new item is selected. Connects to changeTheme() and updates the theme using setType(). Figure 6-5 displays one of the different themes. Also, changing the theme resets the graph's settings. Emits the custom background_selected() and grid_selected() signals to update the corresponding QCheckBoxes.

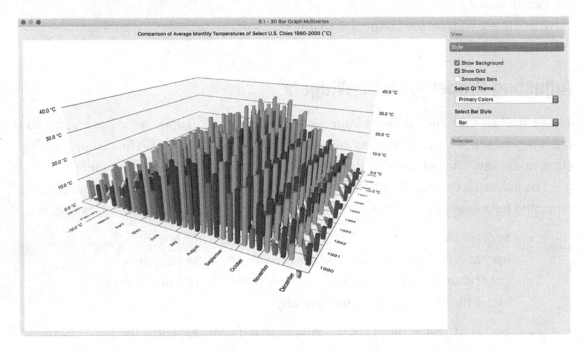

Figure 6-5. *Example of selecting built-in themes to represent the different series in the graph*

- bar_style_combo – Triggers the changeBarStyle() slot when a different bar style is selected. Uses the Python function isinstance() to check if the combobox object from the sender() is of the type QComboBox. Gets the itemData() about the selected style and sets the mesh style for all series.

- second_series_cb – When the state changes, calls showOrHideSeries(). Checks the state of the checkbox and its text to determine which series to display or hide.

- third_series_cb – Same as second_series_cb.

- selection_mode_combo – When the index of the combobox changes, calls changeSelectionStyle() and uses isinstance() to check if the combo_box object from sender() is a member of QComboBox. Uses itemData() to determine the selection_style for the graph.

An example of hiding the secondary series and changing the selection mode is shown in Figure 6-6.

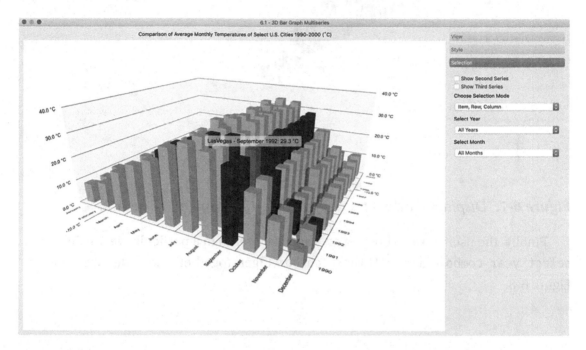

Figure 6-6. *An example of hiding the series for the Spokane and Richmond datasets and changing the selection mode*

- select_year_combo – If the current index changes, calls the selectYears() slot. Checks first if the user has selected the All Years option. Uses setRange() to set the axis for the graph.

- select_month_combo – Signal emitted when the index changes and calls the selectMonths() slot. The process for selecting the month is similar to select_year_combo.

Figure 6-7 shows the result of selecting the year 1997 using the select_year_combo widget.

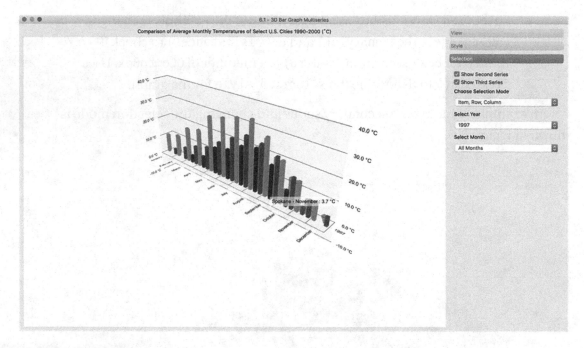

Figure 6-7. *Displays the data for a single year, 1997, and all 12 months*

Finally, the user can also hone in on a specific month in a particular year using the `select_year_combo` and `select_month_combo` widgets together. This is demonstrated in Figure 6-8.

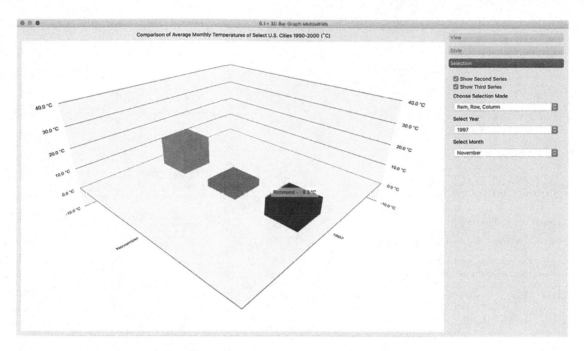

Figure 6-8. *Displays the data for all three series in September 1997*

There are still many other features that could be adjusted, such as the font style or size of the labels or the shadow quality in the scene.

Summary

There are numerous options for interacting with and visualizing the underlying data in our world. In previous chapters, we have explored methods for creating GUIs to interact with two-dimensional datasets, databases, and image and video formats. However, the data displayed using 2D charts, tables, and images loses the interactivity that a three-dimensional environment can offer.

With PyQt, you can display your data using 3D bar, scatter, and surface graphs. These tools are dynamic and interactive from the start and can be further exploited using PyQt's widgets and the signal and slot mechanism. The examples in this chapter demonstrated how to visualize the climatological data for different cities around the globe using the PyQt classes for creating 3D bar graphs.

In Chapter 7, you will be introduced to the PyQt networking classes used for accessing and sharing data across networks.

CHAPTER 7

Introduction to Networking with PyQt

We are connected like never before through a web of networks. They are the way we communicate, connect with families and friends, do business, send photos, and play video games with people we have never met. They let us share breaking news and listen to incredible stories from places all around the world. We have become so used to networks in our daily lives that most of us probably don't even notice them very often. To build this vast collection of intertwined systems, we need fast technologies and a set of rules to maintain them.

Ideas spread faster because of networks. The Internet is one of the largest networks humans have ever created. Your projects, photos, and videos can be uploaded and shared and liked by others. Projects coded in this text could all be connected to other applications in some way. Even if you want to create and share a small application that only runs locally on someone's computer, you still need a means for others to find and have access to downloading and installing your application.

In this chapter, we will

- Learn some of the fundamentals about networks.

- Find out about the classes in PyQt5 for networking.

- Use the `QtNetwork` module and `QWebEngineView` class to create a simple web browser that displays requested HTML code.

- Build a PyQt GUI that uses the Python `smtplib` module for sending emails.

© Joshua Willman 2021
J. Willman, *Modern PyQt*, https://doi.org/10.1007/978-1-4842-6603-8_7

What Is Networking?

A **network** is a group of computers linked together to share resources, allow for communication within the group, and to permit the exchange of information among its authorized members. Systems that create a network are a combination of both hardware and software working together to allow everyone with access to communicate and request information securely. Networking is involved in telephone calls, text messaging, streaming videos over the Internet, and so much more.

For a network to function properly and to remain secure, it must rely on a set of **protocols**, rules that decide how data is shared between different nodes on the same network. Regardless of the underlying hardware, these devices still need to be able to work together. There are a number of protocols, including **Hypertext Transfer Protocol** (**HTTP**) for displaying web pages and exchanging information between clients and servers. **Transmission Control Protocol/Internet Protocol** (**TCP/IP**) is another useful Internet protocol for transferring information over an IP network. This only skims the surface of networking, but it's enough to get us started in this chapter.

PyQt Networking Classes

PyQt5 offers both high-level and low-level networking classes in its **QtNetwork** module. The lower-level classes allow for a developer to work closely with TCP/IP clients and servers. These classes include functionality for working with both TCP, QTcpSocket and QTcpServer, and UDP, QUdpSocket. TCP is more reliable than UDP and therefore used most often in client–server applications. The QTcpSocket class can be used to execute standard network protocols.

At the high level, classes such as QNetworkAccessManager, QNetworkRequest, and QNetworkReply are great for working with HTTP. These three classes work together, with network applications only having one instance of QNetworkAccessManager. QNetworkRequest acts as a container for information about the request, including the **header** (contains protocol information about the data it is carrying) and the **body** (contains the actual data). The QNetworkAccessManager class keeps network requests in order and keeps track of a request's progress using signals and slots. With a request made, QNetworkReply sends information back to the managing class, sending updates about the progress of a request.

Please have a look at `https://doc.qt.io/qt-5/topics-network-connectivity.html` for more information about Qt's networking classes.

Example 7.1: Requesting HTML from a Web Page

For this chapter's first program, we will create a simple application to show the process for using the different QtNetwork classes for getting and posting data over HTTP. **Hypertext Markup Language (HTML)** is the language that creates the documents designed for being displayed on a web browser. HTTP has its own set of methods for requesting data. There are a few different ones, but the general two are GET for collecting information or resources from a server and POST for sending data to the server.

If you ever want to view the HTML code for a website in your browser, simply right-click the page and select the appropriate option from the context menu that appears. The application you are going to build is seen in Figure 7-1. This example displays the HTML code for a web page and updates automatically every time a new web page is viewed.

Figure 7-1. *The GUI for displaying a web page and viewing the underlying HTML code*

Before jumping into this section's example code, we'll need to install a few additional Python and PyQt modules.

Installing Beautiful Soup

The first package we will be installing, Beautiful Soup, is typically used for **web scraping**, the process of collecting useful data, such as images, text files, and even videos, from the Internet. Accessing this data often means parsing through a web page's HTML code looking for the specific bits of information that we need to download. We won't be web scraping in this example. Instead, we will use Beautiful Soup to parse the code and make it easier to read.

To get Beautiful Soup using the PyPI wheel, run the following command:

```
$ pip3 install beautifulsoup4
```

Debian or Linux users may need to use the following command to install the library:

```
$ sudo apt-get install python3-bs4
```

To check that everything is working properly, open up Python 3 and enter

```
>>> import bs4
```

The Beautiful Soup library already supports the HTML parser used by Python. If you are interested in seeing what other HTML parsers are supported, check out `lxml` or `html5lib`.

The documentation for Beautiful Soup can be found at `www.crummy.com/software/BeautifulSoup/bs4/doc/`.

Installing PyQtWebEngine

You may also need to install the **PyQtWebEngine** module, a collection of Python bindings for the Qt WebEngine library. With PyQtWebEngine, you are able to create applications that can embed a web browser into the graphical interface. Current versions of Qt WebEngine are built upon Google's Chromium software. For our purposes, we only need to display a web page and the HTML that constructs that page in a QtWidgets-based application. It sounds like a daunting task, but it really isn't.

To get started installing PyQtWebEngine, open up your computer's shell interface and enter the following command:

```
$ pip3 install pyqtwebengine
```

To test that the installation was successful, open up the Python 3 shell and try importing the package with the following line of code:

```
>>> import PyQt5.QtWebEngine
```

That's all there is to it! You are now ready to get started creating applications that connect to the Internet. More information about the PyQtWebEngine module can be found at https://riverbankcomputing.com/software/pyqtwebengine.

In Listing 7-1, we will explore how to use HTTP request methods to retrieve and view the HTML code for a web page.

Listing 7-1. Code that demonstrates how to perform HTTP requests with PyQt networking classes

```python
# request_html.py
# Import necessary modules
import sys
from bs4 import BeautifulSoup
from PyQt5.QtWidgets import (QApplication, QMainWindow, QWidget, QSplitter,
QTextEdit, QToolBar, QHBoxLayout, QAction)
from PyQt5.QtNetwork import QNetworkAccessManager, QNetworkRequest,
QNetworkReply
from PyQt5.QtWebEngineWidgets import QWebEngineView
from PyQt5.QtCore import Qt, QUrl, QSize
from PyQt5.QtGui import QFont, QIcon

class DisplayWebContent(QMainWindow):

    def __init__(self):
        super().__init__()
        self.initializeUI()

    def initializeUI(self):
        """Initialize the window and display its contents."""
        self.showMaximized() # Window starts maximized
        self.setMinimumSize(1000, 500)
        self.setWindowTitle('Ex 7.1 - Request HTML')
```

```python
        self.setupWindow()
        self.setupToolbar()
        self.show()

    def setupWindow(self):
        """Set up the widgets in the main window."""
        home_page_url = "https://www.google.com"

        # Create the view instance for the web browser
        self.web_view = QWebEngineView()
        self.web_view.setUrl(QUrl(home_page_url))
        self.web_view.urlChanged.connect(self.loadHTML)

        self.html_text_edit = QTextEdit()
        self.html_text_edit.setText("Loading HTML...")
        self.html_text_edit.setFont(QFont('Courier', 12))

        # Create splitter container and arrange widgets
        splitter = QSplitter()
        splitter.setOrientation(Qt.Vertical)
        splitter.addWidget(self.web_view)
        splitter.addWidget(self.html_text_edit)

        main_h_box = QHBoxLayout()
        main_h_box.addWidget(splitter)

        main_container = QWidget()
        main_container.setLayout(main_h_box)
        self.setCentralWidget(main_container)

    def setupToolbar(self):
        """Create the toolbar for navigating web pages."""
        toolbar = QToolBar()
        toolbar.setIconSize(QSize(24, 24))
        toolbar.setMovable(False)
        self.addToolBar(toolbar)

        # Create actions
        back_act = QAction(QIcon("icons/back.png"), "Back Button", toolbar)
        back_act.triggered.connect(self.web_view.back)
```

```python
        forward_act = QAction(QIcon("icons/forward.png"), "Forward Button",
        toolbar)
        forward_act.triggered.connect(self.web_view.forward)

        # Add actions to the toolbar
        toolbar.addAction(back_act)
        toolbar.addAction(forward_act)

    def loadHTML(self):
        """Send a GET request to retrieve the current web page and its
        data."""
        # Retrieve the url of the current page
        url = self.web_view.url()

        request = QNetworkRequest(QUrl(url))

        # Create QNetworkAccessManager to send request; emit finished()
        # signal to connect to replyFinished() and display the page's HTML
        self.manager = QNetworkAccessManager()
        self.manager.finished.connect(self.replyFinished)
        self.manager.get(request)

    def replyFinished(self, reply):
        """Get the reply data. Check for any errors that occurred while
        loading the web pages."""
        error = reply.error()

        if error == QNetworkReply.NoError:
            # The function readAll() returns a byte array containing the
            # requested data
            data = reply.readAll()

            # Use BeautifulSoup to "prettify" the HTML before displaying it
            soup = BeautifulSoup(data, features="html5lib")
            beautified_html = soup.prettify()
            self.html_text_edit.setPlainText(beautified_html)
        else:
            error = "[INFO] Error: {}".format(str(error))
            self.html_text_edit.setPlainText(error + "\n" + reply.
            errorString())
```

```
if __name__ == '__main__':
    app = QApplication(sys.argv)
    window = DisplayWebContent()
    sys.exit(app.exec_())
```

The final GUI displaying a web page and the HTML code is shown in Figure 7-1.

Explanation

We begin as normal by importing the modules we need for the application. We will import BeautifulSoup from bs4. From QtWidgets, QSplitter will be used as a container for the QWebEngineView (the widget used to view and interact with web pages) and the QTextEdit widgets. The application's QToolBar will contain two buttons for moving between previously viewed web pages.

From QtNetwork, the network operations will be performed by QNetworkAccessManager, QNetworkRequest, and QNetworkReply.

Let's first see how the main window is arranged in setupWindow(). When the application first opens, the user will be directed to Google. The next step is to create the QWebEngineView instance and set its URL to home_page_url. Whenever we move to a new website, the urlChanged() signal is emitted. This calls loadHTML(). We'll talk about this function a little later.

The HTML we request to view from each website is displayed in html_text_edit. Both web_view and html_text_edit are contained in a QSplitter widget.

Setting Up the Toolbar

The example's toolbar is very simple. It contains two buttons, back_act and forward_act, to navigate through web pages like in a normal web browser. Other tools, such as the navigation bar, are left to the reader to implement. The QWebEngineView already has built-in functions for navigating the Internet. The following code from Listing 7-1 illustrates how to implement the button for moving back to previously viewed web pages:

```
back_act = QAction(QIcon("icons/back.png"), "Back Button", toolbar)
back_act.triggered.connect(self.web_view.back)
```

The button for moving forward is set up in a similar manner.

Sending a GET Request

While this example only demonstrates how to perform GET requests, the QNetworkAccessManager class also allows you to perform other HTTP operations. GET requests are useful for receiving data and not affecting the contents of the web page.

When a user views a new website, the new `url` is retrieved using the following code from Listing 7-1:

```
url = self.web_view.url()
```

This `url` is passed to `QNetworkRequest`. The next thing is to create the application's `QNetworkAccessManager` instance to manage the sending and retrieving of data from the request. Since QNetworkAccessManager works asynchronously, we should call `readAll()` immediately after the `get()` method. The `readAll()` function is used to read and return data in an array of bytes; `get()` posts the `request` and returns a `reply` for reading. However, the request has not been made at that time. So we need to connect the `manager` to the `finished()` signal and perform the reading action in the slot connected to the signal, `replyFinished()`. A simple download from a network can be accomplished using the following code from Listing 7-1:

```
manager = QNetworkAccessManager()
manager.finished.connect(self.replyFinished)
manager.get(QNetworkRequest(QUrl("https://www.google.com")))
```

The next step is to use Beautiful Soup to make the returned `data`, the HTML code, readable to a human. The `html_text_edit` will then update and display the returned code.

Project 7.1: Email Sender GUI

Python already has a number of built-in classes that make it easy to get started connecting to servers, sending email, and working with different network protocols. In this project, you will see how to create the PyQt application shown in Figure 7-2 and find out how to use the Python module `smtplib` to send emails using the SMTP (Simple Mail Transfer Protocol).

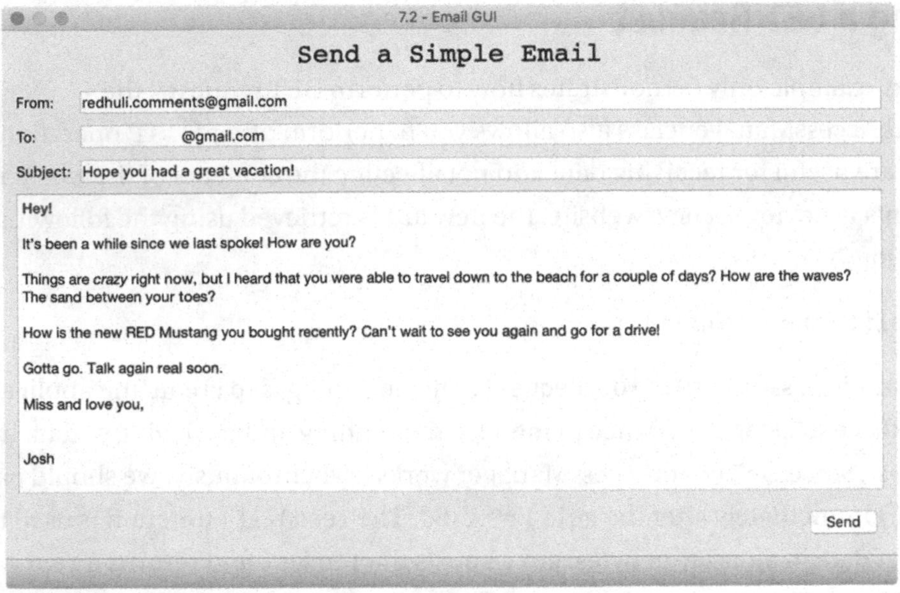

Figure 7-2. *The email sender GUI. QTextEdit widgets can be used for creating and displaying rich text*

Let's first have a look at the network protocol we will need to use in order to create an application that sends emails.

What Is the Simple Mail Transfer Protocol (SMTP)?

There are different kinds of communication protocols that set the rules for what kind of data can be transferred between nodes in a network. **Simple Mail Transfer Protocol (SMTP)** is used when sending emails between users. Clients who want to send an email open the TCP connection to the SMTP server, whose main purpose is to send, receive, or relay mail between users sending mail on the server.

Setting Up Your Gmail Security Settings

Since we are using Gmail in this project, we will need to work with Google's security settings. Otherwise, you will get an error, and your email will never be allowed to send. Log in to your Gmail account, and at the top of the page where your user icon is, click it, and then click Manage your Google Account. On the next page, look for Security (as of this writing, it's on the left of the window). This link will also take you directly to the Security page: `https://myaccount.google.com/security`.

250

Now, there are two ways to send an email using Python. The first is to turn on access to less secure apps. It's not recommended, but for a short application like this, it shouldn't be a problem. Just be sure to turn access off again when you are finished.

The second option is to proceed with two-step verification. This takes a few minutes, and when you are finished, you will be given a 16-character password. While running the program in Listing 7-2, when you get to the dialog shown in Figure 7-4, use the secure password you received for verification and not your normal password. This will allow you to send your email and keep your email account secure.

Email Sender GUI Solution

This example will demonstrate how to use the Python module `smtplib` for connecting to the SMTP server and sending an email. To create a secure connection, we will be using **Secure Sockets Layer** (**SSL**) for establishing an encrypted link between the client and the server.

The GUI created in Listing 7-2 is also relatively simple, composed of a few QLineEdit widgets for inputting the sender's and recipient's email addresses and the subject heading, a QTextEdit for creating the body of the email, and a QPushButton to send the email. After clicking Send, users will be prompted for the password to their Gmail account. If the email is successfully sent, a message will appear in the status bar at the bottom of the window. Otherwise, an error message will be displayed.

The `smtplib` library in this application is also set up so that it always sends rich text.

Tip   When you send a large message or if you have a poor Internet connection, you may notice the GUI freeze for a few moments until the request is complete. One way to alleviate this would be to use PyQt's low-level networking threading classes instead of `smtplib`.

Listing 7-2. Code for the email sender application

```
# Import necessary modules
import sys, smtplib
from email.message import EmailMessage
```

```python
from PyQt5.QtWidgets import (QApplication, QMainWindow, QWidget, QLabel,
QPushButton, QLineEdit, QTextEdit, QDialog, QMessageBox, QDialogButtonBox,
QStatusBar, QGridLayout, QHBoxLayout, QVBoxLayout)
from PyQt5.QtGui import QFont
from PyQt5.QtCore import Qt

class PasswordDialog(QDialog):

    def __init__(self, parent):
        super().__init__()
        # [INFO] This line only checks if sender and recipient line edits
        # are not blank. There are other checks you could make, such as if
        # the @ symbol exists, or if the email extension is valid.
        if parent.sender_address.text() != "" and parent.recipient_address.
        text() != "":
            self.setWindowTitle("Submit Gmail Password")
            self.setFixedSize(300, 100)
            self.setModal(True)

            enter_password_label = QLabel("Enter Password:")
            self.enter_password_line = QLineEdit()
            self.enter_password_line.setEchoMode(QLineEdit.Password)

            # Create nested layout for widgets to enter the password and
            # for the QDialogButtonBox
            password_h_box = QHBoxLayout()
            password_h_box.addWidget(enter_password_label)
            password_h_box.addWidget(self.enter_password_line)

            buttons = QDialogButtonBox.Ok | QDialogButtonBox.Cancel
            button_box = QDialogButtonBox(buttons)
            button_box.accepted.connect(self.accept)
            button_box.rejected.connect(self.reject)

            dialog_v_box = QVBoxLayout()
            dialog_v_box.addLayout(password_h_box)
            dialog_v_box.addWidget(button_box)
            self.setLayout(dialog_v_box)
```

```
        else:
            QMessageBox.information(self, "Missing Information",
                "Sender or Recipient Information is Empty.", QMessageBox.Ok)

class EmailGUI(QMainWindow):

    def __init__(self):
        super().__init__()
        self.initializeUI()

    def initializeUI(self):
        """Initialize the window and display its contents."""
        self.setMinimumSize(800, 500)
        self.setWindowTitle('7.2 - Email GUI')

        self.setupWindow()
        self.show()

    def setupWindow(self):
        """Set up the widgets for inputting the headers and body of the
        email."""
        window_label = QLabel("Send a Simple Email")
        window_label.setFont(QFont("Courier", 24))
        window_label.setAlignment(Qt.AlignCenter)

        sender_label = QLabel("From:")
        self.sender_address = QLineEdit()
        self.sender_address.setPlaceholderText("your_email@gmail.com")

        recipient_label = QLabel("To:")
        self.recipient_address = QLineEdit()
        self.recipient_address.setPlaceholderText("friend@email.com")

        subject_label = QLabel("Subject:")
        self.subject_line = QLineEdit()

        # Layout for the sender, recipient and subject widgets
        header_grid = QGridLayout()
        header_grid.addWidget(sender_label, 0, 0)
        header_grid.addWidget(self.sender_address, 0, 1)
```

```python
        header_grid.addWidget(recipient_label, 1, 0)
        header_grid.addWidget(self.recipient_address, 1, 1)
        header_grid.addWidget(subject_label, 2, 0)
        header_grid.addWidget(self.subject_line, 2, 1)

        self.email_body = QTextEdit() # Input widget for creating email
        contents

        send_button = QPushButton("Send")
        send_button.clicked.connect(self.inputPassword)

        bottom_h_box = QHBoxLayout()
        bottom_h_box.addWidget(QWidget(), 1)
        bottom_h_box.addWidget(send_button)

        # Nested layout for all widgets and layouts
        main_v_box = QVBoxLayout()
        main_v_box.addWidget(window_label)
        main_v_box.addSpacing(10)
        main_v_box.addLayout(header_grid)
        main_v_box.addWidget(self.email_body)
        main_v_box.addLayout(bottom_h_box)

        container = QWidget()
        container.setLayout(main_v_box)
        self.setCentralWidget(container)

        self.status_bar = QStatusBar(self)
        self.setStatusBar(self.status_bar) # Create status bar

    def inputPassword(self):
        """Create an instance of the PasswordDialog class and input the
        Gmail account password."""
        self.password_dialog = PasswordDialog(self)
        if self.password_dialog.exec_() and self.password_dialog.enter_
        password_line.text() != "":
            self.password_dialog.close()
            self.sendEmail()
        else:
            pass
```

```python
    def sendEmail(self):
        """Compose the email headers and contents. Use smtplib to login to
        your Gmail account and send an email. Success or errors will be
        displayed in the status bar accordingly."""
        # Define the headers and content of the email
        message = EmailMessage()
        message['Subject'] = self.subject_line.text()
        message['From'] = self.sender_address.text()
        message['To'] = self.recipient_address.text()

        # Convert the text in the QTextEdit to HTML
        message.add_alternative(self.email_body.toHtml(), subtype="html")

        with smtplib.SMTP_SSL("smtp.gmail.com", 465) as smtp:
            try:
                # Login to your Gmail username and password
                smtp.login(self.sender_address.text(), self.password_
                dialog.enter_password_line.text())
                smtp.send_message(message)

                # Display feedback in the status bar and clear input widgets
                self.status_bar.showMessage("Your email was sent!", 5000)
                self.subject_line.clear()
                self.recipient_address.clear()
                self.email_body.clear()
            except smtplib.SMTPResponseException as error:
                error_message = "Email failed: {}, {}".format(error.smtp_
                code, error.smtp_error)
                self.status_bar.showMessage(error_message, 20000) # Display
                error for 20 seconds

if __name__ == '__main__':
    app = QApplication(sys.argv)
    window = EmailGUI()
    sys.exit(app.exec_())
```

The GUI for sending emails can be seen in Figure 7-2.

Explanation

For this example, we do not need to import any classes from QtNetwork since we are using `smtplib` to connect to the server and send the email. In order to create the headers and structure for the email a user writes, the `email` module is imported. `email` can be used to not only handle the contents of emails but also manage the types of data we send through email, whether it's plain or rich text, PDFs, images, or even videos. `email.message` is the main class used to create the email.

The main window is created in the `EmailGUI` class. In `setupWindow()`, the line edit and other widgets are instantiated and arranged in the GUI. The most notable aspect is the `QStatusBar` object created at the bottom of the function. This is the reason why `EmailGUI` inherits from `QMainWindow`. The main window is shown in Figure 7-3.

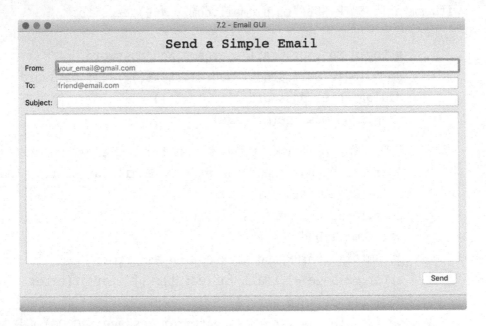

Figure 7-3. *The email sender's main window with placeholder text. While users can only send emails using their Gmail accounts, recipients do not have this restriction*

Once a user has filled in the sender and recipient email address fields and other input areas, they can click the `send_button`. This emits a signal, calling `inputPassword()`. The dialog box shown in 7-4 will appear requesting the user's Gmail password. The `QDialog` is subclassed so the user can accept the password, close the dialog, and call the `sendEmail()` function at the same time.

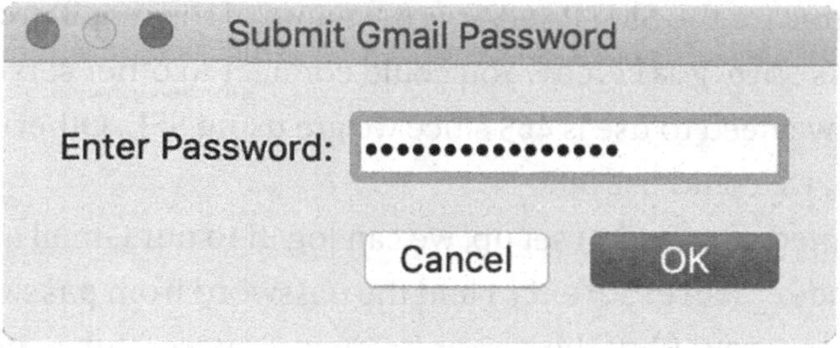

Figure 7-4. *Dialog to enter your Gmail password*

Using the smtplib Module

We begin by setting up the email's headers and body and collecting information from the widgets in the main window. The process for creating the email's subject, sender ('From'), and recipient ('To') is shown in the following code from Listing 7-2:

```
# Define the headers and content of the email
message = EmailMessage()
message['Subject'] = self.subject_line.text()
message['From'] = self.sender_address.text()
message['To'] = self.recipient_address.text()
```

With the email headers prepared, next is the body. For this example, we always format the text of email_body using toHtml(). You could change this part to only send plain text or other data types. HTML is used in case the user wants to give the text some color or style. The add_alternative() function can be used to combine one or more kinds of data into a single body:

```
# Convert the text in the QTextEdit to HTML
message.add_alternative(self.email_body.toHtml(), subtype="html")
```

The last thing to do is to connect to the SMTP server using a secure, encrypted connection. This is done with SMTP_SSL(). Check out the following code from Listing 7-2:

```
with smtplib.SMTP_SSL("smtp.gmail.com", 465) as smtp:
    try:
        # Login to your Gmail username and password
        smtp.login(self.sender_address.text(), self.password_dialog.enter_
        password_line.text())
        smtp.send_message(message)
```

The domain name for the SMTP server is the name of the email provider's domain. For this example, it's `smtp.gmail.com`. You could connect to other servers using different domains. The port we need to use is 465 since we are using SSL. Otherwise, with a regular connection, we could use 587.

With the encrypted connection set up, we can log in to our Gmail account using the username from `sender_address.text()` and the password from `password_dialog.enter_password_line.text()`. If the transmission was successful, a message will display in the `QStatusBar` like in Figure 7-5.

Figure 7-5. *The status bar will either display text letting the user know the email was successful or show errors if something went wrong*

A new email will appear in the recipient's Gmail inbox like in Figure 7-6.

Figure 7-6. *A new email in the Gmail inbox*

The contents of the email will display rich text. An example of this can be seen in Figure 7-7.

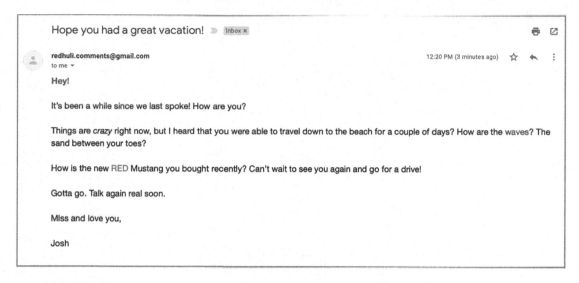

Figure 7-7. *The email's contents. Can't wait to go on vacation*

Summary

Communication, collaboration, and the ways in which we live are reliant on networks. The Internet has changed the ways in which humans view themselves, creating communities that are global and no longer dependent on the time of day or location. Protocols help share information and maintain the security of these networks.

In this chapter, we saw how to construct a web browser that connected to a server using QtNetwork classes and requested the HTML content of a web page. Email is still an essential part of our lives. A GUI application was also constructed using PyQt widgets and the smtplib module to create a working email application.

In Chapter 8, we will take a look at building a chatbot by leveraging artificial intelligence and machine learning algorithms.

CHAPTER 8

Creating a Chatbot

Some of the readers may remember earlier versions of the phone tree system. Still in use today, picking up a phone and dialing a number for assistance usually meant listening to a prerecorded message telling them about their options. Pressing the correct button would lead them to the help they were seeking. However, it was often never that simple.

The phone tree system became overused. The monotone voices would list out your options, and you could swear that the assistance you needed was always the last option. Callers would often be led down a complicated and frustrating path of choosing one option after another, becoming angrier as their problem wasn't being solved. All you really wanted was to speak to a human representative, and when you finally reached the end of the maze of button pushing, the human was usually busy.

As time and technology improved, the systems changed. Callers could speak keywords into the phone, and the voice recognition system would redirect their call. Modern applications now allow users to speak into their phone, order a cup of coffee, and receive a response telling them when it is ready. Enhancements in technology have helped improve the system and, in some cases, migrated toward pop-up windows in your web browser or live chats. Even today, this system is continuing to evolve and improve, as robots are taking the place of human employees in certain positions. Humans are often willing to speak to computers, but only if the conversations feel fluid and similar to talking to a fellow human.

In this chapter, we will have a look at

- Designing a chatbot GUI with PyQt

- Using the ChatterBot library for generating the chatbot's responses using machine learning

In the following sections, you will find out about chatbots.

© Joshua Willman 2021
J. Willman, *Modern PyQt*, https://doi.org/10.1007/978-1-4842-6603-8_8

What Is a Chatbot?

Recent decades have seen businesses move their platforms online, creating a digital society that is fast-paced and difficult for a normal human to keep up with the increasing demands of consumers. Fortunately, some of that work can be offloaded onto intelligent automated computer programs.

Chatbots are computer applications designed to simulate human conversation, giving the impression that you are communicating with a real person rather than a robot. They play an important part in the way that businesses and customers interact and communicate, improving the customer experience while reducing the workload of employees and costs for businesses. Chatbots save employees' time, freeing them to perform more important and critical tasks. With chatbots, businesses are also able to reach more customers while using less resources.

Businesses can use chatbots internally to manage communications among employees regarding system updates, training exercises, or ordering business supplies. For a consumer, chatbots can provide customer services and assistance when making purchases online.

Like any computer program, they are great at performing rudimentary and routine activities efficiently. Many chatbot systems are created so that questions which are commonly and quickly answered can be handled by a chatbot, and complex requests are forwarded to human employees. Chatbots are able to analyze a user's request and return an informative response based on the system's rules.

There are different kinds of chatbots with differing degrees of complexity. Some are only capable of handling basic queries, while others act as digital assistants that learn from the user and deliver personalized responses based on the information collected. Nowadays, chatbots are driven by varying degrees of artificial intelligence (AI) algorithms and can be divided into two categories:

- Declarative chatbots that are rule based and generate automated responses to a user's inquiry based on a set of guidelines. Difficult requests may cause the chatbot to refer the user to a human operator.

- Conversational chatbots that leverage the power of AI and machine learning to deliver personalized, human-like, and predictive responses based on the user's question. These kinds of chatbots are designed to learn from the conversations they have with a user.

The performance and capabilities of chatbots continue to improve as researchers dive deeper into the complexities of the human language.

Brief Introduction to Natural Language Processing (NLP)

Natural Language Processing (NLP)[1] is a field in computer science and AI that allows computers to analyze and derive meaning from the human language, both spoken and written. For the purposes of this chapter, we'll be considering only textual language sources.

Since computers can't read text like a human can, NLP can be used to look for patterns in books and other documents. Understanding language is a very complex task. There are different ways to approach and simplify the process of learning from text.

Sentences can be parsed and deconstructed into their fundamental parts using speech and grammar rules. Algorithms that NLP uses may go about first removing words that don't offer much contextual value, words such as a, is, or are. An algorithm may then split the remaining words into groups, counting how many times those words appear in the text. Using these words or sequence of words, we can then find out how many times they appear across multiple documents and gain insight about the content of the different documents by the frequency of particular words.

We can also use rules and the information learned from training data to generate new text. The two processes of parsing existing text and generating new text are key to creating chatbots that use NLP.

Using large language datasets, we can train chatbots and other natural language systems to create more intelligent computer applications. In NLP, these collections of texts are referred to as a **corpus**. There are already many open source machine learning libraries and datasets available to assist in creating a chatbot application, as we shall see in the next section.

---

[1]If you would like to find out more about NLP, the following text is a great resource to get you started:

Lane, H. (2019). Natural Language Processing in Action: Understanding, analyzing, and generating text with Python. Manning Publications.

The ChatterBot Library

We are going to use the ChatterBot library to construct our chatbot's logic. Using ChatterBot, we are able to use machine learning algorithms that will generate automatic responses from a user's input. The library already has a collection of different corpora in different languages, but you can also build your own conversation datasets to train ChatterBot for your own purposes.

ChatterBot is designed to learn and improve its responses from a user's input. Responses are chosen by finding the closest matching statement that is similar to the input and then selecting a reply from a set of known responses.

More information about training and using ChatterBot is found at `https://chatterbot.readthedocs.io/en/stable/index.html`.

Installing ChatterBot

For this project, you will need to install the ChatterBot library and possibly a few other dependencies. To get started, open the Terminal application for Mac or Linux or the Command Prompt for Windows and enter the following command:

```
$ pip3 install chatterbot
```

To check that ChatterBot is properly installed, open up the Python 3 environment using the command `python3` and enter

```
>>> import chatterbot
```

With ChatterBot installed, let's also install the conversation data from the ChatterBot Corpus:

```
$ pip3 install chatterbot-corpus
```

While installing the corpus, you may run into an error: `Cannot uninstall 'PyYAML'`. To solve this problem, first, run the following command:

```
$ pip3 install chatterbot-corpus --ignore-installed
```

Then, rerun the command to install the ChatterBot Corpus.

ChatterBot is also dependent on a few other packages, so there is a possibility that you may receive errors if the following packages are also not installed. To install spaCy, an open source library for NLP, enter the following command into the command line:

```
$ pip3 install spacy
```

For the final step, you may need to install the English spaCy model. To do so, run the following command:

```
$ python3 -m spacy download en
```

The en model is a shortcut for downloading the statistical model en_core_web_sm. With those steps out of the way, let's see how to set up a simple ChatterBot.

Creating a Simple ChatterBot

This section will introduce you to using the ChatterBot library. Follow along with the code and comments in Listing 8-1 to create a very simple chatbot that follows along with a very basic conversation.

Listing 8-1. Basic code for setting ChatterBot

```python
# chatbot_example.py
# Import necessary modules
from chatterbot import ChatBot # Import the chatbot
from chatterbot.trainers import ListTrainer # Method to train chatterbot

chatbot = ChatBot('Chatty') # Create the ChatBot called Chatty

# Create the dialog
conversation = [
    "Hello",
    "Hi! How are you?",
    "I'm happy. How about you?",
    "Hungry.",
    "Let's have lunch!",
    "Let's go!"]

trainer = ListTrainer(chatbot) # Create trainer
trainer.train(conversation) # Train the chatbot
```

```
while True:
    try:
        user_input = input('You: ')
        bot_response = chatbot.get_response(user_input)
        print('Bot: ' + str(bot_response))
    except(KeyboardInterrupt, EOFError, SystemExit):
        break
```

Of course, the conversation that the chatbot was trained on was very short. An effective chatbot requires a massive amount of training data in order to quickly solve user inquiries and respond to the user. In this chapter's project, you will find out how to load your own files or the ChatterBot Corpus and create a better chatbot.

Project 8.1: Chatbot GUI

For many modern chatbot applications, the user interface has taken on the appearance of chat and messaging applications. The interface for these programs often takes on a very minimalistic style, displaying icons for the people in the conversation, speech bubbles that appear whenever someone sends a message, and an area for inputting text, images, or emojis. Other visual cues are often used, such as different colors for the speech bubbles and a comic bookish tail appearing at the end of the bubble next to the speaker's icon.

Figure 8-1 showcases the chatbot application created in this project.

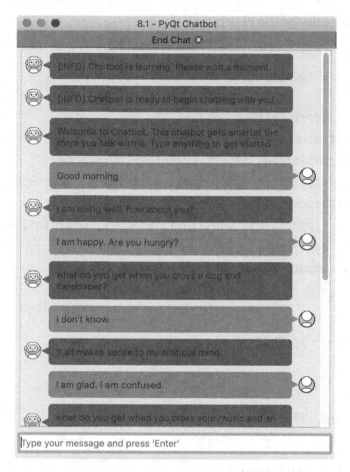

Figure 8-1. *The chatbot GUI – having a friendly conversation with a chatbot*

Chatbot GUI Solution

The chatbot application created in Listing 8-2 has a very simple graphical interface. Users are unable to converse with the chatbot until they click the Start Chat button at the top of the window. After clicking the button, the chatbot will begin training itself in a separate thread. With the training complete, users can begin chatting. Drawing the text and speech bubbles is handled using model/view programming classes.

Listing 8-2. The code for the chatbot GUI

```python
# chatbotGUI.py
# Import necessary modules
import sys
from chatterbot import ChatBot, utils
from chatterbot.trainers import ChatterBotCorpusTrainer
from chatterbot.comparisons import LevenshteinDistance
from PyQt5.QtWidgets import (QApplication, QWidget, QPushButton, QLineEdit,
QListView, QMessageBox, QVBoxLayout, QStyledItemDelegate)
from PyQt5.QtCore import (Qt, QAbstractListModel, QMargins, QSize, QRect,
QPoint, QThread, pyqtSignal)
from PyQt5.QtGui import QIcon, QColor, QImage, QPolygon

style_sheet = """
    QPushButton {
        background: #83E56C /* Green */
    }

    QListView {
        background: #FDF3DD
    }"""

class ChatWorkerThread(QThread):
    # Signal emitted when the chatbot is finished training
    training_finished = pyqtSignal()

    def __init__(self, chatbot):
        super().__init__()
        self.chatbot = chatbot

    def run(self):
        """This function handles training the chatbot. Once the training is
        complete, the training_finished signal is emitted, which allows the
        user to begin chatting."""
        self.trainer = ChatterBotCorpusTrainer(self.chatbot)
        self.trainer.train("chatterbot.corpus.english")
        self.training_finished.emit()
```

```python
class ChatLogModel(QAbstractListModel):

    def __init__(self):
        super().__init__()
        self.chat_messages = []

    def rowCount(self, index):
        """Necessary to include rowCount() when subclassing
        QAbstractListModel. For this program, we only need to update the
        the number of rows in the model,which is based on the length of
        chat_messages."""
        return len(self.chat_messages)

    def data(self, index, role=Qt.DisplayRole):
        """Necessary to include data() when subclassing QAbstractListModel.
        Retrieves items from the list and returns data specified by the
        role, which in this case is displayed as text."""
        if role == Qt.DisplayRole:
            return self.chat_messages[index.row()]

    def appendMessage(self, user_input, user_or_chatbot):
        """First, append new messages to chat_messages. Doing so will
        update the number of rows and indexes in the model (rowCount()),
        which will then update the data()."""
        self.chat_messages.append([user_input, user_or_chatbot])
        # Emit signal to indicate that the layout of items in the model has
        # changed
        self.layoutChanged.emit()

class DrawSpeechBubbleDelegate(QStyledItemDelegate):

    def __init__(self):
        super().__init__()
        self.image_offset = 5 # Horizontal offset for the image
        # The following variables are used when drawing the speech bubbles
        self.side_offset, self.top_offset = 40, 5
        self.tail_offset_x, self.tail_offset_y = 30, 0
        self.text_side_offset, self.text_top_offset = 50, 15
```

```python
def paint(self, painter, option, index):
    """Reimplement the delegate's paint() function. Renders
    the delegate using the specified QPainter (painter) and
    QStyleOptionViewItem (option) for the item being drawn at given
    index (the row value). This function paints the item."""
    text, user_or_chatbot = index.model().data(index, Qt.DisplayRole)
    image, image_rect = QImage(), QRect() # Initialize objects for the
    user and chahbot icons
    color, bubble_margins = QColor(), QMargins() # Initialize objects
    for drawing speech bubbles
    tail_points = QPolygon() # Initialize QPolygon object for drawing
    the tail on the speech bubbles

    # Use user_or_chatbot value to select the image to display, the
    color of the pen and the brush. Set the margins for speech bubble.
    Set the points for the speech bubble's tail.
    if user_or_chatbot == "chatbot":
        image.load("images/bot.png")
        image_rect = QRect(QPoint(option.rect.left() + self.image_
        offset, option.rect.center().y() - 12), QSize(24, 24))
        color = QColor("#83E56C")
        bubble_margins = QMargins(self.side_offset, self.top_offset,
        self.side_offset, self.top_offset)
        tail_points = QPolygon([QPoint(option.rect.x() + self.tail_
        offset_x, option.rect.center().y()),
                        QPoint(option.rect.x() + self.side_offset,
                        option.rect.center().y() - 5),
                        QPoint(option.rect.x() + self.side_offset,
                        option.rect.center().y() + 5)])
    elif user_or_chatbot == "user":
        image.load("images/user.png")
        image_rect = QRect(QPoint(option.rect.right() - self.image_
        offset - 24, option.rect.center().y() - 12), QSize(24, 24))
        color = QColor("#38E0F9")
        bubble_margins = QMargins(self.side_offset, self.top_offset,
        self.side_offset, self.top_offset)
```

```
        tail_points = QPolygon([QPoint(option.rect.right() - self.tail_
        offset_x, option.rect.center().y()),
                        QPoint(option.rect.right() - self.side_offset,
                        option.rect.center().y() - 5),
                        QPoint(option.rect.right() - self.side_offset,
                        option.rect.center().y() + 5)])
```

```
    # Draw the image next to the speech bubble
    painter.drawImage(image_rect, image)

    # Set the QPainter's pen and brush colors; draw the speech bubble
    and tail
    painter.setPen(color)
    painter.setBrush(color)
    # Remove the margins from the rectangle to shrink its size
    painter.drawRoundedRect(option.rect.marginsRemoved(bubble_margins),
    5, 5)
    painter.drawPolygon(tail_points)

    # Draw the text in the speech bubble
    painter.setPen(QColor("#4A4C4B")) # Reset pen color for the text
    text_margins = QMargins(self.text_side_offset, self.text_top_
    offset, self.text_side_offset, self.text_top_offset)
    painter.drawText(option.rect.marginsRemoved(text_margins),
    Qt.AlignVCenter | Qt.TextWordWrap, text)

def sizeHint(self, option, index):
    """Reimplement to figure out the size of the item displayed at the
    given index. Uses option to figure out the style information, in
    this case, the margins of the speech bubble."""
    text, user_or_chatbot = index.model().data(index, Qt.DisplayRole)
    font_size = QApplication.fontMetrics() # Calculate the size of the
    text
    text_margins = QMargins(self.text_side_offset, self.text_top_
    offset, self.text_side_offset, self.text_top_offset)
```

```
        # Remove the margins, get the rectangle for the font, and add the
        margins back in
        rect = option.rect.marginsRemoved(text_margins)
        rect = font_size.boundingRect(rect, Qt.TextWordWrap, text)
        rect = rect.marginsAdded(text_margins)
        return rect.size()

class Chatbot(QWidget):

    def __init__(self):
        super().__init__()
        self.initializeUI()

    def initializeUI(self):
        """Initialize the window and its contents."""
        self.setMinimumSize(450, 600)
        self.setWindowTitle("8.1 - PyQt Chatbot")
        self.setWindowFlag(Qt.Window)

        self.chat_started = False

        self.setupWindow()
        self.show()

    def setupWindow(self):
        """Set up the widgets and model/view instances for the main
        window."""
        self.chat_button = QPushButton(QIcon("images/chat.png"), "Start Chat")
        self.chat_button.setLayoutDirection(Qt.RightToLeft)
        self.chat_button.pressed.connect(self.chatButtonPressed)

        # Create the model for keeping track of new messages (data), the
        list view for displaying the chat log, and the delegate for drawing
        the items in the list view
        self.model = ChatLogModel()
        self.chat_log_view = QListView()
        self.chat_log_view.setModel(self.model)
```

```
    message_delegate = DrawSpeechBubbleDelegate()
    self.chat_log_view.setItemDelegate(message_delegate)

    # Create the QLineEdit widget for entering text
    self.user_input_line = QLineEdit()
    self.user_input_line.setMinimumHeight(24)
    self.user_input_line.setPlaceholderText("Press 'Start Chat' to
    begin chatting...")
    self.user_input_line.returnPressed.connect(self.enterUserMessage)

    main_v_box = QVBoxLayout()
    main_v_box.setContentsMargins(0, 2, 0, 10)
    main_v_box.addWidget(self.chat_button, Qt.AlignRight)
    main_v_box.setSpacing(10)
    main_v_box.addWidget(self.chat_log_view)
    main_v_box.addWidget(self.user_input_line)
    self.setLayout(main_v_box)

def chatButtonPressed(self):
    """When the user begins chatting, the appearance and state of the
    chat_button are set, and the chatbot is created. The user can also
    end the chat."""
    button = self.sender()
    if button.text() == "Start Chat":
        self.chat_button.setText("End Chat")
        self.chat_button.setIcon(QIcon("images/end.png"))
        self.chat_button.setStyleSheet("background: #EC7161") # Red
        self.chat_button.setDisabled(True)
        self.createChatbot()
    elif button.text() == "End Chat":
        self.endCurrentChat()

def enterUserMessage(self):
    """Get the text from the line edit widget and append the message to
    the model. Then display the chatbot's response."""
    user_input = self.user_input_line.text()
```

```python
        if user_input != "" and self.chat_started == True:
            self.model.appendMessage(user_input, "user")
            self.displayChatbotResponse(user_input)
            self.user_input_line.clear() # Clear the QLineEdit's text

    def displayChatbotResponse(self, user_input):
        """Get the response from the chatbot, convert the reply to a string
        and append the text to the model where it will be added to the
        window."""
        chatbot_reply = self.chatbot.get_response(user_input)
        self.model.appendMessage(str(chatbot_reply), "chatbot")
        # Uncomment to get the time it takes for the chatbot to respond
        #print(utils.get_response_time(self.chatbot))

    def createChatbot(self):
        """Create the chatbot and train it in a separate thread."""
        self.chatbot = ChatBot("Chatbot", storage_adapter="chatterbot.
        storage.SQLStorageAdapter",
            database_uri='sqlite:///database.sqlite3',
            logic_adapters=[{"import_path": "chatterbot.logic.BestMatch",
                "statement_comparison_function": LevenshteinDistance}])

        self.chat_worker = ChatWorkerThread(self.chatbot) # Create worker
        thread
        self.chat_worker.training_finished.connect(self.trainingFinished)

        # Feedback for the user. Begin the thread for training the chatbot
        self.model.appendMessage("[INFO] Chatbot is learning. Please wait a
        moment.", "chatbot")
        self.chat_worker.start()

    def trainingFinished(self):
        """Once the chatbot has been trained, display messages to the user
        and start chatting."""
        self.model.appendMessage("[INFO] Chatbot is ready to begin chatting
        with you.", "chatbot")
```

```python
        self.model.appendMessage("Welcome to Chatbot. This chatbot gets
        smarter the more you talk with it. Type anything to get started.",
        "chatbot")
        self.user_input_line.setPlaceholderText("Type your message and
        press 'Enter'")
        self.chat_started = True
        self.chat_button.setDisabled(False) # Enable the chat_button

    def endCurrentChat(self):
        """Display a QMessageBox to the user asking if they want to quit
        the current chat."""
        choice = QMessageBox.question(self, "End Chat",
            "The chat history will be deleted. Are you sure you want to end
            the chat?",
            QMessageBox.Yes | QMessageBox.No, QMessageBox.No)

        if choice == QMessageBox.Yes:
            # Clearing the list will set the number of rows to 0 and clear
            the chat area
            self.model.chat_messages = []
            self.user_input_line.setPlaceholderText("Press 'Start Chat' to
            begin chatting...")
            self.chat_button.setText("Start Chat")
            self.chat_button.setIcon(QIcon("images/chat.png"))
            self.chat_button.setStyleSheet("background: #83E56C") # Green
            self.chat_started = False
        else:
            self.model.appendMessage("I thought you were going to leave me.",
            "chatbot")

    def closeEvent(self, event):
        """Display a dialog box to confirm that the user wants to close the
        application while in a chat."""
        if self.chat_started:
            choice = QMessageBox.question(self, 'Leave Chat?', "Are you
            sure you want to leave the chat?",
                QMessageBox.Yes | QMessageBox.No, QMessageBox.No)
```

```
            if choice == QMessageBox.Yes:
                event.accept()
            else:
                event.ignore()
if __name__ == "__main__":
    app = QApplication(sys.argv)
    app.setStyleSheet(style_sheet)
    window = Chatbot()
    sys.exit(app.exec_())
```

The chatbot desktop application is displayed in Figure 8-1.

Explanation

In order to create the chatbot, we'll first need to import a few classes from the chatterbot library. For this example, we are going to import `ChatterBotCorpusTrainer`, which will let us use the ChatterBot Corpus to train the chatbot. `LevenshteinDistance` is used to help the chatbot select the best response when comparing two statements. The `utils` module is included in case you want to check the amount of time that it takes for the chatbot to respond.

The interface for this application is a relatively basic one, with the main part of the window taken up by the `QListView` widget. Many of the PyQt classes included are used to handle new messages and drawing speech bubbles in the application's window. `QListView` displays a list of items populated from a model, in this case `QAbstractListModel`. The item delegate, `QStyledItemDelegate`, provides the tools for drawing and editing items in the view.

A number of classes are imported from the `QtCore` and `QtGui` modules for drawing the speech bubbles in the list view. `QIcon` is used to display an icon on the `QPushButton` for starting or ending a chat session.

The training process for the chatbot occurs in a separate `QThread`, and the user is notified when training is finished using a custom `pyqtSignal`.

The `style_sheet` is also quite simple, only being used to set the color of `QPushButton` and the `QListView`.

Creating the GUI

The application's main window shown in Figure 8-2 is created in the Chatbot class. Comprised of three widgets, chat_button, chat_log_view, and user_input_line, the application is designed to mimic the appearance of modern chat applications. The model and message_delegate instances are all also created in the setupWindow() function. These will be discussed further in a later section.

Figure 8-2. *The chatbot application when it is first launched*

The chat_button object at the top of the window can be used to start or end a chat session. When the user is not chatting, the button is green and displays the Start Chat text and the chat.png icon; otherwise, the button is red and shows End Chat and the end.png icon. The icons and text are arranged in Listing 8-2 from right to left using

self.chat_button.setLayoutDirection(Qt.RightToLeft)

277

Users can enter text into the QLineEdit widget at the bottom of the window and talk with the chatbot. This functionality is disabled until the user begins a chat session. QLineEdit is used rather than QTextEdit because line edits already have the built-in signal returnPressed().

When the user clicks the chat_button, it emits a signal that calls chatButtonPressed(). This function can either be used to start or end a chat. We check if the button's text is Start Chat. If it is, the appearance of the chat_button changes and becomes disabled. This is to prevent users from creating multiple Chatbot instances and training threads. The next step is to call createChatbot() and begin the process of training the chatbot.

Creating the Chatbot

In createChatbot(), we create the chatbot object and specify its training parameters in the following code from Listing 8-2. Quite a few arguments can be passed to a ChatBot instance:

```
self.chatbot = ChatBot("Chatbot", storage_adapter="chatterbot.storage.
SQLStorageAdapter",
database_uri='sqlite:///database.sqlite3',
logic_adapters=[{"import_path": "chatterbot.logic.BestMatch",
"statement_comparison_function": LevenshteinDistance}])
```

The storage_adapter parameter is used to select or create a database, specified by database_uri, for storing the conversation data. logic_adapters are used to decide how the chatbot selects a reply; BestMatch will select a response based on a selection of known responses. Finally, we use the LevenshteinDistance for comparing and selecting replies.

Next, we instantiate ChatWorkerThread and pass the chatbot as an argument to the class's constructor. Begin running the thread with the following line from Listing 8-2:

```
self.chat_worker.start()
```

Training is performed in a separate thread to prevent the application from freezing. This is especially useful if the dataset you are using is quite large. The chatbot created in Listing 8-2 is initially set up to train using all of the files in the English corpus. You can track the training process by looking at the output in the terminal shown in Figure 8-3. When the training is finished, the `training_finished()` signal is emitted from the secondary thread in Listing 8-2:

```
self.trainer.train("chatterbot.corpus.english")
self.training_finished.emit()
```

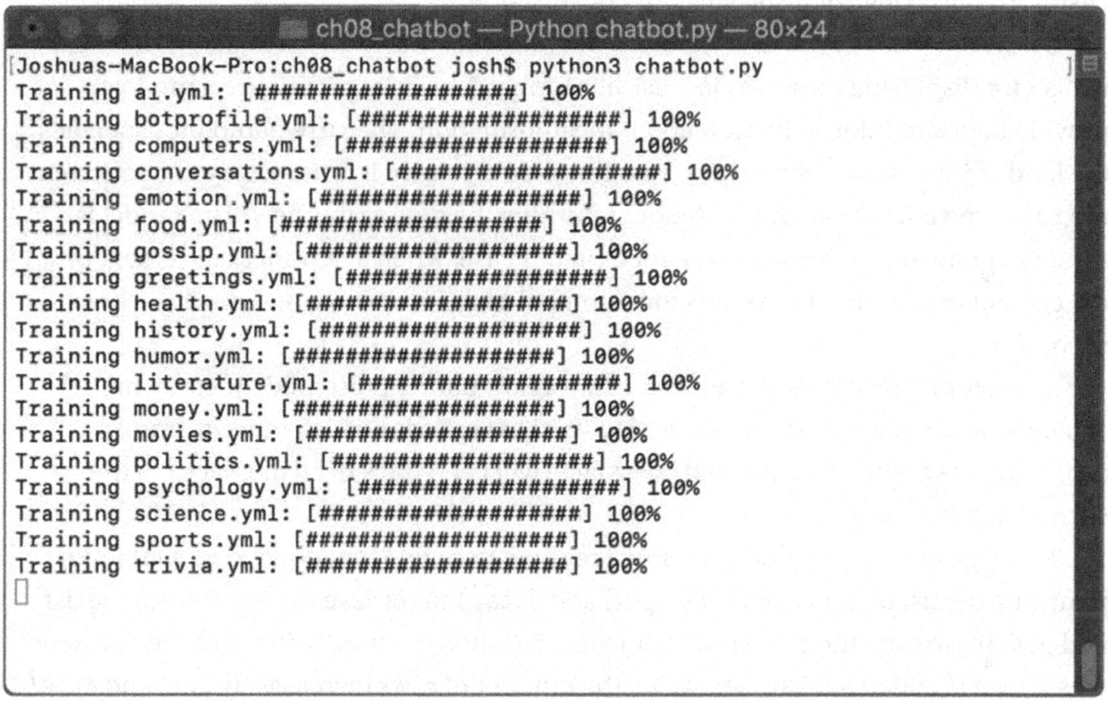

```
● ● ●                  ch08_chatbot — Python chatbot.py — 80×24
[Joshuas-MacBook-Pro:ch08_chatbot josh$ python3 chatbot.py              ] ⊟
Training ai.yml: [##################] 100%
Training botprofile.yml: [##################] 100%
Training computers.yml: [##################] 100%
Training conversations.yml: [##################] 100%
Training emotion.yml: [##################] 100%
Training food.yml: [##################] 100%
Training gossip.yml: [##################] 100%
Training greetings.yml: [##################] 100%
Training health.yml: [##################] 100%
Training history.yml: [##################] 100%
Training humor.yml: [##################] 100%
Training literature.yml: [##################] 100%
Training money.yml: [##################] 100%
Training movies.yml: [##################] 100%
Training politics.yml: [##################] 100%
Training psychology.yml: [##################] 100%
Training science.yml: [##################] 100%
Training sports.yml: [##################] 100%
Training trivia.yml: [##################] 100%
[]
```

Figure 8-3. *Output to the terminal window giving feedback to the user about the training process*

The `trainingFinished()` function notifies the user that they can begin chatting by displaying messages in the `chat_log_view`, enables the `chat_button`, and sets the `chat_started` variable to True. The user can finally begin chatting with the `chatbot`.

Drawing the Messages

With a chat started, the user can now enter text into the `user_input_line` and press Return on their keyboard to display their message in the `chat_log_view`. Pressing Return calls `enterUserMessage()`, where the `user_input`'s text is added to the model using `appendMessage()`. You may have already noticed that this is the same function used to display information in the list view while the chatbot is training. The function takes as arguments a message, in this case user_input, and a string for who is sending the message, either "user" or "chatbot".

Let's pause for a moment and understand how the model, view, and delegate are working together to draw the speech bubbles with text in the interface. A new message is created by calling the model's appendMessage() function. We want to create a customized list view for displaying our conversation.

QListView visually presents data in a one-dimensional list. This makes it the ideal widget for displaying messages in a list-like format. View classes require a model to provide data and inform the view about the information. The role parameter specifies the kind of information the data() function should return. It is necessary to check that the role type is Qt.DisplayRole before returning the data to the view. The model is used to update data whenever is needed (in our case, when a new message is sent or the current chat ends). The view is then notified of these changes and displays them accordingly.

By customizing the model, we can control how data is presented. Abstract models can only be subclassed. Therefore, we create chatLogModel which inherits from QAbstractListModel. The list chat_messages will keep track of all messages in the current conversation.

To create our simple model, we must reimplement two functions: rowCount() for returning the list of items (our messages) and data() to retrieve the items from the list and pass them onto the delegate for drawing. So when the user writes and sends a new message, it is added to chat_messages, the number of rows increases by one, and data() returns the new messages to be updated in the view.

DrawSpeechBubbleDelegate subclasses QStyledItemDelegate and is used to draw new messages in the list view. To do so, we must reimplement the class's paint() function. The sizeHint() function is also included so that items drawn in the list view can adjust for the size of the bubble and the size of the text.

The QPainter class is very useful for drawing on widgets. In paint(), first check if the user or the chatbot is sending a message by checking the data() sent from the model for that row. The correct image, color, margin sizes, and coordinates for drawing the speech bubble's rectangle and tail are chosen based on the value of user_or_chatbot. The QPainter object, painter, is created and the speech bubbles and text are drawn according to their sizeHint(), specified margins, and other values.

With that lengthy process for drawing a single speech bubble complete, we return back to the function enterUserMessage(). The next step is to call displayChatbotResponse(), get the chatbot's reply, and go back through the process again for drawing the chatbot's message in the view.

Note   While chatting with the chatbot, you may begin to notice that the chatbot's response time is taking longer. This is because of how large your dataset is and also due to how ChatterBot processes selecting a response. It is not an issue with PyQt5.

While chatting, the user can end the chat either by clicking the End Chat button and clearing the current chat history or by closing the application. Both of these situations will cause a dialog box to appear for confirming the user's decision. These are shown in Figure 8-4.

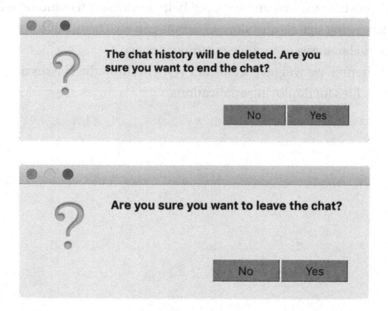

Figure 8-4.   *Dialog boxes. Checks if the user wants to end the current chat when they click the End Chat button (top). Asks if the user wants to close the application while in a chat (bottom)*

Summary

Chatbots probably won't be going anywhere in the future. Rather, they will continue to adapt to new technologies, allowing people to move away from performing mundane tasks and instead move more toward creativity and innovation. Advances in machine learning and NLP will also continue to make chatbots faster and better at engaging and assisting human users.

Current chatbots still lack the ability to handle complex human conversations, but advances in AI and better data sources are helping to integrate chatbots into our everyday lives. In the meantime, chatbots still continue to work in conjunction with human agents to tackle more difficult situations.

In this chapter, we saw how to create a chatbot desktop application. The ChatterBot library was used to build the chatbot's logic. By itself, this application is nothing more than a program that can keep you company if you feel lonely. However, this program could be integrated into a larger application that opens a separate window or a drop-down menu to assist the user when they need help. Information could be relayed back to the main window using signals and slots. Chatbots can also be used to connect to remote servers and query databases or provide customer service.

In the final chapter, we will take a look at PyQt's multimedia classes and see how to create executable files for deploying applications.

CHAPTER 9

Deploying PyQt Applications

You've done it! You finally have your application finished, and you are ready to share it with the world. The good news is that there are plenty of options for packaging your Python code and getting your application ready for distribution. You will, however, need to find the packaging software that best fits your needs.

Before choosing one, you will need to consider a number of factors, including whom your target audience will be, what Python libraries or other third-party modules your application requires, and how do you want to share your code with others, be it through a downloadable standalone application, creating an open source project, or perhaps sharing your code through a software repository such as PyPI.

In this final chapter, we will walk through a simple PyQt GUI created specifically to see how to code and build a standalone application. You will take a look at

- Building a dynamic desktop application for recording audio using PyQt's `QtMultimedia` classes

- Creating resource files using PyQt5's resource system

- Adding interactive application icons in the system tray

- Generating an executable application file using the PyInstaller module

Let's get started by looking at this chapter's project – an audio recorder.

© Joshua Willman 2021
J. Willman, *Modern PyQt*, https://doi.org/10.1007/978-1-4842-6603-8_9

Project 9.1: Audio Recorder GUI

We saw back in Chapter 5 how we can import visual data in PyQt GUIs using computer vision libraries. PyQt has its very own modules that support working with multimedia, including videos, audio, or cameras. The **QtMultimedia** module builds upon the multimedia utilities of the user's computer platform. This means that support for certain PyQt media classes or functionality may be platform specific.

For this project, we will create a GUI application for recording voices, conversations, and other sounds using the audio classes in QtMultimedia. The interface can be seen in Figure 9-1.

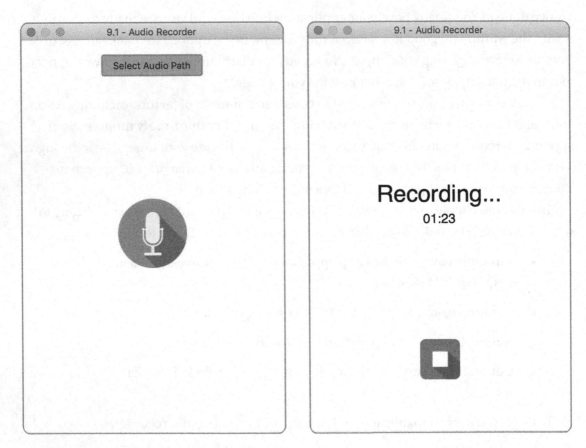

Figure 9-1. *The GUI for the audio recorder application. The left image displays the GUI's first "screen" to begin recording; in the second "screen," different widgets appear allowing the user to stop recording and return back to the first "screen"*

Audio Recorder GUI Solution

The project in Listing 9-1 is not a very elaborate interface. It makes use of a few basic widgets and the QtMultimedia module's classes for working with audio data. When the application begins, the user can select the location where they want their audio files to be stored. After clicking the green start button, the user is shown a set of different widgets giving them feedback about the current recording's time. By clicking the stop button at the bottom of the window, the user can return to the first "screen" and begin recording again. If the user does not specify a new file location, then the previous file will be overwritten.

Listing 9-1. Code for the audio recorder application

```python
# audio_recorder.py
# Import necessary modules
import sys, os
from PyQt5.QtWidgets import (QApplication, QWidget, QLabel, QPushButton,
QMessageBox, QMenu, QFileDialog, QVBoxLayout, QSystemTrayIcon)
from PyQt5.QtMultimedia import QAudioRecorder, QAudioEncoderSettings,
QMultimedia
from PyQt5.QtCore import Qt, QUrl
from PyQt5.QtGui import QIcon, QFont
from AudioRecorderStyleSheet import style_sheet
import resources

class AudioRecorder(QWidget):

    def __init__(self):
        super().__init__()
        self.initializeUI()

    def initializeUI(self):
        """Initialize the window and display its contents to the screen."""
        self.setFixedSize(360, 540)
        self.setWindowTitle('9.1 - Audio Recorder')

        self.audio_path = "" # Empty variable for path to audio file
```

```python
        self.setupWindow()
        self.setupSystemTrayIcon()
        self.show()

    def setupWindow(self):
        """Set up widgets in the main window and the QAudioRecorder
        instance."""
        # Set up two push buttons (the app's first "screen")
        self.select_path_button = QPushButton("Select Audio Path")
        self.select_path_button.setObjectName("SelectFile")
        self.select_path_button.setFixedWidth(140)
        self.select_path_button.clicked.connect(self.selectAudioPath)

        self.start_button = QPushButton()
        self.start_button.setObjectName("StartButton")
        self.start_button.setEnabled(False)
        self.start_button.setFixedSize(105, 105)
        self.start_button.clicked.connect(self.startRecording)

        # Set up the labels and stop button (the app's second "screen")
        self.recording_label = QLabel("Recording...")
        self.recording_label.setFont(QFont("Helvetica [Cronyx]", 32))
        self.recording_label.setVisible(False)
        self.recording_label.setAlignment(Qt.AlignHCenter)
        self.time_label = QLabel("00:00")
        self.time_label.setFont(QFont("Helvetica [Cronyx]", 18))
        self.time_label.setObjectName("Time")
        self.time_label.setVisible(False)
        self.time_label.setAlignment(Qt.AlignHCenter)

        self.stop_button = QPushButton()
        self.stop_button.setObjectName("StopButton")
        self.stop_button.setFixedSize(65, 65)
        self.stop_button.setVisible(False)
        self.stop_button.clicked.connect(self.stopRecording)
```

```python
# Set up the main layout
self.main_v_box = QVBoxLayout()
self.main_v_box.setAlignment(Qt.AlignHCenter)
self.main_v_box.addWidget(self.select_path_button)
# Force select_path_button to be centered in the window
self.main_v_box.setAlignment(self.select_path_button, Qt.AlignCenter)
self.main_v_box.addStretch(3)
self.main_v_box.addWidget(self.start_button)
self.main_v_box.setAlignment(self.start_button, Qt.AlignCenter)
self.main_v_box.addWidget(self.recording_label)
self.main_v_box.addWidget(self.time_label)
self.main_v_box.addStretch(3)
self.main_v_box.addWidget(self.stop_button)
self.main_v_box.setAlignment(self.stop_button, Qt.AlignCenter)
self.main_v_box.addStretch(1)

self.setLayout(self.main_v_box) # Set the beginning layout

# Specify audio encoder settings
audio_settings = QAudioEncoderSettings()
# Depending upon your platform or the codecs that you have
available, you will need to change the codec. For Linux users if
you are having issues use "audio/x-vorbis", and then select the
.ogg extension when saving the file
audio_settings.setCodec("audio/wav")
audio_settings.setQuality(QMultimedia.HighQuality)

# Create instance of QAudioRecorder for recording audio
self.audio_recorder = QAudioRecorder()
# Uncomment to discover possible codecs supported on your platform
#print(self.audio_recorder.supportedAudioCodecs())
self.audio_recorder.setEncodingSettings(audio_settings)
self.audio_recorder.durationChanged.connect(self.displayTime)
```

```python
def setupSystemTrayIcon(self):
    """Set up system tray icon and context menu. User can re-open the
    window if it was closed or quit the application using the tray
    menu."""
    self.tray_icon = QSystemTrayIcon(QIcon(":/resources/images/
    mic_icon.png"))

    # Create the actions and context menu for the tray icon
    tray_menu = QMenu()

    open_act = tray_menu.addAction("Open")
    open_act.triggered.connect(self.show)
    tray_menu.addSeparator()
    quit_act = tray_menu.addAction("Quit")
    quit_act.triggered.connect(QApplication.quit)

    self.tray_icon.setContextMenu(tray_menu)
    self.tray_icon.show()

def selectAudioPath(self):
    """Open file dialog and choose the directory for saving the audio
    file."""
    path, _ = QFileDialog.getSaveFileName(self, "Save Audio File",
        os.getenv("HOME"), "WAV (*.wav)")

    if path:
        self.audio_path = path
        self.start_button.setEnabled(True)
    else:
        QMessageBox.information(self, "Error",
            "No directory selected.", QMessageBox.Ok)

def startRecording(self):
    """Set up the audio output file location, reset widget states.
    Also starts the timer and begins recording. """
    self.audio_recorder.setOutputLocation(QUrl.fromLocalFile(self.
    audio_path))
```

```python
        # Set widget states
        self.select_path_button.setVisible(False)
        self.start_button.setVisible(False)
        self.recording_label.setVisible(True)
        self.time_label.setVisible(True)
        self.time_label.setText("00:00") # Update the label
        self.stop_button.setVisible(True)

        # Start the timer and begin recording
        self.audio_recorder.record()

    def stopRecording(self):
        """Stop recording, stop the timer, and reset widget states."""
        self.audio_recorder.stop()

        # Reset widget states
        self.select_path_button.setVisible(True)
        self.start_button.setVisible(True)
        self.recording_label.setVisible(False)
        self.time_label.setVisible(False)
        self.stop_button.setVisible(False)

    def displayTime(self, duration):
        """Calculate the time displayed in the time_label widget."""
        minutes, seconds = self.convertTotalTime(duration)
        time_recorded = "{:02d}:{:02d}".format(minutes, seconds)
        self.time_label.setText(time_recorded)

    def convertTotalTime(self, time_in_milli):
        """Convert time from milliseconds."""
        minutes = (time_in_milli / (1000 * 60)) % 60
        seconds = (time_in_milli / 1000) % 60
        return int(minutes), int(seconds)

    def closeEvent(self, event):
        """Display a message in the system tray when the main window has
        been closed."""
        self.tray_icon.showMessage("Notification", "Audio Recorder is still
        running.", 8000)
```

```
if __name__ == '__main__':
    app = QApplication(sys.argv)
    app.setWindowIcon(QIcon(":/resources/images/mic_icon.png"))
    app.setQuitOnLastWindowClosed(False) # Closing the window does not
close the application
    app.setStyleSheet(style_sheet)
    window = AudioRecorder()
    sys.exit(app.exec_())
```

The completed application can be seen in Figure 9-1.

Explanation

For this project, we need to import a number of different resources – a few standard
Python modules, some classes from PyQt, and a couple of additional scripts that we
create ourselves. A few notable PyQt classes are QMenu which will be used to create a
context menu, QSystemTrayIcon to supply an icon for an application in the computer's
system tray, and classes from the QtMultimedia module:

- QAudioRecorder – Class for recording audio

- QAudioEncoderSettings – Provides functions for processing digital
  audio and audio encoding

- QMultimedia – Class providing miscellaneous identifiers when
  working with the QtMultimedia module

AudioRecorderStyleSheet contains the application's style sheet settings. We also
need to import the resources script to include images and other resources associated
with our application. Both of these imports will be covered in later sections.

The program's main class, AudioRecorder, inherits from QWidget. This is where we
set up the widgets, the QAudioRecorder instance, and functions for the application's
main window. This application has two "screens" which can be seen in Figure 9-1. When
the application first begins, the user can see two buttons, one for selecting a path to save
the audio file and another for starting the recording process (which is disabled at first
using start_button.setEnabled(False)).

The user selects a directory using the select_path_button. When clicked, it emits a signal that is connected to selectAudioPath(). Once a path is chosen, the start_button is enabled. The user can then begin recording by clicking the start_button and calling the startRecording() slot.

When this happens, a few actions occur: the audio_recorder object calls setOutputLocation() to set the destination of the audio file; the widgets from the first "screen" are disabled, and the widgets for the second "screen" are enabled; audio_recorder calls record() and begins recording.

While recording, the user can see the widgets for the second "screen" – recording_label, time_label, and stop_button. Rather than using QTimer to keep track of the time that has passed, the QAudioRecorder class provides a signal, durationChanged(), that we can use to update the time_label's text while recording in the displayTime() slot. If the user clicks the stop_button, a signal is sent to stopRecording(). Here we use audio_recorder.stop() to stop recording and switch back to the first "screen."

All of these widgets are arranged in the same layout, main_v_box, in the GUI's window.

Using the QAudioRecorder Class

To create a very simple audio recorder using the QAudioRecorder class, let's first create an instance of QAudioEncoderSettings. An audio encoder is needed to convert the analog sounds a user produces to a digital audio format. In the following code from Listing 9-1, you can see how setCodec() is used to specify the audio codec format, in this case wav. The setQuality() function is used to set the audio encoding quality:

```
# Specify audio encoder settings
audio_settings = QAudioEncoderSettings()
audio_settings.setCodec("audio/wav")
audio_settings.setQuality(QMultimedia.HighQuality)
```

Next, pass the audio encoder settings to the QAudioRecorder instance using the setEncoderSettings() function, and set the path for the output audio file:

```
audio_recorder = QAudioRecorder()
audio_recorder.setEncodingSettings(audio_settings)
audio_recorder.setOutputLocation(QUrl(path_to_file))
```

To begin recording, call

```
audio_recorder.record()
```

To end recording, call

```
audio_recorder.stop()
```

The QAudioRecorder object is set up similarly in Listing 9-1.

Creating Application Icons

A very common feature of many desktop applications is to include an icon in your computer's task bar. Sometimes referred to as the **system tray** or the menu bar depending upon what platform you are using, they are the bars located at the top or bottom on your computer's desktop. Information such as Internet connection, date, time, and volume are usually displayed in the system tray. Application icons can also be placed in the system tray for conveniently accessing the application or using menus to perform additional functions.

Note   The QSystemTrayIcon class has support for Windows and Mac, and the icon may not appear if you are using Linux. To check if your system has an available system tray, create a QSystemTrayIcon instance, in this case called tray_icon, and then run print(tray_icon.isSystemTrayAvailable()).

To create a system tray icon, first, create an instance of QSystemTrayIcon like in Listing 9-1:

```
tray_icon = QSystemTrayIcon(QIcon("images/mic_icon.png"))
```

Then, create the menu instance, add actions, and pass the menu instance to setContextMenu(). An example of this is shown in the following lines from Listing 9-1 to create the action for closing the program. **Context menus** act as pop-up menus for conveniently displaying a list of commands for interacting with the application:

```
tray_menu = QMenu()
quit_act = tray_menu.addAction("Quit")
quit_act.triggered.connect(QApplication.quit)
self.tray_icon.setContextMenu(tray_menu)
self.tray_icon.show()
```

Finally, use show() to make the icon visible in the system tray. The application's icon and context menu are shown in Figure 9-2.

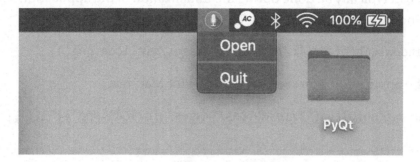

Figure 9-2. *The system tray icon on MacOS and its context menu*

The typical response of a program is to quit the application when closing the main window. With PyQt, app.exec_() runs the application's main loop. Closing the main window will return a value of 0, indicating a successful closing of the application. This is why a PyQt application is closed with the following code:

```
sys.exit(app.exec_())
```

The setQuitOnLastWindowClosed() function is called in Listing 9-1 to demonstrate in this project how you can alter this behavior:

```
app.setQuitOnLastWindowClosed(False)
```

When the window is closed, a status notification message, shown in Figure 9-3, is displayed to inform the user that the program is still running in the background. The notification is created using the showMessage() function in closeEvent(). The user can then reopen the window or quit the program using the context menu shown in Figure 9-2.

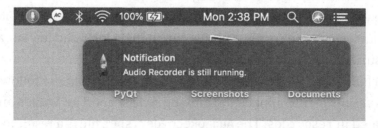

Figure 9-3. *An example of a status notification message on MacOS*

Another common feature is to display the application icon in the top-left corner of the window or, for Mac, in the Dock area. Setting the application icon for Windows and Linux users can typically be done during the initialization of the application's class for the main window with

```
self.setWindowIcon(QIcon(':/resources/images/mic_icon.png'))
```

To set the application icon seen in Figure 9-4 for Mac, use

```
app.setWindowIcon(QIcon(":/resources/images/mic_icon.png"))
```

Note   Windows typically uses ICO format bitmap files (`.ico`) for the icon images, whereas MacOS uses Icon Resource files (`.icns`). Both formats are included in the project's `resources/icons` folder for your convenience.

Figure 9-4.   The audio recorder GUI's icon shown in the MacOS Dock

More information about setting application icons can be found at `https://doc.qt.io/qt-5/appicon.html`.

Creating .qrc Resource Files

You probably noticed a colon and forward slash, `:/`, when loading the icon paths in the previous section and in Listing 9-1 or Listing 9-3. Qt provides a resource management system to store your application's resources, such as images, icons, style sheets, and other data resources, in a binary file. This file can then be included in your application's executable ensuring that the resources we need won't be lost.

Let's take a look at the files we need for the audio recorder. In the following, you can see the Python scripts for the application and the style sheet. The `images` and `icons` folders are located in `resources`. The `AudioRecorder.spec` file is a result of building the application's executable. Finally, you will notice two resource files: `resources.py` and `resources.qrc`. Additional files include `__init__.py` and the `README` text file:

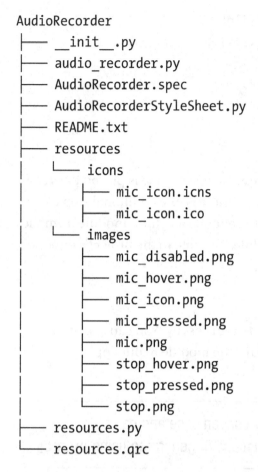

```
AudioRecorder
├── __init__.py
├── audio_recorder.py
├── AudioRecorder.spec
├── AudioRecorderStyleSheet.py
├── README.txt
├── resources
│      └── icons
│              ├── mic_icon.icns
│              ├── mic_icon.ico
│      └── images
│              ├── mic_disabled.png
│              ├── mic_hover.png
│              ├── mic_icon.png
│              ├── mic_pressed.png
│              ├── mic.png
│              ├── stop_hover.png
│              ├── stop_pressed.png
│              └── stop.png
├── resources.py
└── resources.qrc
```

Qt uses resource collection files (.qrc) which are written using the Extensible Markup Language (XML) format for wrapping information between tags. XML's syntax is similar to HTML. Listing 9-2 shows the .qrc file created for this project.

Listing 9-2. Code for the resource collection file used in the audio recorder application

```
# resources.qrc
<!DOCTYPE RCC><RCC version="1.0">
<qresource>
    <file>resources/images/mic_disabled.png</file>
    <file>resources/images/mic_hover.png</file>
    <file>resources/images/mic_icon.png</file>
    <file>resources/images/mic_pressed.png</file>
    <file>resources/images/mic.png</file>
```

```
    <file>resources/images/stop_hover.png</file>
    <file>resources/images/stop_pressed.png</file>
    <file>resources/images/stop.png</file>
    <file>resources/icons/mic_icon.ico</file>
    <file>resources/icons/mic_icon.icns</file>
</qresource>
</RCC>
```

The path to each of our resources we need relative to the `.qrc` file is placed between the `<file>` and `</file>` tags. Since we are using PyQt, there is one additional step to perform before we can use the `.qrc` file – we need to generate a Python module from the `.qrc` file using the `pyrcc5` utility. To create the module, navigate to the project's directory and enter the following code into the command line:

```
$ pyrcc5 resources.qrc -o resources.py
```

This outputs (`-o`) a resource file with the name `resources.py`. You can specify a different name if necessary. The next step is to `import` the module in our application using `import resources`.

Note   The `resources.py` is included for your convenience and can be downloaded from the GitHub link in the "Introduction" or generated using `pyrcc5`.

With the module imported, you can now access files using the prefix `:/`. So the file path `resources/images/stop.png` would become `:/resources/images/stop.png`. There are a few other features for accessing resources using `.qrc`. For example, if you have a long path name, you can use a `file` tag's `alias` attribute to access a file. For example, let's use

```
<file alias="mic-img.png">resources/images/mic.png</file>
```

In the program, this image can be accessed as `:/mic-img.png`.

Once completed, run the program to make sure that there are no issues with accessing the resources. Also, if at any point you update or modify the resources or directories, be sure to update the `.qrc` file and rerun `pyrcc5` to update the binary file. More information about creating resource files can be found at `https://doc.qt.io/qt-5/resources.html`.

Style Sheet for the Audio Recorder

The code for the Qt Style Sheet used in this application is in a separate Python script shown in Listing 9-3. Style sheets can be applied to PyQt applications to create more visually appealing and responsive GUIs. For the audio recorder GUI, the QPushButton widgets will change their appearances if the user is hovering over or clicking the buttons. For the start_button and stop_button objects, different images from the resource files are selected depending upon their states.

Listing 9-3. Code containing the style sheet settings for the audio recorder application

```python
# AudioRecorderStyleSheet.py
# Style sheet for the Audio Recorder GUI

style_sheet = """
    QWidget {
        background-color: #FFFFFF
    }

    QPushButton {
        background-color: #AFAFB0;
        border: 2px solid #949495;
        border-radius: 4px;
        padding: 5px
    }

    QPushButton:hover {
        background-color: #C2C2C4;
    }

    QPushButton:pressed {
        background-color: #909091;
    }

    /* Set up the appearance of the start button for normal, hovered
    and pressed states. */
    QPushButton#StartButton {
        background-color: #FFFFFF;
```

```
        image: url(:/resources/images/mic.png);
        border: none
    }

    QPushButton#StartButton:hover {
        image: url(:/resources/images/mic_hover.png);
    }

    QPushButton#StartButton:pressed {
        image: url(:/resources/images/mic_pressed.png);
    }

    QPushButton#StartButton:disabled {
        image: url(:/resources/images/mic_disabled.png);
    }

    /* Set up the appearance of the stop button for normal, hovered
    and pressed states. */
    QPushButton#StopButton {
        background-color: #FFFFFF;
        image: url(:/resources/images/stop.png);
        border: none
    }

    QPushButton#StopButton:hover {
        image: url(:/resources/images/stop_hover.png);
    }

    QPushButton#StopButton:pressed {
        image: url(:/resources/images/stop_pressed.png);
    }
"""
```

In the next section, you will see how you can package your PyQt applications so they can be easily shared with others.

Sharing Your PyQt Applications

Nowadays, there are so many options for packaging and distributing your Python applications. Older methods for sharing software often involved packaging the code and dependencies together into a single file for distribution. Software created this way could be considered a finished product, where developers did not have to worry about the technical capabilities of the user.

More modern options for deploying software include distributing open source programs that other programmers can download and contribute to on platforms like GitHub or uploading your completed applications to the PyPI repository for others to install using the `pip` package management system. A notable downside to these methods is that you may also need to download other Python libraries, potentially leading to conflicts with other packages that you already have installed. More information about the best practices for packaging Python projects can be found on the Python Packaging Authority (PyPA) website at `www.pypa.io`.

For the purpose of creating desktop applications that users can simply open and begin using right away, we will look at creating standalone executables with PyInstaller.

Creating an Executable with PyInstaller

PyInstaller is an application that can be used to turn your Python scripts into self-contained executables. This means that PyInstaller takes your Python scripts, the Python interpreter, then searches for any necessary modules and libraries (even PyQt5 modules), and bundles them altogether, generating a single folder (or a single executable file) that can then be shared.

While PyInstaller can be used on MacOS, Windows, Linux, and other platforms, it is worth noting that the executable file that is created is specific to the system that it was created on. To create an application for another OS, you will need to run PyInstaller with Python on that OS.

There are also other options for packaging and distributing Python applications. A few examples include PyOxidizer, Briefcase, and the fman build system (fbs). Riverbank Computing Limited also has its own software for specifically deploying PyQt applications – `pyqtdeploy`. If you are interested in using `pyqtdeploy`, have a look at `https://riverbankcomputing.com/software/pyqtdeploy/intro`.

Further information about PyInstaller can be found at `www.pyinstaller.org`.

Installing PyInstaller

To install the most recent version of PyInstaller, open your computer's shell and run

```
$ pip3 install pyinstaller
```

Next, enter the following command into the command line to verify that the installation was successful:

```
$ pyinstaller --version
```

This will print your version of PyInstaller in the console, which, as of this writing, is version 4.0. You are now ready to begin bundling your Python application.

Note   As of this writing, PyInstaller only works with Python versions 3.5–3.7. If you are running the latest version of Python, v3.8, you may need to roll back to a previous installation or choose one of the other packaging applications mentioned.

Building the Executable

To begin creating the executable, first, navigate to the location of your application's main file for running the program. This file is generally called `main.py`. For this project, the main file is `audio_recorder.py`:

```
$ cd path/to/AudioRecorder
```

Creating an executable with PyInstaller is almost effortless if you don't need to specify any options or resources. From the command line, enter

```
$ pyinstaller audio_recorder.py
```

Running this command will create a `.spec` file with the same name as the specified Python file and two new folders – `build` and `dist`. The `.spec` file contains the configuration settings and instructions used by PyInstaller for building your application; `build` contains log files and working files needed for preparing and analyzing the bundle; `dist` contains the folder, or optionally a single file, with the executable that can be zipped up and distributed to others.

We could stop here, but there are a few other options we have for specifying the parameters of the executable that PyInstaller outputs. A few commonly used flags are listed in the following:

- `--windowed, --noconsole` – Creates a windowed application and prevents the shell window from opening up alongside the application (best for GUIs).

- `--onefile` – Bundles the application into a single file that can be distributed to others, meaning that users do not have to install any other packages or even Python to run the application.

- `--onedir` – Bundles the application into a single folder (default).

- `--icon` – Sets the application icon for the executable. On Windows use `.ico`, on Linux use `.png`, and on Mac use `.icns` image files.

- `--add-data` – Specifies additional non-binary files or folders that contain resources, such as images, that the application needs. The option can be used multiple times and will need to be stated for each resource.

- `--name` – Creates a name for the `.spec` file and the executable.

Let's see how we can use them. In the following command, we specify that we do not want the shell window to appear when running the application, set the path to the icon, create a name for the program, and specify the main script:

```
$ pyinstaller --windowed --icon=resources/icons/mic_icon.icns --name
AudioRecorder audio_recorder.py
```

The newly created `.spec` file as well as the `build` and `dist` folders that are created are shown in Figure 9-5. You can also see the contents of the `dist` folder and the application with its icon.

If you run the executable in the `dist` folder, you will notice that our images appear without any problems. This is the reason for using Qt's resource system and the `resources.qrc` file. Otherwise, you would need to specify each resource using the `--add-data` flag or find some other means for importing your data files.

Note   The `AudioRecorder.spec` found on GitHub and in Listing 9-4 reflects this build.

Figure 9-5. *The audio recorder project with its own application icon created with PyInstaller and the default --onedir flag*

One final note, if you wish to create a single executable file in the dist folder, then be sure to include the --onefile flag:

```
$ pyinstaller --windowed --onefile --icon=resources/icons/mic_icon.icns
--name AudioRecorder audio_recorder.py
```

Creating an Executable Using the .spec File

When you run PyInstaller, a .spec file will automatically be generated based on the options you specified. This file can also be created before running PyInstaller using pyi-makespec (included with PyInstaller) and then used to create your executable.

Check out the comments in Listing 9-4 to see which settings were modified when running PyInstaller.

Listing 9-4. The specifications file for the audio recorder application

```
# AudioRecorder.spec
# -*- mode: python -*-

block_cipher = None
```

```
a = Analysis(['audio_recorder.py'],
             # Be sure to set the path name
             pathex=['/path/to/AudioRecorder'],
             binaries=[],
             # Use datas to specify resources not in .qrc
             datas=[],
             hiddenimports=[],
             hookspath=[],
             runtime_hooks=[],
             excludes=[],
             win_no_prefer_redirects=False,
             win_private_assemblies=False,
             cipher=block_cipher,
             noarchive=False)
pyz = PYZ(a.pure, a.zipped_data,
             cipher=block_cipher)
exe = EXE(pyz,
          a.scripts,
          [],
          exclude_binaries=True,
          # Set the name of the executable
          name='AudioRecorder',
          debug=False,
          bootloader_ignore_signals=False,
          strip=False,
          upx=True,
          # Hide the console by setting its value to False
          # Set the icon for the executable
          console=False , icon='resources/icons/mic_icon.icns')
coll = COLLECT(exe,
               a.binaries,
               a.zipfiles,
               a.datas,
               strip=False,
               upx=True,
               name='AudioRecorder')
```

```
app = BUNDLE(coll,
             # Set the name of the app
             name='AudioRecorder.app',
             # Set the icon for the app
             icon='resources/icons/mic_icon.icns',
             bundle_identifier=None)
```

You can recreate the executable using only the files and resources found in the AudioRecorder directory found on GitHub, by opening the `.spec` file, setting `pathex` in Listing 9-4 to the location of AudioRecorder on your computer, navigating to the folder, and entering the following line into the command line:

```
$ pyinstaller AudioRecorder.spec
```

Windows users will need to use `mic_icon.ico`; Linux users can use `mic_icon.png`. You now have a working executable that you can distribute to other people.

What's Next?

Once you have an executable file, your adventure may be over. For some of you though, you may need to occasionally update your application to fix problems, add new features, update the software, or package your executable into an installer. Some of the earlier mentioned tools, Briefcase and fbs, include the tools needed for packaging applications that are ready for distribution to desktop platforms.

There are also other platform-specific tools available, such as dmgbuild for creating MacOS disk images (`.dmg`), InstallForge or Nullsoft Scriptable Install System (NSIS) for building Windows executable (`.exe`) files, and stdeb or fpm for producing Debian source packages (`.deb`) for Linux.

Tip   Before distributing packages, always be sure to check the license(s) of the software you are using. For example, PyQt5 uses two licenses – Riverbank Commercial License and GPL v3. With GPL, you can distribute your applications for free, but not for commercial purposes. More information about the commercial version of PyQt can be found at `www.riverbankcomputing.com/commercial/`. Further details about GPL are located at `www.gnu.org`.

Summary

The best way to build an application is to always be thinking about the user. The user doesn't have to be a single person. They could be a small business made up of a few people or a large business formed by hundreds. It's important to keep in mind that the applications that you build could serve as the solution to simplifying their lives, saving or making them money, or building new relationships.

In this chapter, we utilized PyQt's QtMultimedia module to build a working audio recorder. Using PyInstaller, the next step was to demonstrate how you could build an executable file for distributing your application to others. There is no single solution for packaging and deploying Python code, and it is best to find the solution that fits you and your user's needs.

Qt and PyQt are incredible tools; and, as we have seen in this guide, there are numerous third-party libraries and other software that have support for them when it comes to building applications.

Before you go, I want to thank you. My hope is that the lessons and projects in this book have helped you in some way in solving your own problems. Thank you for following along with me on this journey. Your feedback and questions are always welcome. Good luck!

Index

© Joshua Willman 2021
J. Willman, *Modern PyQt*, https://doi.org/10.1007/978-1-4842-6603-8

Printed in the United States
By Bookmasters